Chasing Unicorns

Roni Askey-Doran

First published by Unicorn Press, June 2005
Second Edition published August 2014

National Library of Australia
Cataloguing-in-publication data:

Askey-Doran, Roni, 1966–
Chasing Unicorns
Second Edition / Digital Edition
ISBN 10: 0-9757600-1-7
ISBN 13: 978-0-9757600-1-7

1. Women's literature – 20th century.
2. Sexual abuse – drug abuse – alcohol abuse – survival – therapy – resolution.
Fiction. I. Askey-Doran, Roni, 1966 – II. Title

This book is dedicated to Lisa and Jane, for your indomitable courage, strength and fighting spirit, and to Robbie, Pamela, Peggy, Scott, and Steve for your love and invaluable support, and to Kelly for all your wonderful help, and also to Margaret and to Mike without whom I could never have caught my unicorn.

Foreword

It was in 1981, when I was the Mayor of Townsville, and officiating at the opening of a share-house for young people who had run away from home, that I first met Roni Askey-Doran. She was only fifteen at the time, although unbeknown to me or anyone else at the opening, and yet, she had already endured over a decade of sustained sexual abuse at the hands of a trusted family member; someone who should have been protecting and nurturing her.

I have had further dealings with Roni over the years in her role as a journalist, and most recently to discuss changing the laws pertaining to sexual abuse in Australia. I am amazed, but not surprised, at her strength and determination to bring her perpetrator to justice and to expose the hurtful truth. I truly admire and commend Roni for being brave enough to share her painful story of childhood abuse with the public and also for her perseverance during her unrelenting quest for justice from which she emerged remarkably successful.

In my role as Queensland's Minister for Child Safety, horrific stories like Roni's cross my desk daily. I am constantly confronted and appalled by accounts of a similar nature and also by the circumstances in which thousands of vulnerable children and young people live their lives. All of these stories are frightening and are very sad descriptions of breakdowns in the fabric of our society. The fact that children can be exposed to sexual abuse is unbelievable to most and yet the incidence of abuse continues to occur all too often and, even more calamitous, the number of sexual abuse victims increases year by year.

Roni's poignant novel, *Chasing Unicorns*, will no doubt have an impact on many people; survivors of abuse, their families and friends, and anyone else who has ever come into contact with the victims of sexual abuse. This insightful literary work, while fictional, closely resembles Roni's own heartbreaking story in many ways. For those countless people who have experienced abuse, hearing Roni tell her harrowing story of survival and justice at seminars across the country will hopefully give you the strength to tell your own story and also let you know that you are not alone in your plight. For the families and friends of survivors, reading this novel may help you discover new ways of listening to and supporting loved ones who have been sexually abused.

For the many professionals who work in the area of abuse and neglect, I hope that reading Roni's novel and listening to her talk about her experiences of sexual abuse and finally winning her long battle for justice, will reaffirm your passion and commitment, and cause you to reflect on your practice to discover innovative ways of working collaboratively to help smooth the path for victims and survivors of abuse.

For the whole community, nationally and internationally, Roni's story is a call to action. By exposing the previously hidden and disturbing aspects of child sexual abuse, Roni challenges us, as a community, to work together to prevent this crime. Governments across Australia, and around the world, have a responsibility to lead the community charge and condemn incidents of child abuse and neglect. We must all work together to create a safety net for our children and send a clear message to paedophiles that abhorrent acts of child sexual abuse will not be tolerated.

For all children, young people and adults who have suffered abuse and neglect, we, as community members, must be steadfast in meeting our responsibilities to provide adequate support and encouragement, and to increase our awareness of the extent and impact child sexual abuse has on its victims and survivors, and their families. We must encourage the reporting of abuse, and promote more sensitive practices in the systems and the processes that sexual abuse victims must endure. We must be resolute in our commitment to creating safe environments for our children and young people, now and in the future.

I applaud Roni Askey-Doran on her strength and courage in telling her painful, yet empowering story, for producing this revealing and touching novel, and also for the significant contribution she has made to increasing the awareness of and intolerance to child sexual abuse within the community.

Mike Reynolds

Mike Reynolds AM MP;
Queensland's Minister for Child Safety and
Member for Townsville (2005)

Note: Mike Reynolds retired from politics in 2009.

Chasing Unicorns

Straddling a wooden chair, Jade faced the wardrobe mirror and glared at her reflection. The barrel of the revolver rested on her bottom lip, crushing the soft flesh against her teeth. Streaks of mascara zigzagged down her cheeks. Tears dripped from her pointed chin onto the polished wooden floor. A smear of red lipstick spread from her mouth across her right cheek like an ugly flesh wound. Nestled between her damp palms, the butt of the revolver rested on the back of the chair. Feeling for the trigger, Jade opened her eyes wide. She wanted her own death to be the last thing she saw.

Jade inspected the girl in the mirror with indifference. A desolate face peered back through thick, curly hair. Her reflection was right; enough was enough.

'Life's a bitch and then you die,' she muttered, closing her eyes to shut out the labyrinthine thoughts whirling through her head.

Now seemed like a good time to die. The bitch part had already lasted a dozen lifetimes. Fragments of recollection flashed through her mind; the shattered ruins of her life, shards of broken childhood, pieces of a teenage jigsaw that would never be complete.

Jade ran a hand through her hair, her long fingernails raking her scalp as if trying to scratch out the horrid memories. She curled the fingers of her other hand closer around the trigger. Her hand shook slightly, the effect of too much bourbon.

A tiny rainbow appeared on the mirror and vanished, then appeared again a moment later. Jade looked out the window at the streetlight. Spears of light reflected through her tears, stabbing the darkness in all directions. She turned back to the mirror and sighed, resigned to her fate. As she squeezed the narrow tongue of steel, she fixed her eyes on the pale face staring back at her from the mirror.

You sad loser, she thought. This is where it ends.

Click.

2

Alec Stonewall drove fast. The narrow road snaked down the mountain. The car hugged the edge of the cliff that fell away from the road. The tyres held a tenacious grip; squealing around hairpin bends. Stones tumbled through the air, landing in dense forest far below as the wheels hurled them from the bitumen. As he neared the bottom of the mountain, Alec sped up. He knew this road as well as he knew the lines on his face. The long curve stretched out ahead. As he approached, he would aim straight for the tree.

It was an ancient Moreton Bay fig, its trunk thick with age, branches gnarled and knotted, bearing the scars of hard-won survival. After the impact there would probably be nothing left of him or the car. He'd filled the fuel tank, anticipating it would explode into a fireball, and he'd be cremated on the spot. He didn't know if the tree would survive the impact. He hoped it would. In any case, there was no one to come and lay flowers or tie ribbons of memoriam at its scorched base.

Alec eased back into his seat, preparing for death. He was calm. Lucid. In control. For a fleeting moment, he wished he could evoke his raison d'être. Life had dealt him a dud hand. When he reached the gates of hell he was going to demand a reshuffle. He pressed the accelerator. This way, he thought with grim satisfaction, it will look like an accident.

The radio on the dashboard crackled. The spiral cord dangling from the handset brushed against his hand. Alec ignored it. He was close now. He grasped the steering wheel tighter.

Here it comes. Blissful death.

Unable to shut out the sound, he heard the voice on the radio.

'I know that address!' he whispered, looking out for the tree as the car raced towards its destiny.

Then, he saw it. Alec focused on the centre of the broad trunk. The wheels gripped the camber, tilting gently to the left as he rounded the curve. A few more seconds ….

The call on the radio was repeated.

'Arrggh!'

Frustrated, he slapped the steering wheel with the heel of his palm, pulling the car gently to the right. The tree whizzed by. He passed the corner and flew down the straight road at high speed.

Alec spoke calmly into the handset, '503 to VKC. On my way.' He switched on the siren and sped into town.

3

Carl carried Lizzie up three flights of stairs. Despite being a dead weight, she was light in his arms. Her face looked angelic as she slept. Her neck stretched back, revealing smooth creamy skin. Her short skirt had rucked up around her hips, exposing smooth thighs that made promises they couldn't keep. Firm breasts were outlined under her skin-tight top. Inhaling her perfume, Carl trod lightly, making no sound as he approached the door of the apartment.

'Here we are,' he whispered in her ear, before hoisting her over his shoulder so he could take the key from his pocket.

He stepped over the threshold and silently closed the door behind him. He took the girl into the bedroom and gently laid her on the huge waterbed. Her limbs sprawled as he lowered her onto the down-filled quilt. Her handbag tumbled over the side of the bed. Leaving her prone, he went to fasten the locks on the front door. He took his time, knowing Lizzie would be out for a while. The door secured, Carl went to the kitchen and made himself a scotch and soda.

A few minutes later, he looked in on Lizzie. She hadn't stirred. He pulled the heavy curtains across and walked over to the bed. He picked up the bag and emptied it onto the quilt. There wasn't much; battered photo ID, lipstick, hairbrush, house keys, mobile phone, a little money. He switched the phone off, put everything back in the bag, and placed it on the sideboard.

'A little while longer,' he chuckled, heading to the bathroom.

He lathered his skin with a loofah, rubbing the coarse fibres over every inch of his trim body. Next, he washed his short grey hair, using the same handmade witch hazel soap. Then, he rubbed himself dry. After wrapping a clean towel around his waist, he shaved. Aside from a jagged scar under his chin, he liked his face. It was square and proud, almost regal. Carl stood for a moment, admiring his features in the wide mirror.

He dampened a face washer and returned to the bedroom, sipping his drink as he walked. Lizzie still hadn't moved. Carl set his glass on the bedside table and lay on the bed beside his prize. He wiped the foundation and blusher from her cheeks, and gently ran the cool cloth over her face. He rubbed off her pink candy lipstick, and wiped the cloth across her forehead. Satisfied her face was clean, he tossed the face washer aside.

'It's time to wake up, baby,' he crooned, brushing a stray strand of hair from her cheek.

Lizzie didn't move.

Carl pulled her long slim legs toward him and undid her denim mini-skirt. It came off easily. So did her yellow panties. He threw the garments on the floor. He sat her up and pulled her lycra top over her head. Her arms fell to her sides as he flung the strip of fabric away. Then, he undid her yellow bra and slipped it over her arms, adding it to the small pile of clothes. Still, she didn't awaken. He left the bright platform heels strapped to her feet. Women in shoes turned him on. Carl shifted her to the centre of the bed and admired her nakedness. He traced her breasts with one hand, lazily running his fingers over her flawless skin. He undid the knot in his towel and let it fall to the floor.

'C'mon, baby, it's time to play,' he whispered, leaning over to kiss her lips, her neck, her ears.

She mumbled and stirred slightly.

Carl moved in. He took one of Lizzie's hands and held it tight. With his other hand, he caressed her stomach, running his fingers down to the tiny patch of light pubic hair, and leaning in to kiss her mouth. Her eyelids fluttered. She groaned a little. He squeezed her hand and gently stroked her cheek.

'That's it, baby. Wakey, wakey.'

He moved down to cover her nipple with his mouth. She opened her eyes. Lizzie tried to move her head, but couldn't. She felt dizzy, nauseous. Carl shifted up on one elbow to look into her eyes as they focused.

'Well, hello,' he murmured, moving to cover her body with his.

She groaned, and tried to move her limbs. Nothing happened. She opened her mouth to speak. Her tongue felt weighed down. Carl kissed her neck. He wound his fingers through hers, then lifted himself up onto one elbow to get a better view of her face.

'Now you're awake, we can play,' he grinned, piercing her dark eyes with his.

'Where am I?' she croaked, slurring, her mouth dry. 'Who are you?'

The Rohypnol was beginning to wear off. She was coming around.

'You're home, Lizzie. Your new home. I'm your Daddy now,' purred Carl.

Eyes wide with terror, she gasped. Her head pounded. She could hear her heartbeat in her temples. Impatient now, Carl pushed her legs apart with his knees. She struggled to move. Her body didn't respond. Her mind fought against him, but her limbs wouldn't obey.

'Oh, no. Please, no. Please. I'm only fourteen,' she pleaded, almost incoherent. Tears rolled down the sides of her face into her hair.

'Relax baby, the fun is just beginning,' he drawled, reaching under the pillow for the white scarf to tie around her mouth.

'Jade? Are you in there?' Alec banged on the door. 'Jade? Open up!' Two uniformed police officers stood expectantly behind him. Constables Jaems and Keaton had responded to the radio call after neighbours had reported screaming and crashing. In his rush to get there, Alec had screeched to a halt outside the building and almost run over the officers.

'Jade? Open the door! It's Alec!'

Standing in the hall, Alec felt a cold surge of fear. He didn't know Jade well, but he was worried. He had surprised himself; for the first time in three years, he actually gave a damn. It was probably too late. Impatient and alarmed, Alec kicked open the door. He burst into the flat with a loaded pistol in his outstretched hand yelling, 'Police!'

Silence screamed back. A dozen red roses tied with a white silk scarf lay neatly arranged on the floor outside the bedroom door.

Alec knew Jade from Nero's, where she worked as a barmaid six nights a week. Since his unexpected divorce, the morose detective had patronised the drinking hole on the nights Jade worked. On Jade's night off, Alec took a bottle home and caught up on lost sleep. Jade was good to him. She listened sympathetically to his drunken woes, often helping him into a waiting taxi. Sometimes, after a particularly interesting discussion, Alec would be sober enough to walk her home after work. The little he knew about Jade Randall could be etched onto a pinhead; he never asked, she never told. On some level they were kindred spirits, or perhaps two lost souls wandering through the same abyss.

Stepping carefully over the roses, Alec pushed the door open and walked into the bedroom. He saw Jade's unmoving body sprawled on the rug near her bed. Despair washed over him. Assuming she was dead, he caressed her pale face before placing his fingers on her neck to feel for a pulse. Her body was warm. Alec was surprised to find Jade still breathing. Her pulse was weak. She reeked of bourbon.

The room was eerily quiet. In the tranquil pre-dawn, a light breeze tickled the filmy lace curtains. An empty bourbon bottle rested on the remains of a pillow beside Jade's head. A Colt .38 revolver lay on the floor under an upturned chair near the mirror. Clothes were strewn across the room. Underwear pulled from the bureau drawers spilled out onto the floor. The hand-stitched patchwork bedspread had been shredded. A pair of dressmakers' scissors was embedded in the wall near the window. Feathers spilled from pillows. In one corner lay a pile of smashed glass and broken porcelain ornaments. A large spider-web crack graced the centre of the mirror. A long, wooden shelf, laden with books, records, CDs and cassettes, had been yanked from its brackets. Some of the books had been ripped in half. A ribbonless Doors cassette lay near Jade's head. Several shattered CDs were strewn about. Shredded newspaper littered the floor. Pieces of broken furniture were scattered around the room. A Janis Joplin poster on the wall above the bed was intact, but a large hunting knife stuck out from the rock singer's nose.

'Call an ambulance!' Alec shouted to one of the uniformed officers behind him. He glanced around at the mess. 'Jade? Wake up! It's Alec! Jade? Wake up! Hell!' The place resembled a bombsite. 'What the hell happened here?' he asked the walls.

Stepping back through the door, Alec picked up the roses and put them on a table near the sofa. The living-room looked normal. Staring back at Joplin's defiant smirk, and the knife she now wore like a piece of bizarre jewellery, he assumed there had been a fight. Alec donned latex gloves and inspected the gun, wondering if it was Jade's or if it belonged to someone else. Five of the six chambers were full. Alec returned the weapon to its place on the floor. He shot off photos of the bedroom in disarray, and of Jade, in case she didn't make it.

Ambulance officers arrived in a flurry of efficiency to take the unconscious woman to Saint Augustine's. While the uniformed police talked to the neighbours, Alec sifted through the debris. A forensic scientist dusted the apartment for fingerprints and collected evidence.

Alec looked around the living-room, and plucked at his uncomfortable latex gloves. Jim Morrison stared seductively from his wooden frame above the television. Large posters of Marilyn Monroe and Elvis Presley occupied one wall. James Dean, Jimi Hendrix and Kurt Cobain looked down from another. A defiant Bonn Scott raised his fist above the bookcase.

A search of the kitchen drawers revealed a cache of cocaine—maybe twenty or thirty grams. Alec stuffed it in his pocket. He'd flush it down the toilet later. The last thing Jade needed was a drug-bust. He knew he'd lose his job if he was caught. It didn't matter. He didn't want to lose his only link to sanity, however fragile. He thought of the tree. How close he had come. If it weren't for Jade he wouldn't be standing there.

Aside from the bedroom, the apartment was neat and clean. There were no signs of forced entry. Whoever made this mess knew Jade, Alec concluded. He stood in the middle of the room, allowing his thoughts to float into space. The puzzle would bother him until Jade woke up. Even then, he wasn't sure she'd tell him anything.

'Alec?'

Jamie Forester stood in front of Alec, snapping his fingers. Alec had known Jamie at school. As kids they hadn't hung out much, but when they'd both ended up at the same police station, they'd become a team of sorts, antagonising each other regularly. Jamie had studied forensic science. Alec joined the force because his Dad had been a cop. Sometimes they swapped favors and worked on special projects. Forensics fascinated Alec, and Jamie admired Alec's gung-ho attitude. They were like chalk and cheese, with a wary respect for each other.

'Alec! Hello? Earth to Alec!'

Alec's head snapped up. 'Yeah? What?'

'I'm taking everything to the lab. I'll let you know in a couple of days.'

'Sure.' Alec's thoughts drifted away again.

'Alec, I found traces of cocaine on the kitchen bench. Don't know anything about that, do you?' He glanced sideways at his colleague. 'If you ask me, it looks like a drug and alcohol binge gone wrong.'

Alec blushed slightly and looked at his shoes. He felt the little packet in his pocket. He knew Jamie knew, and he knew Jamie wouldn't snitch.

'What do you think?' Alec asked, indicating the bedroom.

'I don't know.' Jamie shrugged. 'Not yet, anyway. You know this lady, don't you?'

'Yeah. She works down at Nero's. I go there sometimes.'

Jamie sighed and nodded, understanding. 'Don't get in too deep, Alec. You nearly drowned last time.'

'I'm still drowning,' admitted Alec.

'Really? I hadn't noticed!' Jamie's sarcasm slapped Alec in the face.

'Gimme a break!'

'You've had three years,' the scientist snorted. 'That's a pretty good break. It's over, pal.'

'Yeah, well—'

'Look at all these pictures …' Jamie pointed at the frames and grimaced. 'Notice something about them? They're all dead, Alec. Every one of them. Rich, young, famous. They had it all. Lived hard, died young. They played Russian roulette with drugs and alcohol, and lost. These are probably her role models. If you ask me, your lady is a little twisted.'

'Are you done here?' Alec felt irritated. He didn't want to hear anything negative about Jade. He didn't know her well enough to criticise. And yet, despite her aloofness, he knew her so well.

'Yep,' said Jamie, and walked towards the door. 'See you tomorrow.'

'Jamie? Just one thing … keep it to yourself for now, will you?'

'Sure.' Jamie stopped and turned. 'Alec?'

'What?'

'Do you mind if I take these roses?'

'No. If they're not evidence, they're yours.'

'Great. Now my wife will forgive us both.' Jamie gathered the flowers and danced out, winking cheekily as he vanished into the dark hallway.

The uniforms filled in Alec before leaving. The neighbours hadn't heard any shots. They'd awoken to glass breaking and things being smashed against the wall. A short time later, the screaming started. That's when they'd called the police. Suddenly, the noise had stopped. One of the neighbours had knocked on Jade's door to see if she was okay, but no one had answered. No one had seen or heard anyone coming or going. Jade usually kept to herself. She wasn't rude or aggressive, just quiet. Shy, maybe. She didn't have a boyfriend that anyone knew of, but there had been a guy a couple of years ago. Nick Troxell. A decent boy, they'd said. No one had seen him for a while. Jade was pretty much a loner.

As dawn broke over the city, Alec surveyed the trashed room again. A crystal ornament hanging in the window caught the sunlight and cast dots of bright rainbow colours around the walls.

'What happened, Jade?' he asked the miniature rainbows.

Alec drove toward Saint Augustine's Hospital, mulling over the possible scenarios. Jamie thought it was a drug and alcohol binge. The neighbours said no one else had been there. After studying her artwork, the uniforms decided Jade was a lonely psycho. Alec didn't believe that.

'Why?' he asked himself. 'What happened in there tonight?'

He parked near the emergency ward and walked toward the building, his jaws clenched. The sun shone brightly in his face. Detective Alec Stonewall was determined to get to the bottom of this. Nearing the door, he shuddered. Just a few seconds later …

Hearing Jade's address on the radio had made him realise what he was doing. Shaking the horror of his own near-suicide out of his mind, he marched into the emergency ward.

5

Jade slept peacefully, her long red hair tangled around her wan face. Alec pictured her almond-shaped green eyes glancing furtively at him from across the bar at Nero's. The secrets of the world were hidden in those melancholy eyes. He sat on a hard chair beside the gurney and held her hand.

'What happened to you, Jade? Tell me what happened. Did you do this to yourself? Did someone else do it? Jade, I need to know.'

Jade's presence calmed him. He looked into her face. She appeared tranquil. Watching the gentle rise and fall of her chest soothed him.

When Alec's wife left him just over three years ago he had shut his heart down. Melanie had broken him, spoiled him forever. She had been the love of his life, but clearly she'd loved other things. People were hard work, thought Alec. Relationships were impossible and in the end, no matter what you did, you got hurt. The day he came home to find his house empty, his bank accounts cleared out, and his wife gone, had been devastating. She'd taken everything. She hadn't even left a note. If that was life, then to hell with it, he'd rather die.

The last three years had been a half-hearted attempt to kill himself. Death by bourbon. Jade had served the poison and listened to the death throes. He'd almost wiped himself out permanently tonight. Before he'd found Jade unconscious, he hadn't known her last name.

Hell, I'm a selfish creep, he thought.

Jade had somehow reached inside him and turned on a light. She had penetrated the thick walls he had erected to protect himself. He didn't know how. He didn't even know her, not really. She'd never given him any reason to believe she gave a damn about anything. Maybe that was it. Maybe it was because she cared less than he did. It seemed like such a waste of a good heart. Something deep inside him needed her to care.

A doctor marched into the room and rustled some papers.

'Are you family?'

'No. Police. I'm investigating the case.' Alec flashed his badge.

The doctor raised his eyebrows and stared pointedly at Alec's hand holding Jade's.

'Is it customary for the police to hold hands with patients under investigation?'

'I know Jade. She's a friend. And I'm also investigating what happened to her tonight.'

'Very well.' The doctor clicked his tongue with disapproval.

To hell with him, thought Alec. What does he know about Jade, or me? He stretched to his full height and stepped foward 'What can you tell me, Doctor err …?'

'Doctor Lerner. Miss Randall has taken quite a bit of cocaine. She's also extremely inebriated. Her blood alcohol level is point three-eight-nine. I assume from her breath she was drinking bourbon. I'm treating her for alcohol poisoning. Aside from a scratch on her forehead, there are no external injuries. She has no marks or bruising. There are no signs of violence. Her throat is inflamed, which indicates she may have been shouting for some time before she became unconscious.'

'Does it look like a suicide attempt?'

'Not on the surface. She'd have to take a lot more narcotics to kill herself, even combined with the alcohol. It looks like a binge. How well do you know her? Is she prone to this kind of thing?'

'She works in a bar downtown. I've never seen her drunk. Come to think of it, I've never even seen her have a drink,' answered Alec, his hackles rising at the doctor's clipped tone.

'Hmm. Very strange.' The doctor looked down his bumpy Roman nose at Jade and creased his bushy eyebrows together. 'Pretty girl.'

Alec felt instinctively protective of Jade. He didn't like the doctor's smarmy attitude.

'Is her life in danger?'

'No.' Doctor Lerner smiled patronisingly. 'She'll live to regret this night.'

'What knocked her out?'

'Hard to say, Detective. My current diagnosis is an alcohol-induced coma, which will wear off in time. It's also possible she has suffered some kind of trauma or shock.'

'Any idea when she'll wake up?'

'No. Maybe in a few hours. She's on a saline drip for re-hydration but she'll have a humdinger of a hangover when she comes around.'

'Is that it?'

'She'll also have a sore throat. Was she screaming at something?'

'Apparently … That's what the neighbours said.'

'Detective …um?'

'Alec Stonewall. Here's my number.' He handed the doctor a card. 'Will you call me when she wakes up? Anytime night or day.'

'Right, Detective Stonewall. Has her family been contacted?'

'No. I don't think she has any family. I doubt she'll have visitors. She's a a loner. I'll come back later and see how she's getting on.'

'Certainly, Detective Stonewall.'

'Thank you, Doctor.'

As he walked out to the car park, Alec decided to track down the ex-boyfriend to see what he could find out about Jade. Maybe he would have some insight into Jade's uncharacteristic binge.

Nick Troxell was easy to find. He worked as a broker at the stock market. Made a decent living. Owned a big house and an expensive car. Lived in a nice neighbourhood. He had no rap sheet. Not even a parking ticket. To any normal girl, Nick Troxell would probably have seemed like the catch of the day. For some reason, Jade hadn't wanted him. For an even more obscure reason, Alec wanted to find out why. Jade was not a normal girl. She was extraordinary. This was getting personal. Alec called Nick's office.

'Is she in trouble?' Nick asked with a worried tone.

'She'll be fine. She had an … um … accident. She's in hospital and recovering well,' Alec lied.

'Which hospital? What happened to her?'

'I was hoping you'd help me figure that out. Can we meet and talk about it?' Nick agreed to meet Alec in a café not far from his office.

Nick was tall and blond with a tanned, chiselled face and gleaming white teeth. He had a scar on his forehead above his left eye that gave him a slightly piratical appearance. A hint of worry creasing his brow, Nick strode into the café looking for Alec. The detective waved him over to the table.

'What happened? Where is Jade? Is she okay?' Nick asked before he sat down.

'She'll be fine,' replied Alec as he stood to shake Nick's hand.

Over coffee they talked about Jade. Alec watched Nick as he spoke. Alec had hated the stockbroker on paper—according to the report, he was too perfect—but he quickly changed his mind as he talked with the open, friendly man. Nick was obviously still in love with her; his blue eyes lit up and smiled whenever he mentioned her name.

Nick explained that they'd been together for two and a half years. He would have walked over broken glass for her. As the relationship between them blossomed and they got closer, part of Jade seemed to want to be further away. The night Nick had proposed to her, Jade had flipped out and thrown him out of her apartment.

'She wouldn't return my calls or let me see her after that,' said Nick, still devastated that she'd shut him out so completely.

She'd had him ejected from Nero's for trying to see her. That was two years ago. After a while, he gave up and went away to heal his broken heart. She had said she couldn't 'take that kind of pressure'. He hadn't understood what she'd meant. Jade had had problems with men in the past and it had taken her ages to trust Nick. He gave her all the time she needed, but she always wanted more, and was always on edge. It was like part of her wanted the relationship to work, but another part of her was determined to sabotage it. She couldn't handle being happy and having everything perfect in her life. She'd said it was asking for disaster.

'Jade's a special girl, but she carries a lot of pain,' said Nick, wondering if he should visit Jade in hospital.

'What kind of pain?'

'Did you know she was abused as a kid?'

'Really?' replied Alec, his mind ticking. 'No, she never said anything about it.'

'She told me one night in the middle of an argument,' Nick said, running his finger around the rim of his coffee cup. 'Later she said it came out by mistake, and she had never meant to tell me. I couldn't get her to talk about it again.'

'Why not?'

'She just clammed up.' Nick shrugged. 'She did that a lot. All the time we were together, Jade never mentioned family. It's like they never existed. When I asked, she refused to hear the questions. She'd change the subject. She must have a family.' Nick looked Alec in the eye, wondering if Alec knew anything about her family, hoping he might read it in the detective's face. 'A mother or father or someone, but she never talked about anyone. She never spoke of her childhood, she wouldn't share stuff about herself.'

'Why do you think she wouldn't marry you?'

'I don't know. I've thought about it a lot. We loved each other. I thought she was my soul mate. I thought I was hers. She's seriously messed up. She always was. But I didn't care. I figured we'd work it out eventually. Even now ...' he sighed. 'If she walked in that door right this minute and told me she'd changed her mind,' Nick grinned shyly, feeling a little silly that he still held a candle for Jade, 'I'd marry her this afternoon.'

'Do you think she'd ever want to hurt herself?'

'Has she tried something?' Nick became agitated. 'What happened to her?'

'I don't know yet. I'm exploring all the possibilities. It's possible. It's also possible that someone attacked her. Is she capable of hurting herself?'

'I guess there's a chance she might. Jade suffers from depression. I tried to get her to see a therapist, but she freaked out and wouldn't go.' Nick's eyes revealed his pain and confusion. 'She never tried to hurt herself when we were together.'

'Her neighbours said Jade was always skittish with you. You never hurt her, did you?'

'No! Never. I worshipped the ground she walked on. Jade was afraid of being happy. It scared the crap out of her. It was like she even hated the idea of happiness. It made her uncomfortable. Sometimes it seemed as if she preferred to be miserable. Stupid, isn't it?'

'No, not really.' Alec knew how that felt. 'Does she drink a lot?'

'Sometimes, but not often. We used to go to the marina and have a few drinks with friends.'

'Did she ever get drunk?'

'Rarely. She hated being out of control. There was this one time, a couple of years ago, just before we broke up. We were at a party with friends. She wiped herself out. She curled up in a dark corner in the garden with a bottle of tequila and cried. Our friends were worried. She wouldn't come out. She drank the whole bottle,' Nick said, a combination of amazement and confusion in his voice. 'I took her home to sleep it off. When I asked, she didn't want to talk about it. I put it down to a fit of depression and let it go.'

'Do you own a gun, Mister Troxell?'

'No, why?' Nick's ears pricked.

'We found a revolver in her apartment,' explained Alec. 'I just wondered if she got it from you.'

'Jade hates guns. Why would she have one in her house?'

'I'm not sure yet. I'm trying to figure it all out.'

'Why don't you ask Jade?'

'I will, Mister Troxell. I will,' assured Alec, concluding the meeting.

On his way home, Alec stopped at Jade's apartment. There was something he wanted to look at. He wasn't sure what it was, but he knew he'd know it as soon as he saw it.

He let himself in with the key he'd taken from the dresser earlier. Going from room to room, he noticed Jade had no photographs. No pictures of herself as a child. No smiling family in frames. No photographs of Nick and her together. There were no photo albums, no shoeboxes filled with happy holiday snaps or hilarious teenage antics. That was it! A girl with no photographs.

How strange. What was she hiding?

6

Lizzie opened her eyes and looked around. It was dark, with no shadows on the walls. She listened for sounds. Nothing. She felt sure she was alone. She reached the edge of the bed, and slid her legs over the padded leather, finding the carpet with her feet. In the darkness, she searched for her clothes. On hands and knees, she scanned the floor with her fingers.

Lizzie had run out of tears. She didn't know how long she had been here. Two days? Three? More? There was no way to tell. Only one thought ran through her mind; she had to get out. Her head bumped against the bedside table. Feeling her way around, she rummaged through the two drawers. Aside from the linings, they were empty. The top was bare; no lamp, no clock. There was another small table on the other side of the bed. That proved fruitless too. She remembered the bathroom; there was a light in there. Still crawling, Lizzie felt along the wall for the doorway.

'Here!' she whispered, as if this discovery was her first victory.

Running her fingers up the wall, she found the light switch. It took several seconds to come on. At first Lizzie thought it was broken, or that he had taken the globe out. Lizzie's eyes hurt with the burst of light. She covered them with her forearm. Gradually she became accustomed to it and put her arm down. Blinking, Lizzie looked around the room.

Aside from being completely black, it was bland. Nothing distinctive at all. No furniture except for the black leather waterbed and its attached side tables. Even the carpet was black. The bathroom was white; white shower, white bathtub, white tiles, white vanity cabinet, a white towel and a bar of white soap. It smelled of antiseptic. Combined, the two rooms looked like part of a chessboard.

'What's that smell?' wondered Lizzie aloud.

The faint aroma reached her nostrils as she approached the sink. She opened cupboards and drawers, unsure what she was looking for. Aside from a few bars of soap, there was nothing there. She didn't recognise the scent, but she remembered that he smelled the same. She shivered involuntarily. He would come back. She didn't know when. Once again she looked around for her things. Her clothes had gone, her handbag too. Even her shoes. She was naked, alone, frightened, and determined to find a way out of this room.

'This is better than nothing,' Lizzie told herself, wrapping a soft bath towel around her cold body.

She walked across the bedroom to the door and tried the handle. As she had suspected, it was locked.

She kicked at the door, screaming for help. It didn't budge. She went to the window and pulled the curtain aside. Three layers of dark glass told her the curtain was just a decoration. She banged her fists on the narrow window, shouting for someone to hear her.

'Help! Please help!'

People in the street below were oblivious to her. Shopkeepers behind thick glass windows couldn't hear her. Nobody knew she was here. She slid to the floor and cried.

'Someone, please. Please help. I want to go home,' she wailed, not feeling nearly as worldly and streetwise as she often behaved.

She promised herself she'd never use a fake ID again. If she got out of here she'd talk to her mother, share her life with the woman she'd ignored for most of the last year. They used to be friends, they could be again. Lizzie didn't know what had changed. She'd been miserable lately. If she could go home, she promised herself, she'd be a teenager, and behave like a fourteen-year-old, instead of trying to be so grown up all the time.

Almost half an hour later, still sobbing and whimpering, Lizzie was exhausted. She picked herself up off the floor and stepped toward the bed. Shuddering with horror, she realised she wasn't willing to lie down on the quilt, no matter how tired she felt. Instead, she walked around the bed on which she had been gagged, tied up, and repeatedly raped. Then, forcing herself to calm down, she ran her hands along the walls, which were also painted black. Near the door she felt one of the panels move. A sliding door. It revealed a large inbuilt wardrobe. The shelves were also painted black. Even with the sliding door open it would have been difficult to see. Inside, a man's suit jacket hung on a wire coat hanger. She put the jacket on over her towel. The rest of the wardrobe was bare. She stepped into the hanging space and sat cross-legged on the carpeted floor. She didn't want to think about where she was or what had happened to her. Instead Lizzie thought about her mother, and how worried she would be.

'I'm sorry, Mum,' whimpered Lizzie. 'I'm so sorry.'

Tears coursed down her cheeks and dripped off her chin. She wiped her nose with the sleeve of the coat. Spent, she leaned against the back of the wardrobe and decided she needed to find a way out. Just before she went to sleep she pulled the door closed with her foot.

At least, she thought, when he comes back he'll think I've gone.

7

'Detective Stonewall! I was told to expect you,' the nurse gushed.

She enjoyed the company of tall, handsome men. Alec had piqued her interest. The nurse charged toward him enthusiastically. In the interests of personal preservation, he tactfully sidestepped.

'There's been no change. She's still sleeping,' continued the nurse, quickly regaining her professional composure.

'Is that normal? Is she okay?'

'Yes, she's fine. We are monitoring her. If anything changes, you'll be the first to know.' Nurse's pale eyelashes batted double-time.

Alec pretended not to notice. 'Can I see her?'

'Of course, come this way. We've moved her to a ward. She'll stay there until she wakes up.'

Beaming, the nurse led him to the ward, her shoes clopping efficiently down the corridor, her ample hips swaying seductively as she moved. Alec followed, careful not to get too close to the vast rump bouncing around like two pigs fighting under a blanket.

As they went into the ward, Alec noticed wires attached to Jade. Green lines blipped and danced on monitors on either side of her head. A drip disappeared under the covers. Her face was angelic.

'What knocked her out?' Alec hoped the cause of Jade's strange coma had finally been diagnosed.

'We don't know, detective. It could have been many things. We're keeping an eye on her heart and her brain. She could wake up any minute, or she could remain unconscious for days, even weeks.'

'She's been out for about fourteen hours now. There's been no change since she was brought in?'

'You know, for a detective investigating a crime, you seem quite concerned about her.' The amorous nurse was put out by his lack of attention.

'I'm also a friend. Here's my number. Please call me the minute anything changes. I'd appreciate it.' Alec gave her a glimpse of his lady-killer smile.

'Sure honey, I'll call you anytime you like …' the nurse smiled, showing a row of crooked teeth, and then winked. He'd astutely given her his office number; the switchboard, not his direct line.

At his desk the next morning, Alec waited impatiently for the phone to ring. It didn't. Jamie Forester came in and sat on his desk.

'My wife loves you.'

'What? Why?' The last thing Alec needed was someone to love him.

'The roses, she loved them. Thanks. I love you, too.' Jamie puckered up and leaned over to kiss the detective.

Alec put up a protective hand. 'Cut the crap. What have you got?'

'The prints on the gun were hers. They were on the bottle and the books, cassettes and records, on the cigarettes and everything else we bagged. They were everywhere. One set of prints. No one was in her house last night. Not until we arrived anyway. She was alone. Whatever she was doing, she was doing it alone. The gun hadn't been fired, the shells were empty, but there was saliva on the barrel; hers. I checked it against the saliva on the bottle.'

'And what is that supposed to mean?'

'Don't kid yourself, Romeo, she had the gun in her mouth.'

'But you just said it wasn't loaded. Maybe she was just mucking around.'

'Maybe. Who knows? When you're that drunk, you might not look to see if empty shells are real bullets. The chamber would look loaded. Maybe she thought it was. Maybe it was a suicide attempt. That would explain the roses. A last tribute to herself.'

'How do you explain the mess?'

'I don't know, Alec. Haven't you asked her?'

'She's still out.'

'Wow! A real live sleeping beauty. Maybe you should hot-tail it down there and give her a kiss, you ugly old frog-prince.'

'Go to hell, Jamie. I've got work to do.'

'Okay, but we did find one thing you might be interested in.'

'What?'

'A bunch of newspaper clippings.'

'Which means?'

'You see, at first I thought she'd ripped up a newspaper. After I matched all the prints, and came to my own conclusion, I was going to throw them out. Then, I took a closer look. All the dates are different. There are about fifty articles. She's obviously been collecting them. I'm putting them back together for you. It's like a complicated jigsaw puzzle. My kind of game. Do you want a squizz?'

'Is the pope a freaking catholic? Of course I want to see them!'

'They'll be done in a few hours. You'd better come to me this time.'

'Sure, I'll come down after lunch. By the way,' Alec lowered his voice, 'is there some way we can lose the gun?'

'Maybe. Leave it with me.'

Alec caught up on his paperwork then went down to Nero's to talk to Jade's boss. Herman was probably the ugliest looking man on the face of the earth. His scarred and pock-marked face resembled a million-year-old lava flow. He'd been burned as a child, then teenage acne had left him a lifelong legacy. A broken, hooked nose and a deep scar across his cheek did nothing to improve the scenery. Built like a concrete outhouse, Herman doubled as security at the bar. He had a permanent 'don't-mess-with-me' expression on his scowling face. Actually, Herman was a lamb trapped in a monster's body. All his staff loved him and had affectionately renamed him Munster. He shouldered the nickname with good humour and ran a tight but friendly ship at Nero's.

Jade hadn't shown up for work last night and Herman was worried. She hadn't called in sick or answered her phone when he called. It wasn't like Jade to disappear. She always said when she needed extra time off.

Herman was happy to see Alec. They had a mutual agreement; when Alec was in the bar, he was off duty. Whatever happened around him was none of his business. Unless, of course, Herman suddenly needed a cop on the premises. In return, Alec was a respected patron and no one ever caused him any trouble. Jade took care of him and he sometimes got discounted drinks. It suited Alec to have a place where he didn't have to be anything but himself. Now, as a detective very much on duty, he gave Herman a brief version of events, editing here and there for Jade's benefit.

'Did you get whoever attacked her?' Herman's eyes narrowed to slits.

'At this stage, there's no evidence to suggest she was attacked. Herman, you leave this to me. Don't do anything dumb, okay. I'll sort it out. Jade will be back on her feet in no time. I'll let you know when she wakes up.'

'Sure, Alec. But if you don't find the mutha-fu—'

'Herman, are you listening to me? She wasn't attacked. What do you know about Jade's family?'

'She's got no family I know of. Never talks about one anyway.'

'What about friends?'

'You know Jade. She keeps to herself. There was a boyfriend a while back. He hasn't been around for a long while.'

'Nick. Yeah, I talked to him. Nice guy. Head over heels in love with her.'

'Yeah. I remember him. He did this to her, did he?' Herman's lip curled in anger. 'You know, revenge or something?'

'No, he didn't hurt her. Did he used to come here?'

'Yeah, every night Jade worked. Just like you …' Herman laughed. 'You're sweet on her too, aren't you?'

Alec ignored the remark. He wasn't sure what it was he felt for Jade.

'Are you going to ask her out?' Herman persisted.

'She deserves better than me. I'm a rotten cop and a broken drunk.'

'She could do worse.' The bar owner patted Alec on the back. 'You could always get off the booze, straighten out a bit.'

'You'd go broke if I did, Herman. I'm your best customer.'

Alec stopped by the hospital on his way to Jamie's lab. Still no change. He stood gazing at Jade while she slept. A stray red curl lay across her cheek. The monitors around her head blipped. The doctor was baffled. She had no injuries, her vitals were normal, and she seemed healthy in every other way. Aside from a little excessive drug and alcohol consumption during a one-night binge, there was nothing wrong with her. All anyone could do was wait until she woke up. She alone had the answers to the mystery. The doctor promised to call the second her condition changed. Alec returned to the station, and descended to the forensics lab.

'Take a look at these.' Jamie had spread the news clippings out on the worktable.

He'd painstakingly taped the jagged pieces of each article back together. They were laid out in chronological order. Dating back five years, Jade had kept over fifty articles from various newspapers around the district. The last one was dated two days ago; the day her world had gone pear-shaped.

'How is Carl Rutherford connected to Jade Randall?' Jamie asked.

'I don't know. There must be a link. Why else would she keep all this stuff? I'll check out his rap sheet.'

Jamie scanned the clippings. Carl Rutherford was the subject of each article. Rutherford was a king of the construction industry with a string of prominent neoclassical-style buildings to his credit all over the country. Hailed as an innovative leader in modern construction, he had been awarded various industry prizes for his innovative ideas and unusual concepts. He had a large collection of trophies and commendations lining his office wall. The fifty-four year old builder had enjoyed a long, distinguished career. Photos of Rutherford with his family graced many of the tearsheets. In others, Rutherford stood next to mayors, puffed up politicians, and a vast range of tagalong VIP's and beautiful people. Rutherford was a pillar of society. He gave to charity, sponsored sports teams, owned racehorses. He had fancy houses all over the place. Nice cars, nice boats, nice toys. The guy was rolling in money. This wasn't a picture Jade fitted into. She was so far removed from Rutherford's scene that Alec couldn't even imagine her in it. It didn't make sense.

'Here, Alec, check this out. This was about two years ago.' Jamie handed one of the articles over.

Alec skimmed over the words. 'Acquitted on a rape charge. The girl was a drug addict, a prostitute, hooking to pay for her habit.'

'Doesn't mean he didn't do it,' snorted Jamie, the original skeptic.

'Wait. Where's that other one?' Alec looked over the pile of clippings that had been taped together.

'Here.' Jamie picked it up. 'It's dated five days ago. Rutherford was questioned, but not charged, over a rape. The girl was fifteen at the time of the alleged offences. She'd be nineteen now. According to his PR people, it's another hoax by some bimbo to squeeze money out of him.'

'So Rutherford could be a rapist. He likes them young, and he has enough money to beat the rap. I still don't see the connection with Jade.'

'Ask her. She must have a reason for collecting this stuff.'

'I wish. I've just come from the hospital. She's still down for the count.'

'I'm not surprised. She drank enough bourbon to knock out a herd of elephants for a week. Not to mention the cocaine.' The scientist looked over his spectacles at the detective, his lips pursed.

Alec scanned the clipping again to avoid Jamie's piercing gaze. 'What about the gun? Can we lose it?'

'Yep. No problem. I haven't officially logged it. I've checked it out. It's not connected to any other crimes. I couldn't trace any other owners or licences for it. None of the dealers have touched it. The serial numbers have been scratched off. It's a ghost. It came out of thin air.'

'Well, let's put it back into thin air, shall we? I don't think Miss Randall will need it. I'd still like to know where she got it.'

'Sure. I'll dump it in the river on my way home. I've wiped the prints.'

'I'll run a sheet on Rutherford and let you know what I find,' Alec said, and headed back to his desk.

Carl Rutherford. The name flickered on the computer screen.

Alec waited for the Soundex data to be collected. A few seconds later, he scanned the information. Two arrests for rape. He got off both times. Aside from that, Rutherford was clean as a whistle. Too clean.

'No one with that much money is that clean,' muttered Alec, addressing the computer. 'He probably pays some lackey to pick up after him.'

Alec dug deeper. Rutherford's wife, Julia, and his son, Robert, were clean. No criminal records. Everything above board.

'Hogwash! No one is that spic and span.'

Alec had a gut feeling he'd find something if he looked hard enough. There had to be a connection between Rutherford and Jade Randall.

He did another check. Jade Randall. Nothing. She didn't exist. He tried again and found a Juanita Randall. All the stats fitted. He checked out Juanita. No criminal record. Arrested at an anti-nuclear protest, but not charged. Arrested at a protest for detained refugees. A car crash a few years back; t-boned a delivery van after she ran a red light. Alec remembered Jade talking about it just after they met. So, Jade was Juanita. Interesting. He read the last two sentences. A couple of speeding fines. Jade was the type of clean you'd expect from the average citizen.

Alec had reached the outer limits of his computer skills. He called Ryland Thomas, the police computer geek who could detect stains in your grandmother's underpants if he had the right software. A little harmless hacking was one of his hobbies.

The phone rang half an hour later.

'Alec! Piece of cake. Julia Rutherford is Juliana Randall. Get this, Jade Randall is Juanita Randall. Apparently, she changed her name at high school, though not in any official capacity. Does she really have emerald green eyes? She's gorgeous!' He let out a short whistle. Alec waited impatiently, rolling his eyes but saying nothing. Ryland continued, 'Juanita vanished off the face of the earth when she was sixteen. Jade turned up in the city a few months later and went to work.' Alec was all ears. 'Anyway, baby Juanita lost both parents to a car accident when she was an infant. They were Maria and Steve Randall. He's Juliana Randall's brother. Aunt Juliana raised the orphaned kid. Then, Juliana married Carl Rutherford and changed her name to Julia. They had a son, Robert. He's five years younger than Jade. So, Carl Rutherford would be Jade's uncle and Robert would be her cousin. She probably thought they were her real parents and Robert was her little brother when she was a kid. She kept her own last name, Randall. It's all there in black and white. By the way, Julia is Rutherford's second wife. First one died almost thirty years ago.'

'Thanks, Ryland. I owe you one.'

'My pleasure. This chick is one hot lady ... she can toast my crumpets anytime—' Alec hung up before Ryland finished his wolf whistle.

Alec began putting all the pieces together. Uncle Carl was filthy rich, but Jade lived in a dumpy apartment building on the west side. Why? Did she run away? Did he throw her out? None of Jade's friends knew she had family. She never talked about them. Why? And why did she change her name? Was it because of Rutherford? Why did she collect all those newspaper clippings? Had the rape article set her off? Was it something else? Had she tried to kill herself or was she just playing around with an unloaded gun? Why did she trash her own place? There was only one person who could answer his questions. Alec headed back to the hospital.

8

When Jade opened her eyes, the first thing she saw was the sheer white curtain billowing in the breeze. Warm rays of sunlight shone onto her face. Her body felt light. Everything was white and fuzzy. She thought she'd woken up in heaven, after all. The room was eerily quiet.

Finally, she thought, I've made it.

'Welcome back, sleeping beauty.'

She turned her head at the familiar voice. Alec was there. How strange. For a surreal moment, she wondered how he had died. It seemed odd that they were in heaven together. Smiling, she was reaching out to touch him when she saw the tube coming out of her arm. There are no tubes in heaven. Shocked, she sat up and stared at Alec.

'I'm not dead, am I?'

'No, Jade, you're not dead,' he replied, relieved she'd finally come back. He'd been coming and going for three days, monitoring her progress.

'Aargh! I wanted to be dead!'

'There are people around who don't want you to be dead.'

'Yeah, right. Like who?'

'Like me ... And Herman ...'

Jade rolled her eyes. She glanced around the white room. She looked again at the tube in her arm, registered the sticky patches and wire dotted across her chest and the machines blipping near her head. She realised she was in a hospital bed.

Damn! She cursed mentally. I thought I'd succeeded this time. Everything had seemed so right. Why me?

'What do you care, Alec?'

'Jade, I want to know what happened.'

'Oh, go away! Leave me alone! Why can't I just die and get it over with?'

Jade turned over to face the window, rattling the bed, but Alec didn't leave. He considered alerting the hospital staff that she'd woken, but decided against it. They'd come in good time. Instead, he scraped a chair across the floor and, with a sigh, sat down.

Jade's thoughts went around in circles. *How did I manage to stuff this up? I had the gun, the bourbon, the coke. My bloody head doesn't even hurt. Damn it! How can you fire a gun into your mouth and not wake up with a sore head? How the hell does anyone wake up after that? I'm probably the only loser on earth who can't shoot straight into the back of my own head. I'm such an idiot.*

Then, she remembered. It hadn't gone off when she pulled the trigger. Jade let the tears roll down her face.

'Jade, I'm not going away. I want you to talk to me.'

Jade ignored Alec. She figured he'd go away when he needed a drink. She lay still under the sheets, gathering her defences.

'Aaah! Miss Randall, awake at last. Did you have a good sleep?'

Jade ignored the doctor. He strode over to the bed and stood in front of the window, looking down his huge nose at his reluctant patient. He inspected the beeping machines before checking her vitals and then made a few notes on her chart. She didn't know how the doctor felt, but for her it was loathe at first sight.

'Everything looks fine. You slept off your wild night and no doubt caught up on a bit of extra rest. You can get dressed and go anytime. I'll have nurse unhook you and bring the discharge papers.'

'Are you making me leave?' Surely the doctor couldn't make her leave, she thought.

'Miss Randall,' the doctor began curtly, 'this is a hospital. It's a place for sick people. You are neither sick nor injured. Now, if you need a rehab centre I can give you a number to call. If you don't have a home to go to and want a hotel, I can get you a phone book. Right now, I need your bed. There are sick people right outside that door who are in need of medical attention.'

'Screw you!'

'No, thank you, Miss Randall, I don't have time.' He turned to leave, his face impassive. 'The nurse will be here soon.'

Five minutes later, Jade was dressed, discharged, and on the street. Alec had said nothing while the nurses shuffled around the room, humming and unhooking. Jade had signed the papers they shoved in front of her and stalked out of the room. Alec was right behind her. She said nothing when he caught up and walked by her side. They marched down the corridor together toward the front door.

'I'll give you a ride home,' he said.

'Damn it, Alec! Why does my life suck so badly?'

'Maybe it wouldn't suck so much if you shared the crap around a little.'

'YOU are telling ME to share? Ha ha! That's funny! Besides, what's to share?'

'Nick told me you had plenty to share. He said you were a great girl.'

'You saw Nick?' She stopped dead and gaped at him.

She couldn't believe it. Alec had seen Nick. Why? What could they possibly have to talk about? Bloody meddlers! Why couldn't Alec mind his own business?

She clamped her lips shut and continued toward the door. As they emerged, Alec led her through the car park. They climbed into Alec's car and drove through the busy streets. Traffic was awful; everyone was going home from work. Jade didn't want to talk to Alec about Nick. Or about anything else. Nick had been the love of her life. She still missed him. He'd wanted to marry her and turn her into a respectable woman. He just couldn't see ...

Jade knew herself better than anyone. She was damaged goods. A total psycho. Who knows what would have happened. She would have destroyed him. Nick didn't need her in his life, screwing it all up. He had everything going for him and he'd chosen a scumbag like her. Why? There are so many nice girls, beautiful girls, normal girls.

Why me? she'd often thought. He could have gone out with anyone. Was it pity?

She couldn't trust the love. It was too intense. Too close. It had scared her. When she was little, people had told her they loved her.

And then they had hurt her. How can you trust love? She was terrified of getting hurt. She was terrified he'd find out about her. About who she was. Who she is now. She was sure he'd have thrown her away like garbage if he'd known. She had to do it first. Sending him away had hurt so much. Still hurt.

She hadn't seen Nick since that terrible night at Nero's when she'd asked Herman to make him leave. She remembered the look on his face, his broken heart. She'd cried herself to sleep for weeks afterward. It was the second most painful thing that had ever happened to her. Nick was probably married to someone else by now. Someone who deserved him. A twinge of pain pierced her heart. She would always love Nick.

'A penny for them,' whispered Alec.

'I wouldn't tell you what I was thinking if you gave me a million dollars,' she sneered.

'Jade, your attitude stinks. That's probably why your life sucks.'

'Who the hell are you to say that? I'd say your life sucks too, don't ya think?'

'Jade, gimme a break. I'm here as a friend as well as a cop. Just tell me what happened.'

'No! Go to hell.'

Alec was fed up. He didn't need Jade to make his life more difficult. He was already living on the edge. His eyes narrowed. He clenched his jaws. Okay, he decided, if this is how she wants to play …

'Fine!' he retorted. 'I'm gonna go to hell. And here's what else I'm gonna do. I'm gonna hand it over to the drug squad. And I'm gonna give them the gun. Unlicenced, numbers scratched off. Five shells in it. Your prints on it. I'm gonna give them the cocaine I found in your kitchen drawer. I'm gonna tell them you have a big mouth, a lousy attitude, and a little brain and I'm gonna go home and get some sleep.'

'What do you mean?' Jade turned to face him.

Finally, he had her attention. 'I mean, Jade, that this is a police matter and there are consequences. You're looking at two years for possession of an unlicenced weapon and probably another ten for the dope, depending on the common purity ratio. If you're lucky, the judge will sentence concurrently. You'll score free lodgings at the Grey-Bar Hotel for a decade. Never mind, it's not really as bad as they say. Are we done? Here's your street.' He didn't even feel guilty about the exaggeration.

'What are you talking about? Do you mean prison?'

'No doofus! I mean Club Med! What do you bloody think?' He pulled up in front of her apartment building.

'But … why?'

'You're in trouble, Jade. You don't wanna play with me, fine. I can live with that. I'll hand your case to someone else.' He shrugged indifferently.

'I'm a police case?'

'Hello! Good morning! Yes! You are a police case!'

'But, why?' she asked again, aware she was beginning to sound like a five-year-old.

'Because, you idiot, your neighbours called the police when they heard you screaming. Because when the police arrived, there was an unlicenced gun on the scene, and illegal substances. Because you were unconscious when we arrived …'

'We?'

'Yes, we,' he said, his voice tinny with fury. 'I was first through the door. It was me who found you unconscious on the floor. I thought you were dead. You have no idea—' He paused a moment, recalling the wave of emotion that had overcome him at the sight of her sprawled on the floor. 'And because, Jade, while you've been floating around in fairyland, there are people investigating this incident.'

'Who? The police?'

'No, the freaking Marx Brothers! Of course, the police. So far, it's just me and a trusted colleague. But since you won't talk to me, I'm handing it over. Now, will you get out of my car? I'm tired and I wanna go home.'

Jade needed to think about these revelations for a second. She didn't want to go to prison. Alec was glaring angrily, waiting for her to get out of his car. Her gut told her not to blow him off. He would take care of her, no matter what happened. In a way, she'd known that for years. She'd been hiding for too long. It was time to come clean. At least a little. She may as well talk to Alec; there was no one else to tell. Besides, she decided, she didn't have to tell him everything. Right now, he was her best friend.

'Alec?'

'What?' he snapped, impatient to get home.

'Um … okay. Look, sorry. Come upstairs.'

'Why? So you can jerk me around some more?' He wasn't buying her instant soft touch.

'No, so we can talk. I'll tell you what happened.'

'No nonsense?' He was still suspicious.

'No nonsense,' she promised, sincerely.

She looked him in the eye. Whatever she told Alec would have to be the truth. He'd know if she was lying. She just had to decide what bits of the truth she wanted to tell him. She'd pissed him off and that wasn't good. Knowing him, he'd probably taken some risks for her. Alec followed her up the stairs. Jade opened the door and let him in. She tossed him a placating smile. Scowling, he plopped on the sofa. He still looked sullen when she brought him a mug of coffee.

'Okay, talk. I'm listening.'

Alec was an attractive man. He was tall with broad shoulders and taut biceps. Despite three years of alcohol abuse he still looked reasonably fit. Dark, curly hair framed his square face. He had gentle hazel eyes which revealed the sadness in his heart. He didn't smile much but, on the rare occasions he did, he had a great smile. A real lady-killer grin. The dimple in his chin was more prominent when he was angry.

It was difficult for Jade to look at Alec and see a policeman. She'd never experienced that side of him. Now here he was, telling her she could go to prison if she didn't tell him what had happened on Sunday night. It was surreal. Alec the drunk could save her life. She wanted to laugh. It seemed absurd. He sat on the chair opposite, his jaw working. He looked irritated and impatient. Out of the blue, Alec the drunk had vanished and a new man had taken his place. Alec the cop was clean-shaven and had neat hair. He spoke with authority and had good posture. His presence was commanding. It demanded respect. Alec the cop was a completely different person to the Alec she knew. She was surprised to discover she liked him.

'Jade, I don't have all night,' he said harshly.

'I know, I'm sorry. I was just thinking that it's usually me serving you. Now you're here, as a cop, trying to help me. Isn't that a little weird to you?'

'Yeah, it's very weird.' Alec sounded bored. 'Now cut the crap and talk to me before I call Inspector Rowland.'

9

'Stupid woman! What was she thinking?' Jamie blurted angrily. Jade's failed suicide attempt had hit him close to home. On top of that, all this overtime was eroding the frayed threads of his fragile marriage.

'I don't know,' sighed Alec. 'I haven't got the whole story yet.'

'It's not surprising, really, considering she worships the dead.' Alec shot Jamie a look. 'The posters in her apartment. All of them are dead. It's like she's got some kind of death wish. Die young, leave a pretty corpse ...'

'She does,' Alec agreed.

Alec scratched his head. Jade had completely confused him. As he'd left her apartment, he'd made her promise to call if she felt suicidal again. He'd taken the drugs from the bathroom cabinet, but there was a knife in the kitchen. Walking to his car, he'd felt nervous. He'd had barely any sleep. First thing in the morning, he'd called to see if she was alive. She'd been asleep when the phone rang, and was annoyed he'd woken her up. He was happy that she was peeved. That meant she was still breathing. Alec arrived at work with a smile on his face.

Jamie and Alec were reading over the newspaper articles again. Jade had told Alec how she had tried to kill herself, but not why. She hadn't checked the gun to see if it was loaded. The empty cartridges had fooled her. When the gun clicked the first time and nothing happened, Jade had tried again. She'd pulled the trigger six times and then gone berserk with rage, tearing her house apart and screaming at the top of her lungs until she'd collapsed. The combination of bourbon, cocaine, stress, shock, terror and rage had knocked her out for a few days.

'It's got something to do with this stuff. Somehow Carl Rutherford is a part of the puzzle.' Alec sucked on the end of his pen and stared at the tiny black dots on the photo of Carl.

'Did Jade admit to knowing him?' asked Jamie.

'I didn't get that far.' Alec shrugged. 'She's a hard nut to crack.'

'What about the police report?'

'I talked to the uniforms. Domestic disturbance. It's been dealt with.'

'So, the police work is over?'

'The department has seen all they need to see. The evidence for a suicide attempt no longer exists. They're satisfied, case closed. But I'm not finished. I want to find out what made her crazy like that.'

'Have you asked Rutherford?'

'No. I'm steering clear until Jade tells me something about him.'

'My gut tells me there's a connection between these articles about the rape cases and Jade flipping out.'

'Her ex-boyfriend mentioned she'd been abused.'

'Really?' Jamie nodded thoughtfully. 'What's the bet Uncle Carl had something to do with that?'

'Maybe. So, what do you think?' Alec speculated. 'He abused her. She ran away from home and changed her name. She tried to have a normal life, then started collecting newspaper articles about him and his success. Then, one day she reads about the rape of another woman and sees he's gotten away with it, so she goes nuts?'

'I'm only guessing, but yeah, something like that. It would make sense.'

'Let me see that first article. Look at the date. Two years ago. That's about the same time she broke off with her boyfriend. He said she flipped out and went off the rails and he hasn't seen her since.'

'This is dated last week. She went berserk on the weekend. It adds up.'

'As far as we all know she has no family; the people she works with, her boss, her ex, even me. She has no photographs, no mementos. It's like everything that isn't in her life today has been erased, except these newspaper clippings.' Alec gestured at the table.

'You see? There's another clue. Time to bring in the big guns I reckon.'

'What big guns?'

'Lazarowitz. She could talk to her and maybe get a statement.'

'Lazarowitz? Debra Lazarowitz would chew Jade up and spit her out before breakfast. Besides, the police report—'

'Alec, Jade Randall clearly has a big problem. From everything we've uncovered so far, it looks to me like this problem started a long time ago. Maybe she needs to confide in another woman.'

Detective Senior Sergeant Debra Lazarowitz was not Alec's idea of another woman. She had more balls than a football team and enough testosterone to supply an army battalion. A marshall arts expert, Debra could kill with her bare hands and exuded more macho than Rambo. He secretly called her Pointy McNipples.

'Jamie, you are kidding. Debra Lazarowitz is not another woman. That's like sending King Kong to peel a banana when it can be done by a chimp.'

'She has a degree in psychology. She's a sexual assault counsellor, and she has the best record for miles around for her success in getting victims to open up. She's also got a spotless reputation for getting a slice of justice for the victims.'

'Even though she breathes fire?'

'She's a specialist in this field, Alec. She's one of the best.'

'Okay, but I want some more time with Jade first.'

'You devil, you! I knew you had a thing for her!'

'Don't be a creep, Jamie. I can't go to Lazarowitz with a handful of hunches. I'll need something solid. Jade is the only one who can tell me what's going on. I'll go talk to her again.'

After work, Alec drove over to Jade's house. She wasn't expecting him.

'What do you want?'

You, Alec thought, but he didn't dare say it. The idea of it frightened him. He wasn't even sure that was what he really wanted.

Jade wasn't pleased to see Alec so soon after the previous night's humiliating confession. She'd cried on his shoulder and blurted out everything about getting drunk and putting the gun in her mouth. She'd refused to tell him why she did it, and clammed up when he asked about her family. After he left, she'd promised she wouldn't try to hurt herself and then spent the night pottering around her flat, trying to put her little home back together. When she realised all the newspaper clippings were gone, she crawled into bed and cried herself to sleep. She assumed the police must have thrown them away, thinking they weren't important, not realising what they were. They were the only link she had to her childhood. The only connection she had with her past. She didn't entirely understand why she needed to keep this link alive, but it had been important to her. Now it was gone. And Alec was back, standing in her doorway and grinning like he'd just gotten away with a major crime.

'I want to talk to you,' he said.

'We talked last night,' she replied.

'Yes, we did. And now we're going to talk a little more.'

'Why?'

'Because there is more to your story and I want to hear it.'

'What if I don't want to tell it?'

'Then, you can tell it to the drug squad.'

'That's blackmail!' Jade's eyes flashed angrily.

'Call it whatever you like.' Alec shrugged.

Alec stepped through the door and made himself comfortable on Jade's sofa. She stood holding the door open, staring over her shoulder, aghast at his effrontery. Jade wasn't to know that Alec had flushed her cocaine stash down his toilet, or that the gun had vanished forever. Dealing with the police frightened her, but as long as it was Alec she had to deal with, and no one else, she could handle it. Jade knew he would do his best to keep her out of trouble. She shut the door and walked over. Standing in front of him, she glared and curled her lip in a mock display of rage.

'Sit down!' Alec knew she was faking and laughed. 'Now, what kind of pizza do you want? My treat.'

'Vegetarian. I don't eat animals.'

'I'm so relieved. For a minute there I thought you were going to chew my butt!' Alec grinned and picked up the phone. He chatted his day until the pizza arrived. Jade said little, but laughed at his jokes. They ate in silence for a while, until Jade got up to get a drink.

'Bourbon?'

'No, thanks, I'm on the wagon.'

'Really? Are you?' Jade was surprised.

'I haven't had a drink since Monday.'

'Wow! Five whole days! I haven't been at work for five days. Do you think that's a coincidence? Aren't the others good enough to serve you?' She was being sarcastic.

'I've decided to get my act together. I'm serious. I'll have a soda.'

'Okay, in that case forget the bourbon. I'll have a soda too.'

Jade put on a Doors CD. She sat eating pizza and sipping soda for a while, looking over at Alec, trying to figure him out.

Who was he now, Alec the drunk, or Alec the cop? Neither. Tonight's Alec was different to those guys. He'd come disguised as Alec the man.

'How can one man be so many different people?' she asked.

'What do you mean?'

'Well, until last night you were just Alec the drunk, and then you turned up at the hospital as Alec the cop. Tonight, unless I'm mistaken, it seems you're Alec the man. It confuses me. Who are you now?'

'Who do you want me to be?'

'I want you to be you, and I want to know who you are.'

'Fair enough. Well, I'm me. Alec the … I don't know. What about Alec the friend?'

'Friend? Friends don't blackmail each other.'

'Not usually, unless they really have to, for their friend's personal safety.'

Alec liked the idea of being Jade's friend. It meant there was no pressure; he could be himself. Friend. He liked that word. He liked the way it made him feel. As Jade's friend he felt comfortable and relaxed. It was pleasant.

'Friend, huh? So a drunken, washed-out cop wants to be my friend?'

Jade liked that too. She didn't have many friends. She had always liked Alec, but they'd never talked like this before. If he ever tried to hit on her she would punch him all the way to Antarctica.

'Yeah. Why not? Friends?' Alec stretched his hand out toward Jade. She took it in hers and they shook hands as friends. He was her first real friend. She had a warm feeling about it.

'Talk to me, Jade. Tell me why you want to die so badly.'

'Oh! Straight for the jugular! Let's not waste any time getting to know each other.'

'Jade, I've known you for three years. You know just about everything there is to know about me, including all the crap you wish you never knew. Call it occupational hazard if you like. After all this time, everything I know about you could fit in this bottle cap. So, talk to me.'

Jade was afraid. She'd been hiding herself for years. No one knew who she was or where she'd come from. She was just Jade, take it or leave it. Most of the people she knew didn't even know her last name. She liked it that way. Anonymity was an asset. Now she was being asked to give it up.

'Um … What do you want to hear?'

'Start with telling me why you are so determined to die.'

'My parents died when I was a baby. I never knew them. My Aunt Julia brought me up. For a long time I thought she was my mother, but … Wait a minute! You know all this stuff! You're a cop. You must have looked it up when I was in hospital!'

'I'm a techno-dumbo. Not good with computers—'

'But you have colleagues who are—'

'Okay, yeah,' he admitted. 'I looked up some stuff, but nothing in the records told me why you want to die. Stop stalling, Jade, fess up.'

Jade took a deep breath. Gathering strands of courage from her deepest reserves of strength, she wasn't sure if she could put it into words. Terrified he might reject her, a knot of tangled thoughts whirled around in Jade's mind as she tried to figure out what to say. Instinctively, she felt she could trust Alec. Breathing slowly, trying to stay calm and clear-headed, Jade labored to find the words.

Alec could see she was struggling with it. He waited, knowing it would come when she was ready. He tried to look encouraging and supportive, but was positive he looked as if he was badly constipated.

He figured Jamie's theory had a ring of truth in it and if it was true, he could understand her desperation to keep it to herself. As he waited for Jade to speak, he decided it was time for both of them to come out and face the world and its demons. It would do them both good to get the past out into the open. Maybe after that, the elusive happiness they both seemed to be searching for wouldn't feel like such an impossible dream, after all.

'He got away with it,' Jade whispered.

Alec almost didn't hear it. It took him a moment to understand what she'd said. Looking over at her, he was shocked to see she looked like a frightened little girl. The Jade he knew was self-assured and confident. This was a side of Jade he'd never seen.

'Who got away with what, Jade?'

'He raped those girls. I know he did. He raped them and then he made them look like liars. He got away with it.'

'Who did? Who got away with it?' Alec knew what she was going to say. He needed to hear it from her.

'Uncle Carl. He did it. I know he did. He …'

Tears streamed down Jade's face. She couldn't speak. Alec's heart broke for her. He reached over to stroke her hair.

'It's okay, no one is going to hurt you. You can tell me about it. Tell me what he did.'

Alec felt helpless. In the face of his own pain he had turned to bourbon, but when someone else was hurting, he was lost. He reached out his arms and put them around Jade's shoulders.

'He … um … he …' Jade leapt into his arms and cried into his shoulder.

Alec felt awkward. He stroked her hair and tried to comfort her. She sobbed for a few minutes and he let her cry.

'It's okay. Everything's going to be okay.'

Jade mumbled something into his damp shirt. Alec couldn't hear what she was saying.

'Jade, tell me again. What did he do?'

'He raped me.'

Alec's jaw clenched tightly shut. He couldn't believe his ears.

She curled up into a ball with her head on his lap and sobbed uncontrollably. Alec patted her back and tried to think of something to say that wouldn't sound dumb. Half an hour later, she was still crying and he hadn't thought of anything to say.

10

Ryland Thomas was waiting for Alec when he arrived at the station.

'I've got something you might be interested in.'

'Great, whaddya got?'

'I've been doing some digging around,' began Ryland.

'Obviously we're not giving you enough to do down there ...' Alec suggested, cheekily.

Ryland pulled a face. 'Maria and Steve Randall died when Jade was ten months old. They'd only been married a few weeks before the accident. Steve Randall was not Jade's biological father. Maria and Steve had applied for legal adoption, but they died before it was finalised. Maria's father, Devereaux, kicked the bucket a few weeks after his daughter. Steve's parents didn't want anything to do with a baby that wasn't his. So, Jade went to his sister who was estranged from the family. The Randalls made up later, around the same time Julia married Rutherford.'

'Ah ... So Julia Rutherford isn't her aunt. Then, who is Jade's father?'

'David Rivers. Here's a copy of Jade's—or rather Juantita's—birth certificate. It appears Rivers was getting ready to marry Maria when her father showed up with his shotgun and scared him off. There was an injunction taken out against the father, but Rivers never saw Maria again. He joined the army and went to Vietnam.'

'Did he make it home alive?'

'Oh yeah, he's alive,' Ryland answered, fidgeting with his pen.

'What are the chances David Rivers doesn't know he has a daughter?'

'Pretty good, I'd say.'

'Do we know where he is now?'

'Yeah ...' Ryland hated to be the bearer of bad tidings.

'That doesn't sound encouraging.'

'It isn't. He's in prison.'

Alec sighed and shut his eyes, pinching the bridge of his nose. 'For?'

Ryland grimaced. 'Attempted murder.'

'Damn!' Alec slapped his hand on the desk. He couldn't believe Jade's luck. She had clearly been in the queue for charm and good looks when they were handing out the functional families. 'Well, let's look on the bright side. Until a few minutes ago, Jade didn't even have a father. Where is he? I'll go and have a chat.'

Ryland handed the notes over and turned to leave. 'You want me to check him out before you go out there?'

'Yeah, that would be useful. Hey! Thanks, man, you've been a great help. I appreciate it.' Alec grinned at him, and picked up the phone.

Alec drove three hours to reach the state prison, a bleak grey building, with bare fields spread out around it, in the middle of nowhere. He wondered if they were mine fields no one ever lived to talk about. That would explain why no one had ever successfully escaped from this prison.

The detective followed routine security procedures and was taken to an interview room. He waited ten minutes before the prisoner appeared.

'Mister Rivers.' Alec was struck by the resemblance. There was no mistaking Jade's father.

'Who are you?'

'I'm Detective Alec Stonewall. I want to talk to you about something that happened over twenty-six years ago.'

'Twenty-six years? I was in Vietnam.'

'Before that.'

'What do you want, Mister Detective?' David Rivers tensed, ready for a fight. He didn't want to remember the past. Deep-seated anger covered his pain and he liked it like that. He didn't see the point of dragging ancient history out of its catacomb. It was best left buried.

'Mister Rivers, I have some news for you. I don't know if it's good or bad, that will depend on you, but I came here to tell you in person.'

'Tell me what?' Rivers screwed his eyes up and glared suspiciously at Alec. The last thing he needed today was more bad news. His cellmate was being released this afternoon and he would be getting a new one.

'You have a daughter, Mister Rivers.'

'I what …?' David Rivers' jaw hit the floor. He stared at Alec in shock. Of all the things that could have been said, this was the last thing he'd ever expected to hear.

'You have a daughter.'

'What …? Who …? When …?' David's mind spun in circles. He dug around in his memory, going back twenty-six years. 'Are you sure?'

'Well, we'll need DNA samples and tests to be one hundred percent certain, but yes, I'm sure.'

David sat staring at the detective. Unexpected tears welled in his eyes. Alec was pleased he hadn't brought bad news. He'd been afraid Rivers would reject the idea and tell him to take a hike.

'Does she know about me?'

'Not yet. I haven't told her.'

'You know her?'

'Yes, Mister Rivers, I know her quite well. We're friends. I've known her for about three years.'

'What's she like?'

'She's … Well, she's lovely. She has your red hair and green eyes.'

'Really? She looks like me?' The war veteran and prison-hardened man visibly softened at the thought of a female version of himself.

'Yes, she does. She has your temper too; she's quite fiery.'

'What happened to her … her mother?'

'Her mother was Maria Devereaux.'

'Yes, Maria.' David sighed. 'Where is she? What happened to her?'

'She died, Mister Rivers. Almost twenty-five years ago. It was a car accident. Your daughter survived the crash and was taken in by her husband's family.'

'No! Maria is gone?' David shut his eyes for a moment and thought about the only woman who had ever captured his heart. He subconsciously smiled as memories of his lost love flooded back.

After Devereaux had chased him out of town, he'd joined up and was sent to Nui Dat almost immediately. After two hard tours in jungles thickly sprayed with Agent Orange, he'd returned home an angry, bitter man and started drinking. The measly pension the army gave him had kept him barely alive, and he'd wandered from town to town doing odd jobs here and there. Whenever he got restless, he packed up and moved on. He'd never tried to find Maria. She'd been the love of his life, but he figured she didn't deserve what Vietnam had done to him. He'd stayed away. When Maria had suggested they get married, he hadn't known she was pregnant. His last memory of her was when Devereaux was chasing him with the hunting rifle, taking pot shots at his feet. Maria had been running behind her father in tears, begging him to stop.

'I'm sorry to bring bad news,' Alec said sympathetically. 'Can I ask you something?'

'What?'

'How did you end up here?'

'I got in a fight in a bar one night. Some smart-mouthed guy started it and I finished it. He accused me of trying to kill him. I didn't have enough money to defend myself properly and copped five years for attempted murder. That sleaze-bucket paid everyone in town to testify against me. Somehow he dug up all my service records and convinced the jury I was a trained killer. I didn't have a chance. I guess that's what happens when you give the mayor's son a well-deserved kick in the butt. I'll be out in nine months with any luck.'

'Well, Mister Rivers, I think your luck may have just changed. I'll see what I can do to get you out of here.'

'You'd do that?'

'Sure. Why not? It's about time you and your daughter had a real life.'

'Is she in some kind of trouble?'

'Not exactly. All I can tell you right now is that she's had a rough time. We're in the process of working it out and she'll be fine. I think she'll need all the support she can get. That's why I came to you.'

'So why are the police involved?'

'They're not. Not officially, anyway. I'm her friend. I got in here to see you because I'm a cop, but I came to see you as her friend.'

'Do you think I'll be able to see her?'

'Mister Rivers, she doesn't know about you yet. I'm going to tell her, but I'll need a little time. I can't tell you how she'll react. I'm hoping she'll be her father's daughter,' Alec grinned, 'but I can't be sure. In the meantime, I'm going to get someone working on getting you out of here. You seem like a decent guy to me. Is there anything I should know about before I set you free?'

'Nah. I'm clean and dry. I dried out in solitary when I first got here and I'm not into drugs. I've been working out to stay in shape and I'm studying agriculture. I thought it might be good to find myself a quiet little farm somewhere.'

'Rivers, I mean are you making any plans to hunt down and kill the mayor's son when you get out? I'm not about to put my butt on the line for a time-wasting loser.'

David Rivers smiled, then laughed out loud. 'Now that would be real justice! No. I wouldn't piss on that rat if he was on fire. I'm not going out of my way to land back in here any time soon. No, detective, I'm not planning to take revenge on the deadbeat who put me here. God will take care of him in His own time. I was planning to go and live on the land. Quietly. Alone. No trouble.'

'Okay, as long as we understand each other.'

'I think we do.'

'Good. I have to go. If you need anything, just call,' Alec handed the man his card.

'I'll do that. And thanks.'

'It's nothing.' Alec hated gratitude, it made him uncomfortable.

'Detective Stonewall, it's not nothing. You just changed my life. You came in here out of the blue and made a most amazing difference. That means something. Thank you.'

'I'll see you again, soon.'

On the drive back to town, Alec wondered what Jade would say about her newfound father. He tried to imagine how she would react to the news. He imagined her punching his lights out and diving head-first into denial. Then, he imagined her thrilled at the news, eager to see her father and learn about his life, grateful to Alec for finding him. David Rivers had taken it surprisingly well. Alec was pleased with his positive reaction. He hoped Rivers' daughter would follow suit. She'd grown up thinking her parents were dead. Now she had a father she hadn't even known existed. Alec drove, wondering how he would feel given news like that. Now, he had to go and tell Jade.

11

Jade called Herman to tell him she'd be back at work in a few days. She needed some time to sort her head out. Alec had been great. He'd stayed with her all night, patting her back and letting her cry. At first she was terrified to tell him anything, but he'd been so gentle. He sat and listened to her, not judgemental, not full of advice, just listening, hearing her words. The pain had come flooding back and she couldn't stop the tears. She hadn't cried like that since she was a child. It was cathartic; as if she'd taken a huge load off her shoulders. Alec was right. It was time for them both to get their act together.

If he can do it, then so can I, she thought.

They'd made a pact; as long as he wasn't going to have a drink, she wasn't going to think of ways to kill herself. It was a start. Jade was taping her books back together when the doorbell rang. She assumed it would be Alec. He'd said he would come around after work.

'Hi.'

Jade stood staring at Nick. He was holding a bunch of flowers; daisies and roses peppered with baby's breath. Her heart stopped. She couldn't speak. She stared dumbfounded at the colourful bouquet.

'I wanted to see you,' he said smiling, 'Detective Stonewall told me you weren't well.'

'I … um … I'm … I'm fine.'

'Jade, I'm not going to bite you. I just wanted to see if you were okay. Are you going to let me in or should I go?'

'No. I mean, um … don't go. Come in.'

'Thanks. Here, these are for you.'

Jade had no idea what to say. It had been two years since they broke up. Since she broke up with him. Since she'd abruptly thrown him out of her life and wouldn't let him back. She figured he'd have moved on by now.

'You look great,' she said, taking the flowers.

Damn! she thought, I look like hell on a stick. The best looking man in town comes to visit and I'm the wreck of the Hesperus. She grimaced involuntarily.

Nick walked in and sat on the sofa. She sat at the other end of the couch, the flowers still in her lap.

'Jade, relax. I didn't come here to scare you. I came here to … Well, I don't actually know why I came. I just felt like it. I was on my way home and I saw these flowers and they reminded me of you. I almost walked past the flower stall but then I remembered you weren't well. I thought you'd like them. Does that sound insane?'

'No,' smiled Jade, 'it sounds exactly like this sweet guy I used to know a long time ago. Do you want coffee?'

Leaping off the sofa, she went into the kitchen to put the kettle on. She had to get away from him before she suffocated. Her heart pounded in her chest and blood screamed through her ears. This was the man she had once been in love with. She was still in love with him. It was as if time had stopped. She braced herself against the kitchen bench and took ten deep breaths. Music came from the living-room. He'd put on a John Lennon CD. Jade spooned coffee and sugar into mugs and searched in the fridge for milk. There wasn't any.

Damn!

Nick liked his coffee black. She liked hers white. She made mint tea.

'So, how are you?' She carried the mugs out to the table and sat down at the far end of the sofa.

'I'm okay. Life is … busy.' He took a sip of the fresh brew. 'Hey, you remembered how I like my coffee!'

'Nick?'

'Hmm?' He was sipping coffee and listening to the music with his eyes closed.

'I'm sorry.' It was hard to get the words out but she had to say it.

Nick had treated her like a queen and she had treated him like garbage. She thought she didn't deserve someone like him in her life. She'd hurt him so badly it surprised her that he'd bothered to visit tonight.

Nick put his coffee on the table and looked over at Jade. He smiled, his eyes filled with love. He reached out and instinctively she moved over to sit beside him. He put his arm around her shoulder protectively, just like he used to before she was so mean to him.

'I know. For a long time, I tried to understand why you did it. But it's okay. I think we've both hurt enough.'

The tears started again.

What's wrong with me? She wiped her face. Every time a man comes to my door, I burst into tears.

Nick held her while she cried. She hadn't meant to let him go. She just couldn't be with him the way she was. Was it really two years ago? It seemed like yesterday. Nick planted kisses in her hair while she sobbed into his green, chequered sweater. It was the same sweater his mother had knitted for him when they'd gone to visit his parents at Christmas a few months after they'd met. It was hideous. She'd always hated the colour, but it held so many wonderful memories; the day they fell off the chalet balcony into the snow, the day they'd gone to get Nick's new car, the day the cat he'd called Pickles had turned up on the doorstep, the day he'd proposed.

Oh, damn! she thought. Nick had been wearing this sweater the last time she'd seen him. Sniffling, she plucked at the threads.

'Have you been wearing this abomination since—?'

'Yep,' he laughed, 'I couldn't take it off.'

'How's Pickles?'

'He misses you,' chuckled Nick, ruffling her hair.

'Okay, I'm done crying.' She took a deep breath, 'So, what now?'

'Are you hungry?'

'Starved.'

'Eat in or go out?'

'In.'

'Takeaway or cook?'

'Takeaway.'

'Chinese? Italian? Thai? Indian? Don't care?'

'Thai.'

'Great idea. They deliver.'

Nick phoned the Thai restaurant down the street and ordered a vegetarian feast. Jade went to make some improvements to her appearance.

'I'll need a week to fix this mess!' she told her reflection.

She showered and changed into clean jeans. She was scrubbing the tears away from her face, when a strange feeling washed over her. She felt … calm. As if everything would be fine. By taking life one step at a time, she felt as if she could tackle it for the first time. It felt right that Nick was here now. The friendship between Alec and Jade still had a long way to go, but life had suddenly improved a hundred-fold.

An hour later, half empty takeaway containers lay scattered all over the table in the living-room. Discarded chopsticks lay beside them. Nick and Jade were stuffed to the gills. He'd ordered all her favourite foods. There would be enough leftovers for a week. They sat on the sofa sipping wine. There was a foreign movie playing on television; Emir Kusturica's *Black Cat White Cat*. She and Nick stretched out together on the sofa, laughing at the antics of Roma gypsies romping on the shores of the Danube. Nick's head rested on her lap. It was just like old times. The doorbell rang. This time, Jade was sure it would be Alec.

'Hi,' he said, stepping in the door. He paused mid-step when he saw Nick. 'Am I interrupting something?'

'No. We were just hanging out. I've been expecting you,' Jade said, smiling and ushering him inside. He hesitated.

'Hi Alec, great to see you again,' Nick called from the sofa.

'Hi Nick.' Alec was surprised to find Nick there. Just last night he'd razzed Jade for spending too much time alone, but he didn't think she'd remedy the problem so quickly.

'So, are you coming in?'

'Well, I had something to tell you but it can wait. No, you two have a good time and I'll come by tomorrow.'

'No! No! No! No! No! You can't come here and say you want to tell me something and then leave without telling me,' Jade chided.

Alec looked uncomfortable.

'Hey Alec, come in!' Nick called out.

Nick had liked Alec when they'd met a few days before. He switched off the television and put on another CD. Fleetwood Mac. Before coming inside, Alec hovered on the doorway for a second, as if he couldn't make up his mind.

'So what's up?' Jade was curious about what Alec had to tell her.

He looked at Nick and was clearly unsure if it was okay to talk. Nick smiled and nodded his head reassuringly.

'It's okay,' Jade reassured him. 'Nick and I go way back. Tell me what's going on.'

'Well, Jade, I brought you these back,' he began, handing her the painstakingly repaired newspaper clippings. Jade stared, speechless, at the folder in her hand. 'A friend in Forensics put them back together. We thought you might want them returned. And I have some news for you. I'm not sure how to put it.'

Jade put the folder on the sideboard and narrowed her eyes at the detective. 'Is it good news? Or bad?'

'Well ... I don't really know. That's up to you.'

'Spit it out then,' she coaxed, her eyes bright with emotion.

'Jade ... I found ... Well ... You see there's—'

'Alec? Are you alright?' Concern tinged her words.

'Yes. I'm fine. I'm really worried about you.'

'Why?' Jade was confused. He had her brain dancing in loops.

Alec stood fidgeting for a moment longer and then blurted it out, 'Because I just found your real father.'

Jade's heart stopped and the world went black. The last thing her conscious mind registered was a falling sensation.

12

Nick stood staring at Alec. Jade had passed out on the floor.

'You found who?'

'Her biological father. It's a long story. Help me lay her down somewhere comfortable and I'll tell you.'

They carried Jade to her bed and Alec took her shoes off while Nick got a cool cloth to press on her forehead. She was out cold. Sitting on either side of the bed, the men talked about Alec's incredible discovery. Alec filled in Nick on everything he knew about David Rivers and Maria and Steve Randall.

'All her life she thought her father was dead,' Alec explained.

'So her father wasn't her father, and she'd never known either of them. Wow! No wonder she fainted.'

'That's not all there is to it. For the first ten years of her life, she thought Carl Rutherford was her father.'

'Damn! Three fathers! Poor girl.'

'There's a lot more, but I can't tell you. Jade wouldn't appreciate it.'

'Sure, I understand. Thanks, man.' Nick patted Alec on the back. He appreciated Alec's honesty and that he respected Jade's wishes concerning her dark, secretive past.

Nick and Alec stayed by Jade's side until she came to. Meanwhile, Nick looked around the bedroom he hadn't been in for two years. It had changed. It was darker, with fewer colours, more black. He'd hated the pictures in the living-room, too, but hadn't said anything. Lamps covered with dark blue scarves. The window shades closed. The room had a macabre atmosphere. Jade had enveloped herself in darkness. She was obviously unhappy. Soon, she opened her eyes.

'What happened?' She looked at the men leaning over her.

'You passed out, sweetheart. Are you okay?' Nick brushed the hair away from her face.

'Yeah. I think so. Alec, did you say you found my father? Did I hear right?'

'Yeah.'

'But my father is dead.'

'Jade, it's a long, complicated story. Look, I'm going home. Nick can tell you about it. I told him about your father.'

'You didn't ...' Jade tried to sit up too quickly. Her head spun.

'It's okay Jade. Your secrets are safe. Alec only told me the basics. The rest I'd prefer to hear from you anyway.'

Jade looked from Nick to Alec. She liked that the two men could be friends. She dreaded that soon they would both know everything she'd been hiding all these years. With her eyes, she thanked Alec for not telling Nick everything. Silently, she cursed her luck. Until now, she'd been bumping along in perfect misery and now people all over the place were caring about her.

'Oh, what have I got myself into?' Jade pulled a pillow over her head and tried to think straight.

Alec got up to leave. It had been a long day. He would like to have stayed but tiredness washed over him. He desperately needed sleep. Jade was in capable hands. Nick would tell her what he'd learned. Alec hoped for her sake that she'd take it as well as her father had.

Jade sat on her bed, stunned. Nick was in the kitchen making her a mug of herbal tea. She turned around and lay down, putting her feet on the wall just under Janis Joplin. This was Jade's thinking position. It relaxed her and cleared her head. She often posed questions to Janis and waited for the answers to come. Last time, Janis hadn't answered and Jade had thrown a knife at her nose. The knife was gone now. And Jade needed answers to the questions that buzzed around in her head.

My father is alive?

How can that be?

Who is he?

Who am I, then?

Does that make me not who I think I am?

How did Alec find him?

How much does Nick know?

Should I tell Nick everything?

Should I get out of town and leave no forwarding address?

What's happened to my life?

Should I tell Alec everything?

How much does Alec know?

Why couldn't I just …?

Why me?

Did I do something bad in another life to deserve all this pain now?

I'm soooooooooo confused!

'Here, drink this.' Nick came back with a steaming mug of tea.

Jade spun around and sat up. 'How much did he tell you?'

'Only the part about your father.'

'You'd better tell me what he said then.'

Nursing her mug in both hands, Jade listened to Nick tell the story Alec had told him. Nick repeated almost word for word what Alec had said. He didn't want to confuse Jade any more. Jade stared into her mug, not touching the hot, minty liquid. When Nick finished narrating the life story of David Rivers, he looked up at Jade. She was gazing at him, her eyes were frightened and her lips were quivering. Nick thought she was about to burst into tears again.

'So,' she concluded, 'I'm a love child.'

Nick didn't know what to say. Usually he never found himself at a loss for the appropriate words, but tonight he hadn't the faintest idea what he should say. Jade broke the silence.

'A week ago, I had no family and no friends. I was ready to leave this earth for more heavenly destinations. Now, I have two friends and a father. Nick, I'm really confused.'

'It's okay. It is confusing. It will sort itself out. Just give it time.' The enormity of what Jade said struck Nick. She'd tried to kill herself. Alec had told him it was possible, but he hadn't believed it. He'd had no idea Jade was so unhappy. A combination of remorse and relief churned through him. He was sorry he hadn't come sooner, but he was glad he had come when he did.

'Should I go and see him?'

'See who?' Nick had been thinking about the consequences of Jade's suicide attempt.

'My new father. Should I go and visit him in prison?'

'Would you like to visit?'

'I'm not sure.'

'Okay. If you decide that's what you really want to do, we'll go and visit him. Take your time, Jade. There's no hurry. I'll be here anytime you need me, and Alec seems to be a good friend, too.'

'How do they know for sure he's my father?'

'Alec said that a trusted colleague had dug deep into your family's history. There were all kinds of files and documents that turned up. He seemed pretty sure David Rivers was your biological father. His name is on your birth certificate. You could do a DNA test if you want to, just to be one hundred percent sure.'

'Maybe we could do that. I like that idea.'

Jade wanted to be certain. This would be her third father. She didn't remember the first one, and the second one turned out to be the devil. If she was going to meet another father, she wanted to be sure he was the real deal.

'Just take it one step at a time. You're not alone. Remember that.' Nick reached out to hold her hand in his. He got up to leave. This had been a long day for him, too.

'Thanks, Nick. Hey, where are you going?'

'It's time I went home.'

'Please stay.'

'Are you sure? It's probably better if I go home. I'll call you tomorrow.'

'You don't have to go. I'd like it if you stayed.' She looked into his eyes. Not promising anything, but promising the world.

He wrapped his arms around her and they lay down to sleep fully clothed. Sometime in the middle of the night, Nick got up to turn the lights off and make sure the door was locked. While she slept, Jade reached for him as he climbed back into her bed. Nick watched her face in repose. She was smiling. This time, Nick decided, he was here to stay. She'd have a hard time getting rid of him.

13

'Do you like to play games?' smirked Carl, squatting in the door of the wardrobe. 'Good. I like to play games too.'

Others had played hide and seek too. The wardrobe was a favoured cubby hole. As soon as he'd walked into the room, he'd opened the door and roused her. He'd have been surprised if she hadn't been in there. She'd been hiding in the closet for most of the week.

'Please, I just want to go home,' Lizzie whimpered, still drowsy from a long sleep. She was curled into a ball in the corner of the hanging space. His coat hung limply off her shoulders. The towel around her body had become loose. Her neck was sore and her legs felt stiff. The lights in the bedroom had been turned on. During her frequent searches, Lizzie hadn't been able to find a light switch. It must be outside, she'd eventually concluded.

'You must be hungry. I brought you some food,' he said, ignoring her oft-repeated plea.

He stood up and walked toward the bed. He took a few takeaway containers out of a plastic bag on the bedside table and turned to face the girl. She cowered in the closet.

'Well, are you coming out of there?' He stood with his hands on his hips, one eyebrow raised.

Lizzie shook her head. She didn't want to come out. She wanted him to close the door and go away. She wanted to go back to sleep where no one could hurt her. She put her forehead on her knees and closed her eyes as the first tears formed. Her mother's face appeared in front of her, then faded quickly.

She felt his grip on her arm. Once again, Carl dragged her out of the cupboard and pulled her to her feet. It happened so quickly, she had no time to fight against him. The towel fell to the floor. She wrapped the coat around her nakedness.

'Lizzie, you must be a good girl for Daddy,' he said, his teeth clenched.

'You are not my Daddy!' she shouted, enraged that he would dare to call himself her father.

Her father, Matty Lawrence, had been killed at work a few years ago. He'd fallen from the scaffolding near the twelfth floor while helping to build an inner-city high rise. That was when the problems with her mother had begun. Lizzie missed her father. He had adored her, and she him. Until he died, Matty had been her best friend. Now this strange man was telling her he was her Daddy. She hated him. At that moment, her hatred of him was stronger than her fear. She lashed out and caught him under the chin with her fist.

'You little witch,' he snarled, grabbing at both her hands.

He tore the coat from her shoulders and threw her on the bed. She landed with a dull thud in the centre of the waterbed. Lizzie screamed, her legs flailing, her arms punching out, her fingernails looking for a target, but he overpowered her. Holding both her arms with one hand, he lay on top of her. She couldn't move her legs. Then, he undid his pants. Overwhelmed, she sobbed until it was over.

'Get in the shower. You stink,' he growled, standing up.

Lizzie curled into a ball in the corner of the bed. She ignored him. She held her head in her hands and cried. Her body shook with grief, pain, fear, helplessness. He marched around the bed and grabbed a handful of her hair, then dragged her to her feet. She shrieked in pain.

'You can scream as much as you want. No one can hear you in here. Now, wash yourself. There is a clean towel on the rack.'

He pushed her into the bathroom and locked the door behind her. Alone again, Lizzie felt a spurt of relief. She had to decide what to do. Lizzie was smart. If she hadn't behaved so badly at school, her grades would have been excellent. She was particularly adept at science. It fascinated her. Physically, she knew this man could kick her butt.

Maybe he's not as smart as I am, she thought. She'd find out.

She turned the water on and stepped under the scalding stream. It felt good. She stood for a long time, letting the hot water run down her body, soothing her aches. She had a long shower. As long as she could get away with. While she was under the water, he was leaving her alone.

In the bedroom, Carl paced the floor. He was angry at himself. He didn't like to lose control. Obviously, he'd stayed away too long. He'd given her time to think. That was bad. He'd have to act fast now. Damn it! He preferred to go slower. She probably wouldn't eat the food he'd brought. Laced with Rohypnol, the spring rolls would have knocked her out for a while, giving him time to prepare. Now there was no time. He'd have to improvise. Resigned to the change in routine, he stripped off and threw his clothes on the bed. Acutely aware he was treading on dangerous ground, Carl unlocked the bathroom door and stepped inside.

Lizzie didn't hear him come in. He leant against the wall and watched her for a while, aroused. She soaped her body over and over, scrubbing with her fingernails, leaving red welts on her skin. He slid the glass shower door across, pleased she hadn't found the concealed lock. Some of them did.

Lizzie screamed and pressed back against the wall, covering herself with her hands.

'Calm down, baby,' he crooned as he stepped into the large cubicle. 'I need a shower too. Besides, you don't have anything I haven't seen.'

Inconspicuously, he flicked the tiny latch on the door, locking it. Every door in the apartment had a lock on it. Some were obvious, others weren't. He'd learned his lesson the first time. Containment was vital.

The girl stood frozen in the corner. He reached out and pulled her toward him. He took the soap from her hands and began to wash her. She stood meekly, letting him run his hands over her body. When she could reach it, she made a grab for the door, but it wouldn't open. He laughed.

'It's locked. Looks like we're stuck here together. Why not enjoy it?'

Lizzie punched him in the chest with both fists, pounding against him. It was futile. She may as well have been hitting a granite wall. He grabbed her wrists and held her hands above her head. Water slapped the back of her head. In this position, she felt more exposed, more vulnerable. She knew he knew that. It made her angry again. She spat on his cheek. He put his face under the stream of water behind her.

'Feisty little thing, aren't you?' he chuckled. Then, his expression changed. He glared into her eyes. Light blue shards of ice pierced through her brown eyes. 'Listen, kiddo. When this is over, you will be a corpse. So, you can decide how long you want to live. Be nice to me, and I'll let you hang around a while. Keep this up and you'll be in the ground by the morning. Understand?'

Carl would never kill her, not like that anyway. He wasn't a murderer. But he knew the threat would hit home fast. It did. Lizzie froze, again. She didn't want to die. None of them ever wanted to die. Her brain worked overtime. The only way to get out of there was to stay alive. If that meant doing what he wanted, she'd just have to live with it. She swallowed hard.

'What do you want?' she stammered, terrified he would kill her anyway.

'What do you want, Daddy?' he corrected, indicating she should repeat the question.

Bile choked her. Thoughts of her father flooded her mind. She could barely get the words out without vomiting, but she did as she was told.

'Turn around,' he instructed, 'face the wall.'

She obeyed, fearing the worst.

'I'm going to wash your back,' he told her, and ran his soapy hands down her spine and over her buttocks.

He reached above the shower wall for the loofah and scrubbed until the skin from her shoulders to her heels shone bright pink. He made her turn around and he scrubbed her front the same way. Then, turning her to face the wall again, he rubbed the soap through her hair, raking his nails through her scalp, massaging her head, washing and rinsing the ends efficiently. She didn't move. When she was clean, he washed himself, scrubbing with the same loofah. Lizzie stayed where she was. Her eyes closed, her mind ticking over. She zoned out, almost unaware of the man in the water behind her. There had to be a way out, she thought. She'd just have to wait for the opportunity. His voice brought her back to the present.

'See those rails above your head?' he asked. 'Hang onto them.'

She looked up and saw the rails. Two small handholds. Silent, she reached up and grabbed them, knowing he was going to rape her again. He pressed her body against the cold tiles. Tears mingled with the water dripping from her fringe. She felt guilty for feeling hungry. And she felt guilty for having enjoyed the sensations when he'd washed her back and her hair. When the rape was over, he stepped out of the shower and handed her a towel. He dried himself and went through to the bedroom, beckoning her to follow.

'This is much better. You've been so good, I'm going to bring you a present,' he said. He dressed himself and buttoned up his jacket.

'Could I have some clothes, please?' she asked, her voice meek, almost whispering.

'Could I have some clothes, please, what?' he said impatiently.

This girl needs to learn manners and respect, he thought.

'Could I have some clothes, please, Daddy?' she replied, a knot forming in her throat. A muscle in her chest constricted. She felt as if she couldn't breathe.

'I'll think about it. I'll be back in an hour. Bye-bye, baby.'

He walked over to kiss her on the lips. She closed her eyes and let him, but didn't respond. Inwardly, she shuddered in disgust.

After he'd gone, Lizzie wrapped the towel around herself more tightly. Gritting her teeth, she went back into the bathroom. She'd watched enough cop shows on television to understand the importance of DNA. From the plughole, she gathered strands of hair and put them in the pocket of the jacket she'd been wearing. Deciding he might find the hair and throw it away, she carefully ripped a small hole in the side of the sleeve lining, and stuffed her little hair sample inside. She tore a section off the rough end of the loofah, knowing there might be skin cells or something else the police could find amongst the fibres. She put it in the hole with the hair. Then, using the plastic fork he'd left behind with the takeaway food, she scraped a small piece of soap from the bar and added it to her little stash of evidence. She plucked a few strands from his towel, and stuffed them into the jacket sleeve. Using a different prong, she scraped under her fingernails, not knowing if anything was coming off. She wasn't sure if the police would be able to use any of her evidence. She broke the prong off the fork and slipped it into the little hole. Then, wincing in pain, she inserted a finger inside herself, and ran it around the walls of her vagina. Carefully, she wiped her finger on the pocket lining; sure the sticky fluid would contain semen. She put the jacket on, knowing he wouldn't find that unusual when he came back. She'd try to take the jacket with her when she escaped.

'The window!' she exclaimed, remembering something she had seen earlier.

She pulled the curtain aside and looked down at the street below. There was a bookshop right across the road. A small café nestled beside it. She memorised the signs facing the street.

Satisfied she'd done all she could, Lizzie looked at the cold food on the bedside table. Spring rolls. Fried rice. Chicken something. She ate the spring rolls and a few mouthfuls of fried rice. Ten minutes later, she was sleeping on the carpeted floor. The dose of Rohypnol would take a few hours to wear off.

When Carl returned, he was delighted to find her unconscious. This was how he liked to do things. He picked the girl up and put her on the bed, letting her towel fall to the floor. He'd brought her a dress and some shoes. He pulled the coat off and hung it in the wardrobe. Then, he sat her up and pulled the flimsy slip dress over her head before laying her back on the quilt. Then, he strapped the stilettos to her feet. He sat on the bed beside her and admired his handiwork for a moment. Red was his favourite colour.

Then, he went out to the kitchen to get the cleaning bucket, and he scrubbed the bathroom, tossed out the used soap and loofah, and replaced the towels again. As he cleaned, he whistled happily, pleased he'd been so clever. It was time to go to stage two.

When she woke up, he'd introduce her to heroin.

14

Debra Lazarowitz sat across the desk from Alec, glaring disdainfully at his dishevelled appearance. His clothes are crumpled, thought Debra. He looks like he needs to sleep. He could have showered and shaved before he'd presented himself in her office. He had no respect. She'd never liked the younger detective. He was smarmy and arrogant, too self-absorbed, and didn't know the meaning of the word 'discipline'. She'd also heard rumours that he was a drunk. That didn't sit well with her. Debra's father had been an alcoholic, and had beaten her regularly. Her sister too. And her mother. As a teenager, the only way she could think of to fight back was to become a cop. Her father had died of cirrhosis of the liver while she was still in training at the academy. She didn't even take the day off to go to the funeral.

'How can I help you, Stonewall?'

'I have this friend …' Alec began, not sure where to start or exactly what to say. It was a touchy subject, and the Senior Sergeant intimidated him a little.

Debra bit her tongue. You have friends? she wanted to ask. 'Yes, go on,' she said.

Unsure how or where to start, Alec blurted out what had been going on with Jade, leaving out insignificant details such as the revolver and the cocaine. He pieced together the puzzle for the Senior Sergeant, laying out the facts, keeping his opinions to himself, letting her make up her own mind. As he explained his investigation thus far, his words flowed more smoothly. When he was finished, he sat back and looked at her face. It was impassive. She never gave anything away.

'Has Miss Randall made a formal complaint?' asked Debra, wondering if Carl Rutherford had been let off too easily in the past. She'd had her suspicions about him last time he'd been brought in for questioning, but had kept them to herself.

'No, but I'm going to advise her to make a statement. I wanted to make sure that I could count on you to be there for her. She doesn't trust easily. She's a bit of a hard-case, actually,' he admitted.

Debra wasn't surprised. Any friend of Alec's would have to be a hard nut. The details of Jade's case piqued her interest. She'd do a little snooping of her own, just to satisfy her curiosity. Alec had told Debra what he knew, but she could dig a little deeper.

'Okay,' she said, matter-of-factly, 'We can only act on this information if Miss Randall is prepared to make a statement.'

Alec nodded. He'd known she would say that. Debra wouldn't dream of not following procedure. Getting the statement would be the hard bit. 'I'll talk to her,' he promised.

'I'll be here for her. You can tell her that. I'll do whatever I can for her. She sounds like she needs help. Have you suggested any counsellors?'

'Not yet. I thought I'd talk to you first.'

'Good.' Debra was pleased. At last, he was showing some common sense. She wrote a name and telephone number on her notepad and tore the sheet off. 'This is Margo Rosewood's number. She's a psychologist, and a whiz with hard-cases. If you can convince Miss Randall to go and talk to her, Margo will do whatever she can to help.'

Alec took the paper and stuffed it in his pocket. 'Thanks.'

'If she agrees to do this, she's going to need all the support she can get. Has she met her father yet?'

'No, she wants to do DNA tests first. Rivers has agreed to that.'

'Fair enough. Well, one step at a time, Alec.' She softened a little. 'This will probably take a long time even once we get moving. Try and get her to see Margo. She's the best in her business. I've known her a long time. We studied together. I'll be here when Miss Randall wants to talk to me.'

'Thank you, Debra,' said Alec, sincerely grateful. He got up to leave. 'Now, I'm going home to get some sleep. It's been a long shift.' And to sweat and shudder my way through another long dry night, he thought, gritting his teeth. It was getting better. The dry horrors were coming to an end. A couple more days, he figured, and he'd be okay.

Debra smiled sympathetically. Long shifts had been part of her life for twenty-five years. Then, an idea struck her.

'Alec, what are you working on at the moment?'

'We have those three murders, the Southeast Shore gangland killings. They're a full-time-plus job.' Alec hated the case. For all he cared, it would save the country a lot of grief and police resources if they were left alone on a football field to wipe each other out.

'There's a case came in yesterday,' Debra began. 'Missing girl. Elizabeth Lawrence. She's fourteen. Hasn't been seen since Sunday night. Her mother is desperate. She might be a runaway. She may have been taken. No one knows yet. I'm short-handed over here. Would you like it? There are more than enough people working on the murder cases. You wouldn't be missed.'

Alec couldn't believe his ears. Debra was going to trust him? 'Sure, yes, I would.'

'Good. You can team up with Orlando Grimshaw first thing in the morning. Get the details from the constable on your way out. Grimshaw will fill you in on the rest when you get here tomorrow.'

'Okay, thanks,' he said, appreciating the chance to prove himself.

Picking up the phone, the Senior Sergeant waved a hand in dismissal, but didn't look up as he walked out of her office.

15

Their footsteps echoed down the long corridor. David Rivers followed the guard, walking two feet behind. Another guard followed David. The doors clanked closed as they passed through each section of the prison. As the trio reached the entrance to the visiting area, two more guards stood watching over the room.

'Hello, Mister Rivers. How are you?' asked Alec, standing to greet him.

'Very well, thanks,' David replied, shaking Alec's proffered hand. He liked Alec. He was one of the good guys. 'The prison system doesn't look kindly on DNA testing, huh?'

'Apparently not, but there are a few ways we can get around that,' Alec told him, keeping his voice low.

Jade's application to have David Rivers undergo DNA testing to determine paternity had been rejected. The Department of Corrective Services said they had no provision for that kind of testing, that it was against regulations, and had suggested she wait until he was released. Nick and Alec knew that Jade would never be able to wait that long. Alec had figured out a way he could help. As far as the prison was concerned, officially, the questioning of David Rivers by police detectives was part of an ongoing investigation.

'Really? I'm a bit nervous about this actually,' admitted David.

'Nothing to be nervous about,' smiled Alec, handing the man a piece of chewing gum. He unwrapped another stick and stuffed it in his own mouth.

David looked at the stick with distaste. 'I don't chew gum,' he said.

'You do now, just for a minute or so,' whispered Alec, nodding and smiling encouragement. 'I can't stand the stuff either, but whatever it takes …'

Realisation dawned on the prisoner's face. 'Oh, I see.'

He put the spearmint gum in his mouth and chewed. He and Alec chatted about the weather, football, election results, David's experiences in Vietnam. Each resembled a cow with a sore tooth chewing a particularly sour cud. Clearly, neither was in the habit of chewing gum. As he masticated the sticky ball, David wanted to ask about his daughter, but didn't dare to hope for too much. He couldn't stand to be disappointed. Alec noticed the barely concealed look of expectation on his face.

'She's giving a sample today. They'll be tested together. Not long to go now. A week or so.'

David nodded in reply. He took in a deep breath and focused on a brown spot on the table. After a few minutes, David put the piece of chewed gum on the wrapper and folded it up. He looked up at Alec.

'Just flick it over here. I'll chuck it in my pocket.'

David flicked the little silver package across the table toward the detective. 'Is that it?' he asked.

'That's it, we're done,' announced Alec, putting his own gum under his tongue. He'd spit it out when he got outside. 'I'll get the sample to the clinic straight away. I'm going there now.'

'Thanks,' David replied, a little overwhelmed by the simplicity of a process that could possibly change his whole life.

David stood up and shook Alec's hand again. A buzzer went off behind his head. He stood passively as the guards returned to lead him back to his block.

Back in his cell, David tried not to think about the result. Despite his efforts to concentrate on his book, he couldn't stop his mind straying back to the question at hand. What if it's negative? he wondered. All this hope wasted. But he wouldn't have lost anything. If it was positive, he'd have gained a daughter. What if she didn't want to know him? Alec Stonewall had said he couldn't promise what her reaction would be. There was no telling what she might do. He only said he'd talk to her. Aside from this quick visit to illegally obtain DNA for the paternity test, David hadn't heard anything from the detective. He was looking forward to seeing Alec again when the results came back. He felt as if it would be the longest week of his life.

At around the same time David was pacing his cell, Jade was sitting in her doctor's office, allowing him to swab her mouth for a DNA sample. Nick sat in the chair next to her, holding her hand. Jade was nervous. Her legs bounced around as she jiggled in the high-backed designer chair. She played with her hair, then cracked her knuckles. Nick said nothing, knowing the only cure for this annoying affliction was time.

'What if it's negative?' she'd asked Nick on the way to the clinic.

'Then, we've lost nothing but some time and a bit of money,' he replied, focusing on the practicalities of the situation.

'And if it's positive?'

'Well, that's bigger, isn't it? You'll have to decide whether or not you want to meet your biological father.'

'Oh, I don't know …' she muttered, unsure if she wanted to meet a stranger who was her father, even though she'd never known the man she'd believed was her father, and the man she'd known as her father wasn't even related. For a moment, she felt like that little bird in the children's book, running around asking everyone, 'Are you my father?'

'How long will this take?' Jade asked the doctor, as he labelled the swabs and put them in vials.

'About a week, maybe longer,' answered the doctor.

'A week!' exclaimed Jade, breathing out hard. She'd thought it would take a few hours. A whole week to wonder about this strange man who may or may not be her father. That was too long. She'd never get through it. Her legs jiggled harder. Nick clenched his jaws. A whole week of fidgeting and jiggling would drive him nuts.

'Is there any way we can speed up the process?' asked Nick, hoping that a few dollars in the right hands could make it all happen faster.

'Sure,' replied the doctor casually, not expecting any response. It was expensive. Most people opted to wait. 'You pay the express fee for speeding up those guys down at the pathology lab, and we'll get you the results in three or four days.'

'From both samples? asked Jade, excited at this newly revealed shortcut.

'Yep, both samples,' confirmed the doctor, nodding confidently. 'I understand Detective Stonewall is collecting a sample from Mister Rivers today. If so, they'll both be tested at the same time.'

'Done,' said Nick, ready to sign on the dotted line. Three days of jiggling would be manageable. He was happy to pay extra for some priceless peace of mind.

'I'm so nervous, I don't know if I should laugh or cry,' said Jade as they emerged onto the street below the clinic.

Nick held her hand. He squeezed it reassuringly. 'When you get the results, you can do both if you like. Until then, how about we take off for a few days?'

'What about work?' she asked, remembering she needed to call Herman again.

'You're still off for now, and I can take the rest of today off and the whole weekend. Probably Monday, too, if I feel like it. I've already told them I have a family crisis to attend to. I'm owed a few sick days. Let's pack some stuff and go somewhere. Promise we'll be back here by Tuesday morning.' He saluted the air, smiling at his ingeniousness.

Jade turned to face Nick. This was one of the reasons she'd always loved him. She adored the spontaneity with which he could abandon real life and dive into fantasy land; a place they could go together.

'A long weekend? Sure, I could live with that.' She grinned, then nudged him in the ribs. 'Family crisis. You really are something!'

'It's true! You're like family to me.' He nudged back, tickling her.

'The only crisis you're going to be having is deciding where we're going,' she chuckled.

'Oh, well I thought we might go up to the mountains, rent a cabin, chill out a little. Do some hiking, catch up on the last couple of years.'

'Nick Troxell, you are a bloody genius!'

If she was going to spend the next three days wondering whether or not she had a living parent, and deciding whether or not she wanted to meet him, then she may as well be having a good time.

As they drove out of the car park in Nick's convertible, and turned toward Jade's apartment, Alec ran into the building with the tiny package of chewing gum.

16

Katie Green stumbled toward the curb as the man approached. The stilettos strapped to her feet wobbled precariously. Her head still fuzzy from the last hit, she was coming down. It felt bad. She wanted to get high. Any trick would do. She needed money. Gerry, her dealer, didn't do credit; he had enough offers of sex to relax him for three centuries. The guy walking her way wore clean black pants and a green striped business shirt. No tie, but polished leather shoes. He looks half-decent, she thought. A bit sexy. She clung to the lamp post as he made his way down the street. Hitching her short skirt up higher, flashing the lace on her tattered red panties, she leaned against the post, pouting seductively with bright red lips. The shoestring strap on her midriff top slid down over her shoulder, and dangled in front of her left breast. The fabric barely covered her nipple.

'Hey mister, wanna play?' she called, winking with long false eyelashes.

He stopped in front of her, frowning. 'Are you Katie Green?' he asked, sure this was the girl.

This time around, she'd been on the missing persons register for almost three weeks. It was the fifth time in four years her parents had reported her missing. Each time she vanished, her mother grew ten years older. Her father had given up on her as a lost cause. He expected the police to turn up one day and tell him his wayward daughter was dead; her body fished out of the river.

Each time she turned up, she was in a terrible state, and she only wanted money. Soon after, she'd disappear in the middle of the night. Her mother would wait a couple of weeks for her to come home, and call the police again. Last time she went home, she'd tried to get herself together. She'd tried to overcome her addiction, and had gone to the police with her tragic story. They'd questioned Rutherford, but his story was convincing. In the end, she was just a hooker with a habit and they didn't believe her. Giving up hope, she took to the streets again.

Alec had a hunch that finding Katie Green would somehow lead him to Elizabeth Lawrence. He couldn't explain it. It was a gut thing.

This girl fitted Katie's description, but didn't much look like the photo he'd been given. The four-year-old photograph was of a teenage girl in a high school uniform, hair neat, eyes smiling. A valedictorian. The girl hanging from the lamp post had aged a fair bit. She looked as if she'd been dragged backwards through a cheese grater. Still, the similarities were striking enough.

Katie straightened up at the mention of her name. Her eyes narrowed. 'Who wants to know?' she replied suspiciously. She never used her real name on the street. No one here knew who she was. As far as anyone was concerned, she was Candy. No last name. How did he know her name? If she hadn't been so stoned, she'd have run away. Her eyes darted furtively around, looking for a way out.

'Katie, you can trust me,' Alec assured her. 'Let's go somewhere we can talk.'

'I ain't goin' nowhere with you 'less you pay first!' retorted Katie. She'd learned the hard way about giving johns credit. Lenny had beaten her up for her trouble.

Alec looked at the girl. Track marks raced down her arms. Her thighs were marked too. Her hair was matted at the back. Her nose had been broken. She was a mess. And she was right not to trust him. He took money from his wallet and gave it to her.

'Fifty bucks?' she sneered. 'Jeez! What'd you do? Rob a bank?'

'I just want to talk to you,' Alec explained patiently.

She shrugged. 'It's your money, pal.'

'C'mon, let's go this way,' suggested Alec, leading her into the park.

He sat on the wooden bench beside her. She looked him up and down suspiciously.

'What do you want? Are you some kind of weirdo?'

'No, I'm a detective. I want to talk to you about the charges that were dropped a few weeks ago.'

'A cop! Dammit!' Katie was frightened. The cops had never done her any favours, even when she was telling the truth. She stood up and walked away. 'Leave me alone!' she shouted over her shoulder.

Alec ignored the remark. He walked over and put his hand on her shoulder. She shrugged him off and tried to run. Her head spun. She felt nauseous. Then, she tripped over a tree root and tumbled to the ground. She was winded. Alec picked her up and sat her on the grass. He sat beside her, pinching the bridge of his nose; he could feel another headache coming on. He fought the urge to abandon the girl to her misery and go to the nearest bar to assuage his own.

'Look, I'm not here to bust you. I'm not going to hurt you. I want to help, Katie. I just want to talk about what happened. Then, I'll go away and leave you alone forever if that's what you want.'

'Really?' she mumbled, looking sideways at the detective. He didn't look like much of a detective to her. He was shaking almost as much as she was. She was suspicious. 'Let me see your badge!' she demanded.

Alec took out his shield and handed it to her. 'It's real,' he reassured her as she inspected it.

'Alec Stonewall,' she read. 'That's you, huh? Alec?'

'Yup, that's me. Alec. And you're Katie.'

'People around here call me Candy.'

'What would you prefer I called you?' he asked, not surprised she'd chosen a cheap name to go with her cheap lifestyle.

'I like Katie. The way you say it makes it sound pretty. But you can't tell anyone,' she warned.

'Not a soul,' he swore, hand on his heart. 'You have my word.'

'A cop's word don't mean much,' she mumbled, picking at the grass near her feet.

'Mine means a lot. But you don't have to trust me right away. You'll see. One day you'll be happy I came to talk to you about this.'

'Will I?'

'Yes, that I can almost promise.'

'Okay, Mister Stonewall, what do you want to talk about?'

'You made a statement saying Carl Rutherford raped you four years ago. I want to talk about that with you.'

'The cops didn't believe me.' She started sobbing. 'They said I was just a dumb street whore, a drug addict who needed money for a fix, and that I'd made it all up.' A tear trickled down her cheek.

'Well, Katie, I don't think you made it up. I read your statement, and I think every word you said is true. If you'll let me, I'd like to try and help you do something about it.'

Katie couldn't believe her ears. Could Alec really help her? She wanted to get off the streets, go back to school or learn a trade, please her parents. She wanted things to be the way they were before. And to get off these horrid drugs. She hated herself, her life, and most of all, she hated the man who had done this to her.

'Can you really do something, or are you just messing with me?'

'No, Katie. It will be tough. We have a lot of work to do. Things will probably get rough from time to time. But I think we can do it. You see, you aren't the only girl he's ever hurt. There are others. I'm going to try and find some of them, see if they'll make statements. Together, there's a fair chance that we can put him away.'

'Really?' She looked at his face, saw the truth, and burst into tears.

'Really. Shhh. It's okay.'

Alec comforted her while she cried herself out. He'd thought she would have been harder to crack. Katie had been on the streets for the best part of four years. But, he thought, inside she's just a little girl. Now, she doesn't have to run away any more. Eventually, Katie pulled herself together. She wiped her face with tissues Alec gave her, then trumpeted loudly to clear her nose.

'Okay,' she said, taking a deep breath. 'What happens now?'

'First, I want you to tell me what happened, starting at the beginning, and then we'll go from there.'

Katie nodded. The last time she'd told this story, no one had believed her. She could hardly blame them. It really was unbelievable. It had happened so long ago. She dug her fingernails into the grass, closed her eyes, took a deep breath, and began to tell Alec about the fateful night when, as a fifteen-year-old high school girl with a fake ID card, she'd gone to the Blue Mango.

17

Ants crawled over every inch of her skin, biting and tickling at the same time. At least, that's what it felt like.

Lizzie sat propped up in a corner of the room, naked except for the jacket she'd taken from the wardrobe however long ago. Her sense of time had long since gone. She shivered uncontrollably, and vomited again, just barely managing to throw her head forward so she wouldn't choke on it. Slime dribbled down her chin to her chest, then onto her stomach, and dripped onto a smelly pool on the carpet. Her body ached. She tried to tear her flesh away, to rid herself of the pain. Huge red welts covered her chest and arms. Some of them were still weeping. The lining of the jacket stuck to her bloodied skin. She craved sugar. There was no food. He'd left nothing behind. She'd eaten a piece of soap, but her stomach had rejected it. She wanted to sleep, but all manner of real and imagined demons invaded her dreams.

Being awake was almost as bad. Monsters leapt out of the walls, shrieking obscenities at her, nose to nose, clawing at her face, her arms, her feet. She screamed in terror, and they vanished back into the dark panels.

She was afraid to close her eyes, and afraid to keep them open. The tips of her fingers were bloody stumps where she'd chewed her fingernails to the quick. She had distinct bruises on her legs and arms, the tell tale signs of an addict.

'Please, come back,' she begged, her voice hoarse from screaming, and from exhaustion. 'Please. I'll do anything you want.'

18

Jade stared at the doctor and gasped, hand clapped over her mouth.

'Can you say that again?' she asked, not sure she'd heard right.

'Miss Randall, it appears that David Rivers is your biological father,' he stated again, slower this time so that she could absorb each word.

'You're sure?' asked Nick, hoping there had been no mistake. He couldn't stand to see Jade disappointed or hurt by high expectations.

'Well, nothing in life is one hundred percent certain, except, of course, death and taxes, but according to the DNA matching at the lab, there is a ninety-eight percent probability that Mister Rivers is Miss Randall's father.' The doctor smiled uncertainly. 'I hope that's good news.'

Jade sat back in the chair and thought about the implications. Tears formed in the corners of her eyes. She didn't know whether to laugh or cry. Nick and the doctor looked at each other, not sure what to say. Jade's lips quivered. Her face felt hot. A surge of emotion rushed through her veins. She tightened her grip on Nick's hand. A teardrop escaped and ran down her cheek. Still silent, the doctor handed her a tissue.

'Do you think I should go and see him?' she asked, wiping her face, a lump in her throat the size of a golf ball.

'That's up to you, honey,' answered Nick. 'Do you want to visit?'

The doctor cleared his throat. He had other patients to see.

'Let's go home and talk about it,' suggested Nick, taking the hint.

Just over three hours later, Rivers approached Alec in the visitors' room.

David Rivers was on edge. Either he had a daughter or he didn't. He took a deep breath and stepped through the security door into the bare room. As he walked toward the table, he tried to read Alec's expression. Alec watched him enter, then looked down at the table as he approached. Every nerve ending in the prisoner's body screamed out in pain. He should have expected this. Against his better judgement, he'd been hoping the test would be positive.

'David,' Alec began, hoping his news was what David wanted to hear.

'She's not mine, is she?' David cut in, sure it would be bad news. The look on Alec's face had told him that.

'No, David. She is. You're her father,' countered Alec, wondering how easily the man had convinced himself that it was too good to be true.

David didn't hear. Only the word 'no' had penetrated the drumming in his ears. His heart sank. He was a fool for believing his life could change that quickly. 'I knew it. I knew I couldn't be anyone's Dad.'

'David,' Alec repeated, 'you are someone's Dad. You are Jade's father.'

'What?' David looked stunned. Wide eyes stared at Alec, disbelieving.

'David, you are Jade's biological father. The DNA came back positive.'

David leaned back in his chair, speechless. His heart pounded. He could hardly breathe. Momentarily, he felt numb. A heatwave of emotion surged through his body, radiating outward to his extremities. Fingertips tingling, he covered his mouth as the tears began. He couldn't focus as the floodgates burst. 'Oh my God!' he spluttered from under his hand.

Alec felt uncomfortable as the man sitting opposite wept. Gradually, David pulled himself together. He wiped a long sleeve across his face, sniffled into the cuff and regained his composure. For a few minutes, Alec intently studied the brown spot on the table.

'Jade?' David croaked, swallowing his uncharacteristic outburst.

'Yes, Jade Randall,' Alec told him. He hadn't been sure if it would be kosher to reveal her identity, but Jade had assured him it would be okay.

'Jade. That's a pretty name.'

'She's a pretty girl.'

'Are you …?'

'A friend. Her boyfriend's name is Nick.'

David nodded, still taking in the prodigious news. He could barely let himself believe that he had a daughter. Jade. He turned the name around in his mind for a few moments. He loved that name. It described something very beautiful. A precious gem.

'Does she want to meet me?' asked David, suddenly desperate to see his daughter. To touch her face, her hair, to make sure she was real.

Alec smiled at the at the man's puppy-like eagerness and chuckled. 'Yes, she does.'

19

'I'm scared,' whispered Katie, her legs crossed at the ankles, her feet tucked under the chair. She was dressed in jeans and a t-shirt. She wore no makeup. Her hair had been washed and brushed and tied back. Her wan face betrayed her anxiety. Her dark eyes darted around the sparsely furnished room, taking in every detail.

'Don't be. Everything's gonna be okay,' Alec reassured her.

He turned and smiled, still amazed at how strong she had become since their first meeting. This was going to be a long, painful experience. Faced with the same prospect, he didn't know if he'd have the stamina needed to follow through. Rehab was only the beginning.

'Miss Green?' a uniformed woman called from a doorway.

Katie looked at Alec. He nodded and smiled reassuringly. She nodded resolutely and stood up.

'Okay, here goes,' she muttered, walking toward the door.

'I'll be right here if you need me,' Alec called as the door closed.

Katie's parents had been relieved the police had found their daughter. Her mother cried a river. Her father had been sceptical.

'How long are you here, this time?' he'd sneered, abruptly turning his back and stalking out to his workshop to bang nails into whatever piece of wood he could find.

'Dad?' she'd called behind him, wanting to tell him that this time it was the beginning of the end of their ordeal. Wanting to say she was sorry for all the pain she'd caused. Wanting him to love her again.

He wasn't ready to hear it. Katie knew words wouldn't be good enough. She would have to prove herself. She looked at her mother, who was still mopping her face with a hankie.

'Mum?' whispered Katie, hoping for more from her mother.

Her mother straightened up, squared her shoulders, and looked her daughter in the eye. 'If you have come to break my heart again, then

I don't want you here,' she said, her voice wavering. 'But if you are going to stay, then you must do some things before we will help you.'

Katie nodded. She knew Alec had come to talk to her parents. They knew most of the story. Alec nodded encouragement at Missus Green. This was killing her, and he knew it. If Alec hadn't insisted on doing things his way, she would never have dreamed for a second of turning her only daughter away from her door, no matter what she had done. Hearing what had happened to Katie had left the woman distraught. After Alec had outlined the sequence of events, Amanda Green wanted nothing more than to hold her child in her arms, and help her any way she could. This tough love stuff was alien to her.

'Alec is taking me to rehab,' Katie began, holding back her own tears, 'I'm going today. The sooner I can get clean, the better.'

Her mother cupped her hand over her mouth. This was more pain than she thought she could bear. Alec patted her arm. The woman swallowed, but couldn't allow any words escape lest she fall apart. She nodded, and tried to smile.

'This is the best way, Missus Green,' reassured Alec, admiring the woman's resolve. He felt partly responsible for her pain and his heart went out to her.

'Bye, Mum. I love you,' Katie said. She turned and walked out the door. Then, put her head back in and added, 'Tell Dad I love him.'

Alec was right behind her. As he closed the front door behind him, he heard Katie's mother beginning to sob loudly. He ushered Katie out the gate toward his car, hoping the young woman hadn't heard. He drove her over to the rehab clinic, and promised he'd wait until she was settled in.

An hour after Katie had disappeared through the wooden door, the uniformed woman came out to see him. Her stern face did nothing to assuage his fears.

'You can see her for five minutes,' the woman proclaimed. 'After today, she is allowed no visitors until she has completed phase one of the program. About ten to twelve days on average. I'll let you know. After that, you can see her every second day for the next month. Then, if her doctors and psychologists feel she is strong enough to cope on her own, she will be released. Is that clear? Do you have any questions?'

Alec couldn't think of any questions. He gave the woman his office number and told her to contact him any time if necessary.

The woman led him through a rabbit-warren of corridors to a small room. Katie was in bed, reading a magazine.

'Hey,' she greeted him, putting the magazine down.

'Hello,' he replied, pleased she looked okay so far. 'I want to give you this. It's my mobile number. If you need me, call. I'll just put it here.' He opened the drawer and dropped the card inside.

The uniformed woman clucked. She'd take it out after he left.

'I'm still scared,' Katie told him, 'but I really need to do this.'

'Yeah, you do. It will be hard, just like I promised. But you'll be fine. You're a strong kid,' he said, pretending not to see her thin, frail frame, her pale face, and the dark circles under her eyes.

'Hey! Who are you calling a kid?' she snorted, her face filled with indignation.

'Sorry,' he apologised, 'You're a strong young woman. You'll kick butt.'

'Thanks, Alec. Thanks for everything.'

'Don't thank me yet. Before this is over, you're going to wish you'd never laid eyes on me,' he warned, knowing that never had truer words been spoken.

'I would never think that,' she insisted, still not fully comprehending the implications of what she was about to endure. Detoxing was only the beginning of the nightmare that was about to become her life.

'I gotta get back to work. You take care of yourself. I'll see you soon,' said Alec, heading toward the door.

'Alec?'

'Yeah?'

'Wish me luck.'

'Good luck, Katie.' He walked over to the bed and kissed her forehead.

'Bye,' she whispered, unaware she was teetering on the brink of emotional hell.

20

'So, what's your objective?' asked Margo Rosewood.

'Objective? I don't understand?' replied Jade, not sure exactly what the question was, or what this odd-looking woman wanted her to say.

Jade wondered if it was the orange scarf the psychologist had wrapped around her head that put her off. Bits of hair stuck out at the top. Margo wore a tie-dyed purple cotton shirt and a long, flowing purple skirt. She wore brown leather sandals, the kind you see in illustrated bibles. Long, gold earrings dangled to her shoulders; shimmering bits of diamond-shaped metal held together with tiny rings that swished to and fro as the woman moved. A pendant, some kind of Celtic knot made from clay and painted bright colours, hung from her neck. She smelled of vanilla and cinnamon. The fiftyish-year-old woman looked like a relic from Woodstock. And yet, somehow, the whole bizarre look worked for her.

'Yes, objective. What do you hope to achieve? Your goal,' she explained, staring intently at her newest patient.

Deb had warned her Jade Randall was a hard-case, but she hadn't expected an idiot. Debra had insisted Margo find time for her. The Detective Senior Sergeant had filled Margo in on the skeletal facts. They'd thought it best if Jade was encouraged to tell the bulk of her story. Over her half-lens spectacles, Margo appraised the nervous woman in the armchair opposite, and fidgeted with her hemline. The psychologist took notes, mapping a course of action. She assumed the task would be tough. If Jade didn't know what she was doing here, how the hell was Margo supposed to know?

'In life? Is that what you mean? I'm sorry. I don't know what you're asking me,' said Jade, exasperated. She felt like a twit. What did this woman want? What was she asking? Why didn't she pose a straight question?

'No, from this. Therapy. What do you hope to get out of our sessions? What are you hoping will happen as a result of your coming here?' Margo spelled it out in the simple terms she usually reserved for her juvenile delinquent patients.

'Oh!' Realisation dawned. 'I haven't given it much thought. I've never been to a psychologist. I mean, I thought only crazy people had therapy,' Jade said, hoping she didn't sound like an imbecile.

Margo smiled. 'I want you to think about it now. Take a moment to reflect. Why are you here? What do you want out of it? What is your objective?' Margo asked in a quiet voice, leaning over to flick the switch on the stereo.

The sound of flowing water filled the room. Birds whistled. Crickets chirped. A brook babbled. Jade wanted to run away. The whole thing seemed absurd. But she'd promised Nick she'd give it a shot.

When Alec first proposed she see a psychologist, she'd been furious. How dare he presume she needed psychiatric help, she'd raged. He'd allowed her to scream at him for five minutes, then dropped the bit of notepaper bearing the name and phone number on the kitchen bench and fled. He'd done his best. The rest was up to her.

She and Nick had talked through the night. She was against therapy. 'I'm not nuts. I just had a bad night.' She tried to sound reasonable.

Nick accepted she'd had a tough time, but suggested talking about it, facing her demons, would do her good. Help her heal. 'It's not just about Sunday night, it's about your whole life.'

She'd been through hell. There were issues she hadn't dealt with. He reasoned that therapy could make a difference. Asking for help, he explained, wasn't a weakness. It was a strength.

'At the very least, Jade, give it a shot,' he'd pleaded.

After all, he'd told her, she had nothing to lose. She'd agreed, and now here she was, with the bird-woman and her ridiculous nest. Still, if she was going to do this, she would have to take it seriously.

She sighed loudly. 'I guess I need some help learning how to come to terms with everything that's happened in my life,' she said.

'Good!' replied Margo enthusiastically, clapping her hands together. 'To come to terms with your life. Yes. That's a wonderful objective.'

Jade was mollified for the moment. At least it made sense now.

Margo was relieved she wasn't dealing with a moron, after all.

'So, where would you like to start?' asked Margo, accustomed to letting her clients take the lead. In her experience, they tended to open up a little more if they weren't being bossed around. But then, she sighed to herself, there were those few who needed a nudge.

'I ... um ... I really ... um ... don't know,' stammered Jade, assuming she would have been asked a series of questions about herself.

'Let's make it simple,' suggested Margo, aware that for many people, this was one of the hardest questions. 'You can tell me as much, or as little, about any part of your life as you like. You can start from the beginning if you prefer, from your first memory. Or you can talk about yesterday and go backwards from there. If it suits you better, you can jump around all over the place, talk about your life at random. It's entirely up to you. Regardless of where you start, whatever you say will never leave this room.'

Jade thought about it. She'd never told anyone about her life. It wasn't something she'd ever felt inclined to share. She didn't feel she was that interesting. Who'd want to know about anything she'd ever done? Her life as a whole was actually quite unremarkable. Biting her lips, she took a deep breath, closed her eyes, and had a quick peek down the long line of skeletons running deep into her past. Whichever one jumped up first, she would talk about. Most of them cowered behind closet doors.

'I suppose the gun and the mirror is the first thing that springs to mind,' announced Jade, opening her eyes.

Margo smiled. Debra had told her a fragment of that story. She was interested in hearing the rest. 'The gun and the mirror?' she said, thinking the phrase sounded like the title of a novel, 'I'm intrigued.'

Jade related the story of the night she'd wanted to kill herself. She didn't leave out any details, admitting how angry and frightened she had been. While recalling the events of that night, she became aware of the gamut of emotions she'd been feeling in the lead up to that weekend. Explaining them to Margo made her feel stronger. She added a few minor facts about Carl Rutherford, and briefly explained her connection to him and his family. She also told Margo about David Rivers, and how she'd decided to go and see him some time in the next few weeks. When she finished speaking, Jade became aware that she had been crying. She snatched a few tissues from the box on the small coffee table between them and blew her nose.

'You've been through quite an ordeal, haven't you?' sighed Margo, visualising the long road ahead. But, the little Jade had told her had helped her to formulate the course she thought they should take. 'Well, now we have a place to start and a direction to go in.'

'We do? But I've hardly told you anything.' Jade was shocked. Now there seemed to be so much more to tell.

'You've made a start, and that's given me an idea of how to best help you,' explained Margo. 'I think it's wonderful that you've found your father. I hope it turns out well for you. I'm sure you'll tell me about it along the way. How do you feel after telling me all that?'

'It's strange. Kind of lighter,' said Jade, a little bemused about her sudden transformation.

A month ago, they'd have had to torture her for information about herself. Now, here she was, telling all to a complete stranger. It felt weird. But it also felt … soothing.

'You know what they say, a burden shared …' mused Margo, then she glanced at the clock on the wall and sat straighter in her chair. 'Jade, our time is just about up for today, but before you go, I want to ask you to consider something and then tell me what you think about it at next week's appointment.'

'Yes?' Jade was curious. Homework from the psychologist, she thought, how interesting.

'I think you should go to the police and make a statement,' stated Margo, all business and matter-of-fact.

'A statement? The police?' Jade was dumbfounded. Is she mad?

Jade had never considered going to the police. To begin with, she thought that no one would believe her. She was just a barmaid with an attitude problem. What if everyone thought it was her own fault? Secondly, Carl knew too many people on the top rung of the ladder. And had enough money to buy whoever he liked. He'd demonstrated that in the past. Anyway, everyone knew that only people with money got any justice. Then, there was his family. What about his wife? His son? Did they number amongst his victims? Or not? Lastly, she was afraid of the demon himself. Surely he would come after her if she went to the police. What if he had her killed, and then dumped her body in the foundations of one of his famous projects? She knew he wouldn't let her die without first subjecting her to all kinds of unspeakable tortures. The concept terrified her.

'I think it will be an important part of your healing process,' Margo continued, 'And I also feel that as long as a man like that is still at large, there is no telling what kind of damage he might do.'

Jade nodded. Who knew how many victims there had been? Guilt flooded through her. Was there anything she could have done to prevent him from spreading like a disease? The thought made her shudder. Her head spun. She understood what Margo was saying, but it was a humungous ask. Even thinking about it would be arduous. Margo saw trepidation in the girl's face, as well as the multi-layered mask of terror, horror, shame and guilt. She understood only too well the whirlpool of emotions Jade was experiencing. Debra had warned her to be gentle. To go slowly. Maybe she'd already overstepped the mark. Margo grimaced inwardly. She resolved to tread softly. In just an hour, they'd come so far. She didn't want to scare Jade off.

'Just think about it, Jade, that's all,' Margo whispered, bringing the frightened girl back into the room with her soothing voice. 'I'm not asking you to do more than that.'

Jade took a deep breath. This scarfed lunatic doesn't understand the enormity of her request. There would be dire consequences. Still, she had promised Nick she'd give it her best shot. 'Okay. I can do that. I'll think about it.'

'Yes. We'll talk about your feelings on the subject next week.'

'Okay,' Jade agreed, not sure if she could think about it again.

21

The bed-head thudded against the wall, chipping fragments from the badly cracked plaster. The mattress squeaked on rusted springs as its occupants jounced wildly up and down. The wooden legs creaked, banged on the floor, and rocked back and forth as the ancient bed frame groaned against its nails, protesting loudly. The tattered quilt slid silently to the floor. Pillows were flung around the tiny room.

'Oh, yes! Oh, yes! Harder!' Julia screamed, raking her nails down his back. She planted her feet under her backside, arching up to meet him. Her body slammed against his, almost winding him, taking him inside her as far as he could go.

He grunted, nearing the end of his strength. She was insatiable. They'd been making love for hours. Once again, he felt tension gather at the base of his spine, building into a surge of power. He pounded into her, his toes gripping the end of the bed. He pinned her arms to the mattress and locked his fingers through hers. The bed shrieked its objections. Julia screamed louder. Sweat ran down his forehead, trickled into his eyes. He grunted. She wrapped her legs around his hips and locked her ankles together. His body became a piston, pumping in and out.

'Baby,' he shouted, 'Oh yeah!'

'Oh, yes!' she shrieked, 'Oh! Oh! Oh! Aarrrrrrrrrgh!'

He buried his face in her neck, his body quivering with the force of his orgasm, hot breath rasping through clenched teeth. She panted underneath him, giggling like a schoolgirl between gasps.

'You are the best,' she whispered, catching her breath. She untangled her fingers from his and ran her hands down his spine, filling her hands with his taut bum-cheeks, finally sated.

'You are going to kill me,' he answered, his breath still ragged, and kissed the perspiration from her neck.

He leant on his elbows and looked into her smiling face. She was grinning like the cat that just ate Tweetie-Pie. He kissed her mouth as he slid down her side and onto the damp sheet. Resting on his elbow, he reached for her again. She turned to face him. He caressed her flat belly, tickling her smooth skin with feather-light fingers.

'Tom Hancock,' she said, 'what would I do with my long, boring afternoons if you weren't here?'

'Well, Julia Rutherford,' he grinned, 'you would probably be bonking the pool guy's brains out.'

She slapped him playfully and laughed. 'Who said I wasn't?'

Tom would not have been surprised to learn that she was going hard at it with the pool guy on his days off. Not that it was any of his business. He had other women too. But Julia liked her sex on tap, and if she couldn't get under the gorgeous gardener, she had no qualms about seducing the pizza delivery guy, the cable TV guy, or anyone else, if they were handsome enough. Obviously her husband wasn't giving it up for her, thought Tom. If he was, the man was seriously lacking in the customer satisfaction department.

Tom didn't often see Carl around the place. On the rare occasions he was present, it was for some yawn-inducing business meeting, or one of the dreary dinner parties that he'd occasionally throw for colleagues, just to show off his gorgeous wife and expensively educated son. Appearing to have a harmonious family was important to Carl. Julia played his silly game of pretence with a great deal of grace and charm, secure in the knowledge that her absent husband didn't have a clue what she got up to when he wasn't around.

'Hello darling, have you had a good day?' she'd ask when he got home. She'd kiss her husband's cheek and place a gentle hand on his shoulder.

'Yes. Yes. Not bad,' he'd reply, patting her hand, bending to kiss it, then heading for the liquor cabinet to make himself a scotch and soda. 'You?'

'Oh, lovely. I spent the afternoon in the greenhouse, tending the roses. They're very pretty this year,' she would tell him, beaming brightly, as a happy woman does.

'Oh, good. Wonderful,' he'd say absently, his mind already elsewhere.

'Goodnight, then,' she'd call lightly, heading upstairs.

He rarely answered; a million thoughts bounced around in his head. He'd have a few drinks, get himself a bite to eat, and head upstairs to his bedroom, at the opposite end of the hall from hers. Julia wouldn't see him again until the following evening, when they repeated a similar routine. Frequently, for days at a time, he didn't come home at all. She never questioned his movements. In fact, she enjoyed his long absences. When he called to say he wouldn't be home for dinner, she often sent the cook home, gave the cleaner the day off, and romped naked around the house, having wild sex on every surface with Tom, or her pool guy, even with the young man who'd installed her billiards table, and a few times with a cute postman who had turned up instead of the usual grumpy withered old man.

'Let's make love. Right here. Right now,' she'd playfully ordered the young, fit-looking postman after kissing him and copping a feel of his trouser fronts. 'I want you inside me.'

'But ... um ... ah ... oh ...' he'd replied, shy and reserved, until she'd led him into the library and pulled him down onto the plush carpet.

Quietly impressed with his debut performance, Julia had enjoyed herself that afternoon. She always told those 'stand-by men' she was a part-time housekeeper, her name was Kathleen, and that the owners of the huge house were out of town.

Occasionally, she dressed down, donning torn black jeans, an old rock'n'roll t-shirt, and a pair of scuffed leather boots. She'd go out, with ruffled unwashed hair and no makeup, to a seedy nightclub. She drank shots of tequila, danced to loud rock music, and found herself a handsome threesome. Sandwiched between two well-equipped men, she giggled and squealed her pleasure until dawn. To combat any controversial rumours that may surface, she held regular Bridge parties, and often invited the incessant, yet mind-achingly dull church and charity women to afternoon tea parties on the front lawn.

Julia had never been in love with Carl, but she liked and respected him. Ten years her senior, Carl had been a close business acquaintance of her father's. He had recommended the marriage soon after the reconciliation with his daughter. Besides, Carl was rich, and could give her everything she'd ever need. She'd given him the son and heir he'd desperately wanted, hosted his parties and treated him well. Ever since the troublesome orphan girl had run away, over a decade ago, her life had been idyllic. As far as Carl was concerned, she was the perfect wife. About twice a year, he visited her bedroom. She accepted this with good grace, and always behaved demurely.

'You're still so beautiful, after all these years,' he'd tell her after very brief, disappointing sex.

'Thank you, Carl. You're not so bad yourself.' Smiling, she would repay the compliment, not even hinting that she hadn't been remotely satisfied.

At forty-seven, Julia was in fine shape. Tom knew twenty-year-olds who would envy her sleek body. It was toned, with light but distinctive definition, and incredibly flexible. Julia could write her own version of the Kama Sutra if she put her mind to it. At thirty-four, Tom Hancock was in excellent shape, but still had a hard time keeping up with her. She'd nicknamed him Tommy Longcock, and occasionally called him Mister Hardcock, much to her own amusement. He knew every inch of her body inside and out. They'd been having this madly dangerous affair for the last two years. Julia thought that Carl would probably kill both of them if he ever found out. She was painstakingly discreet. There were only two keys to the dingy little room in the basement under the greenhouse. She had one. Tom had the other.

Tom had soundproofed the walls and ceiling four or five years previously, when the one-man teenage rampage, Robert Rutherford, had gone through his annoying drumming phase. Even while standing in the greenhouse, pruning her roses, Julia had been unable to hear him pounding away at his set, as if he were Joey Kramer.

When Robbie had gone off to university, just over two years ago, Tom had set up an old double bed he'd found in an op-shop downtown so that he could sneak in and take cat naps during sweltering summer days. He'd been dozing one especially hot afternoon when Julia came down, searching for a book of music Robbie had asked her to send to him while he was travelling in South America. Julia had stood on the last step, scanning the dimly lit room, and seen Tom asleep in short denim cut-offs and no shirt, his broad, hairy chest gleaming with sweat, beads of perspiration gathering on his forehead. She'd locked the door behind her, slipped out of her dress and shoes, and climbed onto the mattress beside him. It was the best sex she'd had in years. They'd had a mutually agreeable arrangement ever since.

'Can I ask you something?' Tom asked, languidly running his forefinger in circles around her still erect nipple.

'Sure. What would you like to know?' Julia propped herself up on one elbow and waited for the question.

He gazed into her eyes, seeking an honest answer. 'Do you ever talk to your husband during sex?'

'Oh, yeah. Sometimes. If he calls …' she giggled.

'You are so bad!' he admonished, laughing. She was always shocking him with funny, off-the-cuff lines.

'Really?' She grinned wickedly. 'Well, then you'd better spank me.'

22

The light came on suddenly, blinding Lizzie. She threw her arms over her face to block out the fierce rays. Quivering in the corner under the window, she whimpered softly. She was naked, her towel lay on the floor near the bed. The jacket was rolled up in the corner behind her.

'Well, what have you been up to?' enquired Carl, pleased she was now totally dependent.

The girl was a wreck. She needed a shower. She looked terrible. Smelled worse. Bedraggled hair, opaque skin, dark rings lining her eyes. She'd become far too thin. Her skin was still covered in open sores. Some of them had healed since he'd clipped her fingernails. He was well and truly over her. It was time to let her go. He decided to go through the last stage quickly, and have her on the street by the morning.

'Please, can I have some more candy?' she croaked, bringing her arms down. She crawled across the floor toward him.

'Excuse me?' he chided, reminding her to use manners.

Usually, she addressed him the way he liked, but when she was strung out, she tended to forget. It hadn't taken long to train her, especially after he'd given her heroin. She'd become hooked very quickly, and as a result, had been extremely compliant. Getting rid of her would be easy.

'Please, Daddy, please can I have more?' she asked again, not caring what she had to say or do. She needed another fix. It hurt so much she would do anything to get it.

'That's better,' he whispered. 'I'll give you a little, just to feel better. Then, you have to shower and clean up. I got you some clean clothes, and some food. You need to eat something. Then, you can have the rest.'

'Thank you, Daddy,' she cried, wrapping her arms around his legs.

He pulled her up to the bed and took the prepared syringe from his pocket. He took the elastic bandage from his other pocket and tightened it around her arm. He injected just a little of the clear liquid.

Instantly, Lizzie relaxed. She smiled and sat up. She hugged him, and put her head on his shoulder. He wrapped an arm around her bony shoulders and rocked her a little. Despite his disgust, he forced himself to treat her gently.

'Now, you must have a shower,' he told her, getting up and pulling her to her feet. He handed her one of the clean towels he'd brought with him. 'When you're done, get dressed. I have a surprise for you.'

'Oh goody, I like surprises,' she laughed, clapping her hands. The drug made her feel calm, happy. It took all the pain away.

While Lizzie was in the shower, Carl went to the kitchen and made a phone call. Satisfied with the arrangement, he returned to the bedroom and laid out the clothes he'd brought for the girl; a short red satiny dress, thigh-high boots, and black lacy underwear, bra and a g-string. He took a small bag of makeup from his briefcase and put it on the bedside table. He locked the bedroom door again, and tidied the room, putting the towel near the door to be taken away, and hanging the jacket in the wardrobe. Then, he sat on the side of the bed and waited for Lizzie to emerge.

She stepped out of the bathroom naked, now accustomed to having bare skin. She'd spent most of the last month with no clothes on, and as the time passed, it bothered her less and less. She stood in front of Carl and twirled, flicking drops of water from her hair as she spun.

'See? Clean!' she announced, looking and feeling much better.

He grabbed her hand and pulled her toward him. She stood in front of him, smiling down at his greying hair. He picked up the underwear and showed it to her. Then, pointed to the boots on the floor. And lastly, he held the dress up for her to see.

'Do you like them?' he asked, pulling her down to sit on his lap.

'They're lovely,' she replied. 'Thank you, Daddy.'

'You're welcome,' he said, kissing her forehead. 'But, there's something I want to tell you. These things, and the heroin, aren't free. You have to pay for them.'

'But I don't have any money!' she exclaimed, vaguely remembering that she'd had a little when she came here, but it had vanished with her bag.

'You don't need money, sweetheart,' he chuckled. He always enjoyed this part of the process. 'You have other assets.'

'Assets?' she repeated, wide-eyed.

'Sure. Assets are what you can use to get things instead of money.'

'Oh. What assets do I have?'

'You have this,' he said, sliding his hand between her legs.

She shivered. Her induction to sex had been harsh, but she'd gradually learned to accept it, even if she didn't enjoy it. It obviously pleased him. And her reward was a floating cloud of dreamlike bliss. So, with stoic patience, she let him do whatever he wanted. Most of the time, when he was on top of her, she was high anyway, so didn't feel a thing. She wondered how sex got turned into a replacement for money.

'Do you want it?' she asked, her naivety turning him on.

She looked better, though still terrible. And it would be the last time. He lay her on the bed, and handed her the boots.

'Here, put these on,' he ordered gently, stepping back to take off his clothes.

Later, after she'd eaten a slice of the pizza Carl had brought, she had a second shower. Washed and dried, Lizzie pulled the skimpy panties over her thin hips. Carl helped her do the bra up and slipped the little dress over her head. She pulled the boots on again and sat down expectantly. He'd promised her more. Another hit.

'In a while,' he said, looking at his watch. 'Our guest will be here any minute.'

He'd told Lizzie they'd be having company. And that he wanted her to look her best. At his coaxing, she went to the bathroom to apply some makeup. She came out at the same time as Carl's phone blipped.

'Are you ready?' he asked, giving her a quick once-over. She'd do. He'd sent much worse looking girls out to work the streets.

'Sure,' she shrugged. She didn't care what happened, she just wanted the needle he had in his pocket. Then, she remembered. 'Yes, Daddy.'

'Go into the bathroom and lock the door,' he said, straightening his jacket. 'Don't come out until I call you.'

She did as she was told. Carl straightened the bed. He tossed the wet towels into the wardrobe and ran a hand over his short hair. He closed the bedroom door behind him and went to open the door of the apartment. Lenny stood on the landing, leaning against the wall. A cigarette dangled from his mouth.

'I got to pick up a package here,' the tall man drawled, lazy eyes appraising the man inside.

'In there.' Carl indicated the bedroom door.

Lenny stepped inside and pushed the door shut behind him. Carl locked it and followed the pimp into the other room. He locked the bedroom door behind him.

'Lizzie, will you come out here, please,' he called.

She opened the door and stepped out. While in the bathroom, she'd made a few small improvements to her makeup. She stood in the doorway, looking at the two men.

'Hi, Lizzie, I'm Lenny.' The stranger spoke softly, not sure if the girl would frighten easily.

'Hello,' she replied uncertainly, looking at Carl. He nodded and smiled, indicating that she should come to him.

Lenny watched her walk across the room. She still had the little-girl thing going on. He had customers who would love that. He wasn't keen on the boots, but they could be replaced easily enough. She looked sweet, innocent. He'd make a bit of money from her before she looked too tired. Addicts aged quickly; he'd have to get his money's worth before she became a liability. That other one, Katie, had only lasted a few months. Just recently, she'd made some trouble for Daddy-O, he recalled, then vanished off the face of the earth. Good riddance, he thought.

'Lenny is your new friend,' explained Carl. 'He's going to take care of you and make sure you get everything you need.'

'Can he give me a hit?' she asked, staring up at the stick-like man in dreadlocks and a worn overcoat that seemed a little too thick for the warm, spring weather.

He looked a lot like a white-skinned version of Snoop Dogg, only tattier. Lenny never displayed his money; it would do him no good to look like a target.

'I sure can, darlin', but you gotta pay me first,' he said, licking his lips.

'What do you want me to do?' she asked, prepared to be obedient.

Carl had taught her that fighting back would only get her a deep hole in the ground. He'd explained that she could pay her way by being nice to everyone she met. Being nice meant letting them have sex with her. A couple of times, Carl had brought friends over. She'd smiled for their photographs, letting them play with her numb body. She knew that if she was nice, she could get high. That was all that mattered to Lizzie now. She would do anything to stay in her warm bubble of oblivion.

As Lenny bent Lizzie over the end of the bed, Carl crept out of the room, closing the door behind him. He went to the kitchen and made himself a scotch and soda. He checked his messages and made a few mental notes, business he could deal with when he got back to the office. He called the housekeeper and arranged for her to come and clean the apartment in the morning. She was the only other person on earth who had a key to his love nest. As far as Clarissa was concerned, the man could do whatever he liked, for as long as he could get away with it. She just hoped his wife never found out he brought his lovers here. Clarissa, the mother of four teenage girls, would have been outraged if she'd known what really went on.

Lenny opened the door and nodded. 'I'll take it.'

Carl went back into the bedroom. Lizzie was having another shower. He'd taught her to be meticulous in her cleanliness. When she emerged, fully dressed, boots and all, she walked over to Carl and gave him a hug, gazing up at him with wide adoring eyes.

'Can I have it now, please, Daddy?'

'Sure, sweetheart. Of course you can.'

She sat quietly on the bed while he wrapped the bandage around her thigh. As the liquid bliss charged through her veins, she lay back, letting the rush overwhelm her senses. Lenny looked on silently as she relaxed into the waterbed, wondering if she knew she'd been sold. Probably not, most of them didn't. The few who did were so high, they didn't care. All that mattered was their next hit.

'Take this,' said Carl, handing the jacket from the wardrobe to Lenny.

Lenny pulled the coat over Lizzie's arms and buttoned it up. It was of the highest quality, but Lizzie had ruined it with blood, vomit and her jagged fingernails. The pimp had insisted he couldn't carry the girl out of the building dressed as she was. It would look suspicious. The jacket would disguise her. Any passersby who noticed them would simply think she was ill. Carl agreed. Giving his favourite jacket to Lizzie was a small sacrifice. Besides, she'd paid for it tenfold.

Carl slid Lizzie's fake ID into her pocket as Lenny went out the door cradling the girl. He closed the door of the apartment and went to the kitchen to get the cleaning bucket. Lenny stepped gently down the stairs, the girl light in his arms. She went out the same way she'd come in; drugged and unconscious. As he went out onto the street, Lenny pulled the designer jacket closer around her, and headed for his car.

23

Jade held her face in her hands while she waited in the visitors' room. The depressing bare walls closed in on her. She shook with fear and anticipation. Her heart felt hollow, as if it was empty. Concentrating on her breathing, Jade tried to keep calm. Her left leg bounced under the table. She heard a distant clank. Her hands moved down slightly, to cover her nose and mouth. Eyes wide with worry, she glanced sideways at Nick.

'It's okay,' he reassured her, patting her arm. 'You don't have to stay if you don't want to. Everything we do here is up to you. You're the one in control.' He leaned over to kiss her temple.

'I'm really nervous,' she said through her fingers, thankful he'd insisted on accompanying her.

'I bet he is, too,' Nick replied as another door clanged shut. 'He's probably more scared than you are. You're going to change his life. Imagine, after twenty-five-odd years, finding out that you have a daughter. A child that the woman you loved had never told you about.'

'You're right,' she conceded, unable to imagine what that must have been like. 'I have to pull myself together.'

She interlocked her fingers and gently thumped her chin with the knuckles of her thumbs, in perfect rhythm with her bouncing leg. The base of the table leg jiggled with her, hitting the floor with a thump every second or so, making the heel of her tapping shoe sound irritatingly out of tempo. Nick rolled his eyes. He'd be so pleased when the jiggling stopped. It drove him to distraction.

A week previously, Jade, Nick and Alec had discussed Jade's impending visit to David Rivers. She wanted to meet her real father, but was frightened he would turn out to be just another terrible man in her life. She didn't need that. But she was curious. She wanted at least to see what he looked like. Her true motive was her mother,

Maria Devereaux. David Rivers was the only person who could tell her anything about her biological mother. If worst came to worst, she'd ask him a few perfunctory questions about Maria, hope that he answered truthfully, and then leave.

The door burst open and he was walking toward her, his eyes moist. His hands jiggled nervously at his sides. Jade stood up abruptly, knocking the chair over. Nick picked it up and stood beside her.

'Hi, I'm David.' He reached out to shake her hand.

Jade couldn't speak. She took his hand and let him squeeze hers. Tears threatened. He looked just like her. Rather, she looked like a female version of him. There could be no mistake, David Rivers was her father. As she looked into his eyes, the same green eyes she saw in the mirror every morning, a hot flash of recognition surged through her. She released his hand and patted her cheeks, concentrated on her breathing, while willing the lump in her throat to dissolve so she could speak.

'I'm Nick, this is Jade,' Nick spoke for her, reaching out to shake the man's hand, knowing she was choked up, unable to speak. 'It's good to meet you.'

'I've heard about you, Nick. Detective Stonewall told me a little. Not much, just the best bits,' chuckled David, the tension seeping out of his shoulders.

'Oh, gosh!' Jade exclaimed, allowing a stray teardrop to sneak down the side of her face. 'Hello!'

Surprising herself, as well as the two men, she stepped toward her father and threw her arms around his neck. Stunned, David wrapped his arms around his daughter and held her to his chest, hugging her tight. David closed his eyes and smelled her hair, kissing it lightly, and let the tears come. Samson couldn't have held them back. Jade howled into her father's shoulder. Nick looked on, helpless, lost, a sharp pain in the back of his throat building to an excruciating crescendo.

'Hello,' David snuffled into Jade's hair. 'Hello.'

24

Jade paced back and forth, coffee mug clasped between her cupped palms. She wished she hadn't said anything. Jeez, I have a big mouth, she thought. She took a sip of the hot liquid. Alec read the same four words on the page of the fashion magazine over and over, and pretended she wasn't glaring at him. When she started pacing again, he reached for his cup and took a mouthful of coffee.

'You know it's impossible, Alec,' snapped Jade, not meaning to sound snarky. She felt … harassed. Everyone had said the same thing.

Alec looked up. Jade stood, hands on hips, right in front of him. 'It's your decision, Jade. I can't force you to do anything. I can encourage you as a friend to do what I think is best for you, but the final decision is yours,' he replied. He'd known she'd never agree.

'There would be such dire consequences. Not just for me. For you too. And for Nick. And probably for David too,' she went on, trying to justify her decision to herself more than anything.

'Well, that's up to you,' began Alec, deciding then and there to lay down his trump card. It was now or never. She was talking herself out of it, and wouldn't change her mind once she'd made it. 'But there is another witness who is willing to testify in court.'

'What?' Jade almost dropped her mug. She plonked onto the chair opposite Alec and gaped open-mouthed at the detective.

'I found another one of his victims, Jade. She's prepared to make a statement and testify. She won't get far if no one will back her up, though,' he sighed dramatically, feeling as if he'd cinched the deal. He just had to nail in the banners.

'How? Where?' she stammered, unable to believe her ears. He'd found someone? One of Carl's victims? This news rocked her world.

'I can't go into details, Jade.' He knew that would make her curious. 'That would contaminate evidence. And betray a confidence.'

'And this person is looking for what? Justice?'

'Yes, she is. She feels it's time. She wants him put away.'

'Alec, she's chasing unicorns,' Jade's inner-sceptic said.

'What do you mean?'

'Well, you hear about them, but no one's ever caught one. They're not real. I mean, there is no justice for those who can't afford it.'

'This girl doesn't need fancy lawyers, and she's determined to get some form of justice, some acknowledgement of the crimes that have been committed against her,' Alec explained.

'Girl?'

Alec laid his remaining cards on the table. 'She's nineteen now. She's in rehab, beating the heroin habit Rutherford gave her as a parting gift. She was fifteen when he abducted and raped her. She's decided to go through with this, and her family are prepared to support her all the way.'

'Fifteen? Oh my god!' Jade crumpled.

The mug slipped through her fingers and landed softly on the rug. She pulled her knees up to her chest and wrapped her arms around them. Lowering her head into the cradle of her arms, she cried. Her body heaved as her pain seeped out in rivers of salty tears. She recalled herself at fifteen. Flashbacks of the years of sexual abuse she'd endured flickered through her mind. She was overwhelmed with guilt. If she'd reported her own abuse years ago, she thought, this poor girl would never have suffered. She should have shot the old pervert when she'd had the chance. Jade wept as agony washed over her. She grieved for her stolen childhood, and for his other victims, whoever they were. For the first time in years, she let go and, in a strange way, it felt good.

Alec moved across to her, sitting on the arm of the chair. He settled a box of tissues in his lap and gently rubbed her back. There was little more he could do. A deep sense of guilt invaded him. If he'd left everything alone, none of this would be happening. Then, he thought of Katie, and how well she was doing in rehab. Something positive must come out of this nightmare, he told himself. It has to. His mind wandered to his current case.

He'd been to the Blue Mango a week ago, and shown Elizabeth's photo around. One of the younger bouncers had recognised her. Apparently, she went there quite frequently. Her school friends had reluctantly confessed that it was one of the places underage teenage girls could get in without having their fake IDs inspected too closely. Not any more. Alec had organised a raid last Friday night. Nearly one hundred people had been arrested; most of them underage drinkers. The owners and management staff had been charged with various licensing infringements, including selling and supplying liquor to minors. The police had been dealing with angry parents all week. The club was shut down for the moment, but everyone knew that wouldn't last long; new name, new owner, business as usual.

All Alec had learned about Elizabeth was that she'd been there several weeks ago, and no one had seen her since.

'I thought I saw Lizzie with a man,' said one of the schoolgirls. 'But I don't know where she went.' She couldn't remember what the man looked like.

Alec had a hunch about where she'd gone—or had been taken. He suspected he'd find Lizzie Lawrence in the same district he'd found Katie Green. He was headed in that direction when he'd decided to call in and see how Jade was before she went to work. It was on his way.

Jade sniffed loudly and brought him back to the present. He handed her a tissue.

'Oh. Thanks,' she snuffled, then blew her nose.

'Are you okay?' he asked, still rubbing her back absently.

'Um … yeah. Sorry, Alec. It just …'

'It's okay. I know this stuff is hard to do,' he said, handing over another tissue. 'Do you want another coffee?' Offering made him feel slightly useful.

'Yes, please,' she said, grateful for his sensitivity.

Alec made two fresh cups, brought them in and settled on the sofa again. Jade had washed her face, but her eyes were still red and her face swollen. Her right foot thumped on the floor as her leg bounced up and down.

'So,' she sniffled, 'going to the police would seem the right thing to do.'

Alec nodded. 'Yes. I think so. But you don't have to do it right away. There's time.'

'He's a powerful man, Alec,' said Jade, her voice filled with the implications of accusing Carl Rutherford of abduction, rape, abuse, and paedophilia. She was afraid of ending up dead. 'The things he is capable of …'

'And you're a powerful woman,' he countered, knowing she could find the strength to get through. He'd be there for her, too.

She'd heard a song called *Powerful Women* on the radio recently. The raw passion in the folk singer's voice had struck a chord in her heart. Maybe that could be my anthem, she thought, making a mental note to find out who the artist was.

Our battle has only just begun.
Women together united we stand
Powerful as we're one.

Jade hummed a few lines of the song. She made up her mind. 'Okay, Alec. I'll do it. I'll make a police statement. Let's put this predator behind bars.'

25

Alec scanned the faces of the working girls as he ambled along the littered footpath.

'Hey mister, need a massage?' called one of the streetwalkers, licking her lips, gesturing obscenely with her hands, winking lewdly.

Alec winced. She was barely out of her teens. He wondered how and why so many of them ended up here. Surely there was another solution to their woes. Katie had been on the streets for six months this time around, before he'd found her. Some of these girls had been here for years. Many of them were beyond redemption, most destined to die with a needle in their arm. He hoped he could find Elizabeth before it was too late. She'd been missing for a month now.

'Woohoo, handsome! Come here, baby, and shake my tree,' cajoled a middle-aged woman. She whistled loudly. The nearby women chuckled.

He approached her warily, ignoring the catcalls, and took the photo from his pocket. 'Have you seen this girl?' he asked, keeping his distance.

'Honey, the only thing I see is you,' she drawled, and puckered her lips.

He sighed, took out his badge and flashed it in her face. He wasn't in the mood to play. If she didn't talk to him, he'd threaten to bust her.

'Now, I asked you a question. I want a straight answer. Don't mess with me. I don't have time for it. Have you seen this girl?' he repeated sharply.

'Okay, okay. No need to get nasty,' she conceded.

She took the photo from his fingers and studied it. The innocent face smiled up at her. The girl in the picture wore a summer dress, and a flower tucked into her hair. The ocean spread out behind her. The prostitute narrowed her eyes and looked harder. Nodding, she called over one of the women leaning on the wall nearby. They whispered to each other. The other woman nodded agreement. She passed the photo to the group of women huddled together. Alec waited patiently while they discussed the girl in the photo. Eventually, it was handed back to him.

'So?' he asked, slipping the holiday snap into his pocket.

'Yeah,' croaked the hooker. 'She's been around here. Newbie.'

'Have you seen her today?' he asked, loud enough for all the women to hear.

Glances passed amongst the group. One of them nodded. A girl in her late teens. Alec stepped toward her.

'When? Where?' he asked, scanning the street for the absent pimp. He knew if he was seen talking to them, they could end up being beaten.

'What are you offering for this information?' asked another woman belligerently, hand on her bony hip.

He glared at her, throwing spears of frustration into her eyes. He had no use for a smartalec. She flinched.

'Your freedom,' he retorted, jaw tense. 'Give me a straight answer, and I won't call the wagon to have you hauled in and charged with solicitation.'

'She was with Lenny,' blurted the young hooker. 'I saw them in Watson Street this morning. Around eleven.' The others glared at her. She'd said too much.

'Thanks,' said Alec, and marched off to find Lenny.

Lenny Morris was a lowlife with whom he'd had dealings before. Lenny had begun his long career as a seven-year-old pickpocket. Out on the streets, he was frequently abused. From there he progressed to shoplifting and then car theft. It didn't help that his mother was a prostitute with a smack habit and his unemployed father was an alcoholic with a violent streak. Once, when he was twelve, his father sold him to a pornographic film producer. As a teenager, Lenny sold dope by the kilo and a vast range of thrill pills, gradually progressing to harder drugs. For a while, in his early twenties, Lenny was a rent boy. These days, he was a drug-dealer-cum-pimp. He'd spent most of his life in and out of prisons, and juvenile detention centres before that. From time to time, in order to save his own skin, he offered tidbits of useful information to the police.

Alec strode purposefully toward Watson Street. He knew Lenny lived around there somewhere. He made a call. Flat Seven B, Number Four was the pimp's last known address. Alec climbed the stairs. A woman answered the door. He'd moved down the street. She didn't know which number.

Alec sat on the bench outside the newsagent, a paper between his hands. He read paragraphs of bad news from around the world, keeping his eyes peeled for his man. An hour passed. Nothing. Alec sighed loudly, looking both ways down the short street. He reshuffled the pages, and went back to the beginning of the broadsheet. He'd wait another hour or so, and then call Debra.

Two figures, huddled closely together, came around the corner. Alec sat up. The girl leaned against Lenny. He half-carried her as she stumbled down the street. Alec waited, on edge. Lenny dragged the little girl in the big coat a few more metres, and stopped in front of a doorway. He searched in his pocket for a key. Alec pounced.

'Lenny,' Alec called out, walking quickly across the street.

'Yo,' Lenny replied, 'I got nothin' for ya taday. Things bin quiet.'

'Au contraire!' Alec said, thinking he'd nail Lenny for his part in this if he could. 'You have exactly what I want.'

'Yeah?' said Lenny, pulling the girl up with his arm around her waist. 'Whassat, man?'

'I believe,' said Alec quietly, 'you have Elizabeth Lawrence, right there under your arm.' Lenny dropped the girl. She sprawled on the footpath. One of the buttons popped off her jacket. Alec sensed Lenny's next move. 'If you run now, I'll hunt you down and bust you all the way to hell and back.'

'Whaddaya want?' Lenny gasped, every nerve in his body poised to flee.

'Aside from the girl? I want to know where you got her.'

'I don' know what ya mean. I found 'er on da street,' he shrugged.

Alec gripped Lenny's skinny upper arm, digging his fingers deep into the bicep. 'Leonard Benjamin Morris, you are under arrest for the—'

'Wait, man. Wait. Okay.' He held up both hands in surrender. 'I don' know the dude's real name. I bought 'er from 'im. He goes by Daddy-O. She was already hooked when I got 'er.'

'You bought her?' Alec questioned, his bile rising. Daddy-O was the same name Katie Green had given. He mentally added sex-trafficking to the list of charges he was planning to throw at Rutherford.

Lizzie was recumbent on the pavement. Another minute wouldn't harm her. She muttered a few words, and reached toward Lenny.

'Yeah. Paid top money,' snorted Lenny, inwardly counting his losses.

'Give me the address,' demanded Alec, his patience wearing thin. Lenny would pay for this too. He'd live to rue the day his mother gave birth to his sorry butt.

'I met 'im in a park, man. Don' know where the dude lives.' He looked shiftily down the street.

Alec knew he was lying. But he already knew where Lenny lived. They'd talk again. He released his grip on the pimp. Lenny took off. He can run, thought Alec, but he can't hide. As Lenny sprinted around the corner, Alec punched the speed-dial button on his phone.

Fifteen minutes later, Lizzie was sitting in the back of an unmarked police car.

'I'll go with Elizabeth, if you don't mind,' Alec said. 'I'd like to take her home first. We'll meet you back at the station.'

Alec handed his keys to one of the detectives and explained where to find his car. The man nodded, happy to help. He knew Alec had put everything into finding this girl, and that her mother would be eager to see her. He'd go when the stake-out detail turned up. They'd wait for Lenny to sneak home, then nab him. He'd be arrested and charged with underage sexual exploitation and trafficking. But that would only be the beginning of Lenny's new nightmare. Orlando Grimshaw climbed into the driver's seat.

'Good job, mate,' he complimented, as he pulled away from the curb.

'Thanks,' replied Alec, 'it's not over yet. I want to find the scumbag who took her.'

'Yeah. We will. We'll get them one way or another. It's probably an organised ring, you know.'

Alec doubted that, but he didn't comment. He turned to see how Lizzie was doing. 'Are you okay back there?'

'Yeah,' she whispered. She was coming back to earth. She wasn't sure what had happened in the last few minutes. Did she have to be nice to these men now? Where was Lenny?

As they drove across town to the Lawrence house, Lizzie gazed out the car window. Shops and parks whizzed by. Lots of traffic. People lined the footpaths. Then, she saw the bookshop.

'That's it!' she shouted, 'next to the café! I know that place. Are you taking me back to Daddy?'

Alec spun around. 'Daddy?'

'Yeah. He lives here. Across from the bookshop.'

Grimshaw hit the brakes.

'Where, Elizabeth?' asked Alec, inspecting the row of apartment buildings opposite.

He got out of the car and opened the door for her. She stepped out onto the street. All the windows looked the same, but she remembered the view from the apartment.

'It was a narrow window. I could see the bookshop and that café,' she said, pointing down the street.

'Show me,' he said, glancing sideways at Grimshaw.

The older detective clenched his jaw. These cases gave him nightmares. He was loathe to let his children out of his sight. The things people did to young boys and girls were unspeakable. He was thinking of asking for a transfer, but felt guilty about abandoning the kids he hadn't yet found.

'Will you give me another hit soon?' Lizzie asked, as they walked toward the bookshop. Her need for heroin was building up again.

'Show me the window, Lizzie. Then, we'll talk about what happens next,' Alec told her, saddened at the condition in which he was going to take her home. Her mother would be frantic.

'I think it's that one,' she said, pointing to a dark window on the third floor.

A neat row of narrow windows marched up the side of the building opposite the shop. They all looked much the same from the outside.

'Are you sure?' Alec asked, taking down the address.

'No,' she admitted, 'but I know the glass in the window is black.'

'Tell me what else you know about this place,' coaxed Alec, leading her back to the car.

He opened the door and she sat on the back seat. As they headed to her house, Lizzie told the detectives about the black room, and the black bed, and the black wardrobe, and the white bathroom.

'I got this jacket from the wardrobe,' she told them, holding up her sleeves for inspection. 'It has secrets in it.'

'Really?' said Alec, playing along. She was a wealth of information, but would have to go through detox and rehab before he could get a statement from her. 'What kind of secrets?'

'Well, when I was still being a bad girl, I made a collection of stuff and put it in the jacket,' she explained. She liked these men. They weren't hurting her. And it had been ages since anyone wanted to talk to her about anything except sex.

'What did you put in the jacket, Elizabeth?' asked Alec, intrigued.

'Well, there's some hair from the shower, and a bit of Daddy's soap. I saw it on television. In one of those American cop shows. They get all this really cool stuff from the crime scene. I got some strings from his towel, too, and—'

'Wait!' cut in Alec, stunned. Grimshaw's mouth dropped open. Alec couldn't believe their luck. With a slight hand gesture, he indicated they shouldn't get too excited in front of the girl. She might get upset. 'You collected DNA samples? Where are they?'

'Oh, I put them in a hole in the sleeve. See?' She held her sleeve up and pulled out a snippet of the lining with her other hand. 'There's some stuff in the pockets too. Can I have a hit now? I don't feel well.'

'We'll have you home in a few minutes,' Alec said, thrilled that a fourteen-year-old girl, after being abducted, had shown enough sense to collect DNA samples before she'd been forced to become an addict. At the same time, he dreaded the prospect of facing her mother.

Grimshaw pulled into the Lawrence's driveway. 'I think you should go and warn her first,' he suggested to Alec, hoping the younger man would take his advice.

'Yes. That would be best, I reckon.'

Turning up on the doorstep unexpectedly, with Lizzie still high as a kite, wouldn't bode well for the future. As Alec opened the door to get out, Donna Lawrence took the wise decision out of his hands. She exploded out of her front door, and ran toward the car.

'Do you have any news?' she yelled, her eyes searching the detective's faces. Then, she saw the figure in the back seat. 'Oh, my god! You found her!' Donna clapped her hands over her mouth and burst into tears. 'You found her! Lizzie?'

Alec opened Lizzie's door and she got out. 'Hi Mum,' she smiled, and walked around the back of the car. 'I missed you.'

'Oh, my baby,' Donna wailed, and scooped her daughter into her arms, laughing and crying simultaneously.

Grimshaw got out of the car and looked over at Alec, who was dumbfounded. The older man shrugged. The best laid plans, and all that jazz, he thought. He braced himself emotionally to deliver the bad news.

Clearing his throat loudly, he tried to get Donna's attention. 'Missus Lawrence?'

Donna didn't hear him. Sobbing, she clung to her daughter, and then led her into the house. Alec followed. Grimshaw tagged behind. Donna took her daughter into the living-room, and sat beside her on the sofa.

'I thought you were lost forever,' she gulped, overwhelmed. She turned to the detectives. 'I can't thank you enough.'

'Missus Lawrence, we need to talk to you,' began Alec, 'but I think Lizzie should get cleaned up and changed first.'

Donna wasn't keen to let go of her daughter that soon. But, she had to admit, Lizzie didn't smell the best. And what was she wearing? Hideous. She looked like a whore. Common sense prevailed.

'That's an excellent idea, Detective Stonewall,' she said. She hugged the girl again, kissing her lank hair. 'Lizzie, jump under the shower, honey. Get some clean clothes on. Your room is exactly as you left it.'

'Okay, Mum,' Lizzie responded, almost robotic, and left the room.

Grimshaw was eager to retrieve the jacket but the girl was gone before he could speak. Alec nodded, gesturing that they'd get it before they left.

'Missus Lawrence, there are some things you need to know,' began Alec, not sure where to begin. It was a long story. Hopefully, Lizzie would have a long shower.

Donna buried her face in her hands as Alec told her what he thought had happened to Lizzie. He repeated what Lizzie had told him. Donna wept as the detective told her about the drug addiction. Several times during his narration, he had to stop so the poor woman could recompose herself. As he concluded his speech, he made some suggestions about detox and counselling that she might want to follow up on. Grimshaw looked on, feeling helpless, yet proud of the way the young detective had handled the situation.

Among the whirlpool of emotions churning inside her, the only one Donna could pinpoint exactly was rage.

'What kind of monster would do this?' She spat. Donna was furious, but she was also extremely practical. She wiped her tears, blew her nose, pursed her lips, and nodded resolutely.

'Do you have any questions?' asked Grimshaw.

'Oh, heaps,' Donna acknowledged, 'but most of them can wait until later. First things first. I need to get my daughter off heroin.'

'There are some really good rehab centres—' began Alec.

She cut him off. 'No. I'm going to do this with her.' She focused on a door opposite. 'I can clean out the spare room. Leave just the bed in there. I'll lock the door so she can't get out. Take some time off work,' Donna said, more talking aloud to herself than addressing the policemen.

Alec shot Grimshaw a look. He wasn't sure if encouragement was the right way to go. Home-based detox was the hardest thing of all. She'd need backup. He didn't know if he could spare that much time. He was already flat out with Katie, and then there was Jade. Grimshaw frowned.

'Missus Lawrence,' he said, 'I really don't think …'

She smiled, nodding. Clearly, they didn't understand. 'Detectives, it's okay. I've done this before. My youngest sister was a heroin addict. Eight years ago, I got her through it like this, and she came out okay. I'll get my daughter through it too. Then, we'll talk about step two. I want the mongrel that did this locked up forever.'

Alec didn't argue. She seemed determined enough. He made a few notes in his book, handed her his mobile number, and then got up to leave.

'Call anytime you need me,' he said.

'Thank you,' she replied gratefully.

'Missus Lawrence,' he added, putting his pen in his pocket. 'I'm going to need the jacket, and the clothes she was wearing. They're evidence.'

'Of course, Detective Stonewall,' she replied, 'I'll get them for you.'

'Incredible strength in that woman,' remarked Grimshaw as they drove away.

'Yes,' answered Alec. And she's going to need every single ounce of it.

26

'Jackpot!' exclaimed Jamie, and reached for the phone.

Ten minutes later, Alec strode into the forensic laboratory and stood across the bench from Jamie, not daring to touch anything in the tangle of tiny evidence bags, microscopes, threads, slides, styrofoam coffee cups, a plastic bag filled with the pieces of the unpicked jacket, another bag containing items of clothing, Lizzie's boots, and jumbled notes cluttering Jamie's worktable.

'What have you got?' he asked as Jamie looked up from the microscope.

'The kid's a bloody genius,' enthused the scientist. 'Bravo to crap cop shows. Just when I was beginning to think television was no longer worth watching …'

Alec felt a twinge of impatience. He wanted to learn what Jamie had uncovered. Instinctively, he already knew, but he couldn't present gut feelings to the Senior Sergeant. Hunches didn't hold any weight when it came to prosecution.

'Well,' Jamie began, 'I've done measurements of the refractive index of the samples and made a comparison of those measurements in our database. So far, analysis of the physiological evidence suggests—'

Alec cleared his throat. He crossed his eyes and tapped his thumb on the bench. Jamie looked up and chuckled at his colleague's expression.

He started again, using layman's terms. 'Let's start with the jacket itself. There's all kinds of crap on it. Vomit, spittle, makeup, perfume, traces of heroin, textile fibres, four different semen samples—'

'Are any of them Rutherford's?'

'We'll come back to that,' he grinned, wanting to save the best for last. 'There's also the loofah. Skin cells, his and hers.'

'Connecting him to her,' Alec concluded.

'We'll need to scrape and swab him for the tests to be conclusive, but we've got them both in the same place. We still have to prove they were there at the same time.'

'Next,' Alec said, wanting to hurry along.

'Okay, the hairs. Some good samples there, with roots still attached. His and hers together. Again, connects him to her, and puts her in the apartment. It's clear they used the same shower, and the same soap. There were hairs in the jacket collar too, from both of them. Now, the soap sample. It's witch hazel,' he explained, displaying his usual bubbling enthusiasm for his job. Alec rolled his eyes. Jamie shook his head in amusement. 'Not much there, but it's the same soap as I found on the hairs. I've done some preliminary tests …' He stopped. No point in explaining details to Alec. He may as well converse in Chinese. 'Water washed it away. I'll do a composite analysis and get a better look. We might find some soap just like it at the scene, if we're lucky. Moving right along, the fork prong had his skin cells on it. Presumably, they came from under her fingernails. Tests indicated … Never mind. The towel has him on it, not her.'

'But it was in her jacket, so it counts right?'

'Nope, it was his jacket first. The towel's out. There's also the time lapse factor to consider. We may still be able to use it for location purposes. If we find the same type of towel in the apartment during the search, I can do a fibre match. I'm not throwing it out just yet. We'll be looking for white cotton towels; expensive ones. I'll be coming with you on this search, Alec,' he stated. 'I can make a more quantitative assessment afterwards.'

Alec nodded silent agreement. Jamie continued his summary.

'There are carpet fibres on the jacket too. I'll hang onto them until we get a sample from the place. First, I want to evaluate the fibre population and assess the distribution of cellulosic and synthetic fibre types. I also need to examine the preponderance of various fibre types on the jacket, and also investigate the retentive properties of the garment.'

'Right,' Alec gave him an odd look. He could never comprehend Jamie's strange vocabulary. 'What else?'

'Partial print on one of the boots. I'll match it after I've done some of the other tests.'

'Is that it?'

'The pièce de rèsistance … I shudder to think what she had to do to get this, but she did very well.'

'What is it?' Alec was excited. There was more than enough evidence to get a search warrant for the apartment. He'd had a property title search done. Ryland came through again. The place wasn't leased in Rutherford's name, but in his secretary's. She'd made all the arrangements, as she usually did, and signed the paperwork. Alec would wait a bit before he went to see her. Presumably, she'd simply followed Rutherford's instructions. Now, he wanted to hear the coup?d'état that would nail Rutherford.

'Semen,' said Jamie proudly, as if he'd collected it himself.

It had matched the DNA sample that investigators had taken from the businessman two years previously, when Rutherford had been acquitted due to the lack of evidence. Alec also suspected that the judge had been paid off.

'Really?' Alec wondered how Lizzie had managed to think of it, considering her circumstances, much less actually get the sample.

'Yep. His semen and her vaginal fluid. Mixed together. It was in the left pocket. Of course, I need to collect more samples from him, to make it all current, but this is the clincher. It proves he had sex with her. The other three semen samples are different. Aside from Rutherford, we're looking for three more men.'

Lenny came to mind. Alec would start with him. 'Will all of this stand up in court?' Alec had lost cases in the past, and couldn't bear the thought of losing this one because of some ridiculous technicality.

'You'll have to check with the prosecutor's office, but I think so. She collected it from her own body. She handed the jacket over voluntarily. We've only tested items and substances found in the jacket. There was no illegal search. I reckon we'll be right, but you should check anyway. Here are my notes.'

'Right. Thanks,' said Alec, striding out the door on his way to the prosecutor's office. 'Will do.'

27

'How do you feel?' asked Alec, leading Katie through the car park.

'Wow. I feel amazing. I'm ready to take on the world,' she answered, sniffing the air as if for the first time in her life.

Alec glanced at Katie. She looked great. She'd gained some weight. Her face had lost its pallid complexion. The dark rings under her eyes had been replaced by rosy cheeks. Her hair shone in the sunlight.

During detox, Katie had been to hell and back. Her first three weeks at the centre had been the hardest; horrors, shivers, tremors, shakes, hallucinations, nausea. She'd screamed and cried, spitting out her hatred at the world. She lamented the day she'd laid eyes on Alec, just as he had promised. She'd howled at the walls, expressing the depth of her anger at her parents. She'd sobbed in despair, feeling abandoned. Her parents had not visited; she didn't want to see them until she'd made a full recovery. The following three weeks of rehabilitation had become progressively easier. During her last session with the counsellor, she'd sworn on her life to attend daily Narcotics Anonymous meetings and talk to her psychologist every week, and to call him for a chat about any problems she had. Satisfied with her remarkable progress, and surprised at her level of determination, the doctor had confidently released her. Alec was taking her home.

'I'm glad you're feeling better. When I showed up, I was afraid you'd throw me out the door.'

'Well,' she laughed, 'There were days I'd have strangled you.'

'I did try to warn you,' he answered, pleased she looked so well. 'Are you ready for round two?'

'Sure am. Lead the way. What happens now?'

'You go to meetings. You see your counsellor. You get a respectable job,' he said, outlining the general plan she needed to follow leading up to Rutherford's anticipated prosecution and the subsequent trial.

'I'm already halfway there. I have meetings at four every afternoon. I have regular appointments with the psych on Mondays,' she said, opening the passenger-side door.

She got in and did up her seatbelt. The world felt alarmingly large after the enforced confinement at the rehab centre. She felt small, but put on a brave face. Alec started the car and drove toward the exit.

'Good,' Alec replied, after pulling out into the traffic. 'You'll need a job too. Something that will show the jury you've made an effort to get your life back together. Rutherford's defence will try to rip you apart. They'll try to turn your chequered past into fodder for the jury. If we're going to win this fight, you'll need to stick to the plan.'

'I was thinking of going back to school,' began Katie, 'but it's halfway through the year, and I don't know if they'll let me in.'

'Do you want some solid advice?' he asked, wondering how much she'd let him boss her around before she told him to get lost.

'Sure,' she grinned. 'You're going to tell me anyway.'

'The next year or so is going to be tough. You have to prepare to testify in court,' he stated. 'You may have to move. Or go into hiding. We don't know yet how far Rutherford will go to protect himself. You also have NA meetings and counselling to attend, and you'll need to sort your head out. This is a long way from being over, Katie. It's going to get rough. I think the school idea is brilliant, but you should wait until it's all over.'

Katie didn't answer. She sat back in her seat and watched as he wove through the narrow streets of the suburbs, on his way to her parents' house. She thought about all she'd been through so far. A mosaic of the last four years appeared in front of her eyes. It was a gruesome picture. She didn't want to look. And yet, she knew she'd have to study it over and over again. He was right, and she knew it. Her education would have to wait. As he pulled up in her parents' driveway, she decided what her next step would be.

'You're right,' she said. 'I'll get a no-brainer job in the video shop or something. Somewhere I don't have to think too much. Just until this is over. Then, I'll finish school and consider university.' She turned to him as he opened his door. 'Thanks, Alec.' Then, grinning cheekily,

'You're a lot smarter than you look.'

'So are you,' he retorted, laughing.

As Katie stepped through the front door of her parents' house, she felt stronger than she'd felt in a long time. The bubble of simmering hatred in her gut kept her determination at a peak. She was going to win this battle, she thought, her resolve hardening as her rapidly aging mother came out of the kitchen to greet her. Amanda looked much older than her forty-eight years. Katie steeled herself. She had to show her parents that the nightmare was over. She filled her heart with happy childhood memories and smiled.

'Hi, Mum,' said Katie.

'Katie!' Amanda exclaimed, inspecting her daughter. She cupped Katie's face in her hands. 'You look wonderful!'

'Thanks,' replied Katie, beaming. 'And I'm going to stay this way.' She walked into her mother's open arms and gave her a hug. A tear fell from Amanda's eye. She hung on to her daughter for a few long moments before letting go. Katie hugged her back. Alec stood by and watched in silence. 'Where's Dad?' Katie asked after a minute or so.

'He's in his shed,' said Amanda, wiping her eyes. 'He's been terribly hurt, darling. You'll have to give him some time.'

'I understand,' said Katie, her heart aching that she'd caused her father so much grief.

Her Dad was her hero. Ever since she could walk, she'd been his precious little girl. He'd taken her fishing, taught her to play cricket, tossed a basketball around the backyard with her, taught her how to ride a bicycle, and shown her how to take care of herself in the schoolyard when the bullies picked on her. Whenever she'd needed him, Gerard had been the first one on the scene. But, even though it wasn't entirely her own fault, she'd destroyed their relationship. Now, it was up to Katie to heal the rift. It would be one hell of a task. But, she decided, she was on this new road to recovery, she was determined to stay on it, and her father would be able to see for himself that his daughter was back for good.

'I'm going now,' said Alec, pleased the reunion had gone without a hitch. He turned to leave. 'Feel free to call anytime you need me. You have the number.'

'Detective Stonewall,' began Amanda, 'I don't know how to thank you for everything you've done. You've performed miracles with my daughter. I can't find the words to express my gratitude.'

'Missus Green, she did most of it herself,' he replied. 'You should be very proud of Katie. Besides, our work has only just begun. Things will get tougher before they get easier. But I'll talk to you about that again soon enough. Now, I have to go to work.'

'Thanks, Alec. You're a champion,' said Katie, placing her arm around her mother's shoulder as the detective strode out the front door.

'Now,' said Katie, turning to her mother with a smile, 'Let's go and talk to Dad.'

28

Five o'clock traffic choked the four-lane road as Jade drove into the city. Impatient drivers honked. Fists came out of windows. Road rage was rampant. She hadn't chosen the best time of day to go into town. It was hot. Tempers flared.

She listened to the radio as she drove, stopping and starting as the obstinate traffic lights allowed only a few vehicles through at a time. On the bridge, she heard her song, her anthem. Elena Higgins, her deep voice resonating like Tracy Chapman's, burst forth over the airwaves:

Have you ever wondered about herstory?
Powerful women and battles fought.
For you and me both to live in this society,
Freedom and choice we've come a long way.

Feeling empowered, Jade sang along, belting out the words, bopping her head and tapping her foot, as she finally got through the last intersection. Jade parked her rusting EH Holden on a side street and headed around to the front of the building. She was still humming Powerful Women as she headed in through the sliding glass doors of the police station.

Debra was expecting her, and came downstairs to greet Jade as soon as the constable at the front desk made the call.

'Hello Jade. I'm Detective Senior Sergeant Debra Lazarowitz,' she said with a friendly smile, extending a hand. 'Just call me Debra. No one can pronounce my last name.' The detective chuckled at her joke.

'Jade Randall,' she introduced herself, shaking Debras hand. 'It's good to meet you.' The detective's cheerful demeanour put Jade at ease.

'Let's go upstairs,' suggested Debra. 'We'll find a quiet room where we won't be disturbed.'

Jade followed Debra up the stairs and then along a series of hallways, into a small interview room. It was set up with video cameras and audio tapes. A small laminated table sat in the centre of the room. Three steel foldout chairs sat around the table. The walls were bare. Debra shut the door behind her. This doesn't feel the least bit friendly, Jade thought, as she took a seat on one of the hard chairs.

Debra noticed Jade surveying the room. 'It's a bit stark, isn't it? I always find these interview rooms depressing. But,' she reasoned with a light chuckle, 'If we made them too cheerful, it would look more like a day-care centre and suspects brought in for questioning probably wouldn't take us very seriously.' She sat at the end of the table, to Jade's left, and placed her notebook in front of her.

'I guess so,' agreed Jade, ready to get down to business.

'I'm just going to turn these on,' Debra said, leaning over to flick two switches. One for audio and one for video. 'We'll record this interview if you don't mind, Jade.'

Jade nodded. 'No problem.'

'Just for the record, would you state your name, current address, date of birth and occupation in a clear voice?'

Studying a red ink-spot on the table as she reeled off the information, Jade gave her details to the machine.

'So, where would you like to start?' asked Debra, after stating the date and time. She sensed Jade's impatience to get on with it.

'I'm not sure,' Jade replied. 'Where is a good place to start?'

'From the little your psychologist, Margo Rosewood, told me when she rang to arrange this interview, I gathered that there was more than one incident of abuse. Would you like to tell me about the first time?'

With Jade's permission, Margo had forewarned Debra about the general nature of the complaint, and had also asked the detective to tread very lightly, but she hadn't gone into any details. That would be up to Jade. Between the little bit of information Alec had been able to tell her, and Margo's brief note, Debra expected the worst.

'I was about four,' she said, her leg thumping nervously against the leg of the table. 'Aunt Julia was pregnant with Robert. Uncle Carl took me to the circus. I didn't know he was my uncle. I thought he was my ... um ... father.' Jade swallowed the lump in her throat. Her voice croaked, trembling slightly, she continued, 'I thought the circus was the best thing ever. Clowns and elephants, fairy floss, hot dogs dripping with mustard. I remember the highwire and the lions. I was scared and excited at the same time. When one of the lions turned and roared at me, I roared right back. Carl laughed his head off. I had a ball, it was such fun ... until we went home. It was dark by the time we left the circus grounds.' Jade's leg bounced double-time. Debra took notes in shorthand, not wanting to disrupt her witness to ask questions; not yet. She was glad of the tapes. Jade paused, took a breath, and went on, 'On the way home, he pulled the car over near the park and turned off the motor. I was sitting in the front seat beside him.' Jade closed her eyes. 'He moved over to the passenger seat and sat me on his lap. I think he must have put the seat back, so it was lying down a little. He took my panties off.' Jade took a sharp inward breath. The memory came flooding back in full-colour. A tear formed in the corner of her eye. She forced the rest back, and kept talking. 'He put his finger inside me, and rubbed until it hurt. I told him he was hurting me. He stopped then. He told me that he didn't mean to hurt me. That he was sorry. I thought it was over. But it wasn't.' Jade paused a moment and struggled against the impending flood of tears.

Debra cursed herself inwardly for not thinking to bring a box of tissues. 'Take your time,' she told Jade. 'We have all the time you need. Would you like some coffee?'

'Yes, please,' said Jade, grateful for the break. She needed a moment to pull herself back together.

'White? Sugar?' Debra asked. Jade nodded. The detective made a formal comment for the benefit of the tapes and flicked the switches off. 'Back in a tick,' said Debra, nipping out to grab a box of tissues and ask someone to bring coffee. A few minutes later, she returned with both. 'Much better,' she remarked, putting the tissues on the table. Sipping coffee, she flicked the switches on again. 'Are you ready to continue?'

'Yes,' replied Jade, inhaling deeply. 'He undid his trousers. He took out his penis and showed it to me. I was still sitting on his lap, close to his knees, with my legs still apart. He told me to touch his penis. I didn't want to, but he said it wouldn't hurt me. He covered my hand with his, and put it on his penis. He said, 'You love Daddy, don't you?' and I told him I did. He said that this was what people who loved each other did. It didn't feel right. I was afraid of him,' Jade whispered, scarcely audible.

'I know this is difficult, Jade, but could you speak loud enough for the tape?' interrupted Debra, scribbling notes that looked like the trail of a crippled chicken staggering across the page.

'Sorry,' apologised Jade, unaware she had lowered her voice. She continued her narration, wanting it to be over quickly. 'He stroked himself with my hand, and I tried to pull away, but he held me tighter. Then, he pulled me closer to him and rubbed his erect penis on my vagina. He was playing with my nipples too. With the other hand. He pinched and squeezed, hurting me. I told him it hurt, but he didn't stop.' Jade's voice became small again. 'He was rubbing harder and harder, and I remember that he told me to tell him I loved him.'

Jade was weeping, letting the stream of tears run down her cheeks as she spoke. As the words came out of her mouth, she was taken back in time until she transformed into the four-year-old girl, sitting in the car with the man she thought was her father, as he abused her. She could smell him, and feel his hands on her. She could hear his words, and see the look on his face. She sounded like a little girl, telling the event as it happened, stumbling and spluttering over words that seemed too big for her age. She felt as if she were there, reliving the incident all over again.

Debra handed more tissues across the table. Absently, Jade took them. She wiped her eyes, blew her nose and went on with her gruesome story.

'I remember feeling shocked, at the time. And afraid. He held my hand tightly, stroking himself, rubbing his penis against my leg, and pinching my nipples.' Debra closed her eyes and shuddered inwardly. A hot ball of rage churned in her gut. Jade sniffled but kept going.

'He yelled at me and ordered me to tell him I loved him. He wanted me to say "I love you, Daddy" but I couldn't. I was too scared. I thought he was going to hurt me. I wanted to go home and I started crying. That's when he stopped.'

Jade stopped speaking. Silence echoed around the walls. Debra opened her eyes. She looked at Jade, who was red-eyed and wiping her face with more tissues.

'Do you want to go on, or continue later?' she asked, ready for a break.

Debra was on the verge of tears herself, but kept them at bay behind the iron mask she always wore to work. Only at home would she allow herself to let go and feel the pain of this courageous woman's testimony.

'I'd like to keep going,' answered Jade, surprising herself, 'but could we get some more coffee? Mine's gone cold.'

'Sure,' Debra said, thankful for a few minutes of respite.

A few minutes later, after sipping her coffee, she settled in to tell the rest of her story. She was here now, she told Debra, and she wanted to get it over with. Debra agreed, but said they only had a couple of hours before she had another job to take care of.

Two hours later, Jade had got as far as her tenth birthday. The tissue box was almost empty. The torn remains of four coffee-stained styrofoam cups sat in a pile in front of her. She'd related incident after incident when Rutherford had sexually abused her; mostly at home, sometimes when he took her out, and occasionally on family trips, during the school holidays. His modus operandi had followed much the same pattern as it had throughout the previous six years. He'd get the child alone and, after molesting her in a range of disgusting ways, force her to perform various sexual acts on him, all the while insisting she call him Daddy and tell him how much she loved him.

Debra was sickened by what she'd heard. She knew Carl Rutherford. She'd been to charity events he'd hosted or attended. She had shaken his hand, talked to him, laughed at his jokes, accepted a fruity cocktail from his fingers. A chill ran down her spine. She shivered, as if trying to shake the essence of the man from her skin.

'I can't go on,' rasped Jade. She felt hollow, almost numb, but aware of a tsunami of pain rushing toward her. It was unstoppable. She wanted to go home before the waves consumed her and she was unable to function.

'Okay,' agreed Debra quickly. She was relieved that she would be able to go home and process what she'd heard thus far, before having to listen to the rest. It was all too much. Debra felt for Jade, and admired her courage in coming forward. That had taken a lot of guts and she acknowledged it.

'I'm sorry,' said Jade, feeling guilty that she was letting the side down.

'Oh, Jade, don't be,' reassured Debra. 'You've been amazing. You have such excellent recall. We've got through so much today. It's a good idea to get some rest now, and start fresh tomorrow. We'll just go at our own pace, and do as much as we can. Like today. Does that suit you? Same time tomorrow?'

'Yes, I can come in then,' said Jade softly. She was exhausted, emotionally drained, as if she had nothing left to give. She'd call Herman and ask for a couple more days off. She couldn't afford it, but she couldn't go to work in this state. It would do her head in. Right now, she just wanted to get home.

29

Outside, the night was clear. Stars battled feebly against the city lights. The huge rising moon lit up the sky as if it were daytime. A stray cat slunk into a dark alley across the street. Jade stepped from the police building onto the pavement like a zombie, operating on autopilot. She hadn't realised she'd been talking to Debra for so long. She ripped the parking ticket off her windscreen and tore it up, throwing the shreds of thin paper into the gutter as she climbed into her dilapidated car.

Half way to her apartment, on a stretch of road lined with businesses, Jade experienced sensory overload. Emotions raced through her, burning her skin as they zinged toward her toes. Memories and visions threw themselves in her face, blurring her sight. She pulled over on the shoulder of the road, unable to see her way ahead, as tears gushed from her eyes like a river in full flood. Enveloped in pain, Jade put her forehead on on the steering wheel and wrapped her arms around its sheepskin cover. She gulped air into her lungs, afraid that if she didn't, she wouldn't be able to breathe. Mucus drizzled from her nose, forming a long thread that reached through the centre of the steering wheel to a wet patch on her knee. Jade cried her heart out, letting the agony of her past escape the confines of her long-locked memory.

Most of the traffic had gone. Everyone was eating dinner, or settling down in front of the television with their families. The road was quiet. Twenty minutes passed.

'Okay,' Jade told herself, her shoulders still heaving. 'Get it together now. C'mon, girlfriend. You can do it.'

She tore a handful of tissues from the container in the glovebox and cleaned herself up, wiping her face, swabbing at the pool of snot on her leg, and blowing her nose like a distant foghorn. She got out of the car, took the lid off the bottle of water she'd bought earlier, and threw it over her face, then dried it with more tissues.

'Look at you, you're a bloody mess,' she chastised herself, not daring to inspect her reflection in the rear-vision mirror as she climbed back into the driver's seat and turned the key.

Jade stopped at the bottle shop on the corner near her place. She wanted a strong drink, a shower, and some sleep. In that order.

'I'll take the tequila, thanks,' she told the attendant, after making her selection. She dug into her purse for the money. 'Do you have any limes?'

He shook his head. 'Is that it?' he asked, his tone surly.

'Yes, thank you,' she said politely, handing over the money. She waited for her change and added cheerfully, 'Have a good night, won't you?' Miserable bugger, she thought as he snarled in reply.

In her apartment, Jade cracked the seal on the tequila. She sloshed some into a shot glass and threw it down her throat. It burned, leaving a trail of fiery liquid sizzling through her oesophagus. She felt the deep rumble of hunger, but was too tired to make herself a meal. Even a bowl of cereal seemed like too much effort tonight. A search of the refrigerator revealed a mouldy loaf of rye bread and some wrinkled capsicums.

'Aha,' she chortled, impressed with her own genius. 'I've still got some cake.'

A few nights earlier, Nick had put the remains of a double-chocolate mud-cake in the back of the freezer. It was still there. Jade took it from its container and put it on the bench to thaw a little, then took her bottle of tequila to the shower. By the time she'd scoured her body and washed her hair, then rinsed and dried off, drinking slugs of tequila from the bottle all the while, she was quite drunk and very morose.

'To hell with that pervert,' she muttered, pushing thoughts of Carl from her mind as she stumbled from the bathroom to the kitchen.

Jade grabbed the gooey chocolate cake off the bench and stuck a fork in the top. She retrieved her tequila from the bathroom, and kicked back the covers before climbing into bed. She pressed the button on her CD player. Janis Joplin crooned at her to *Try (Just a Little Bit Harder)*. Jade stuffed chunks of cake into her mouth, and followed each bite with a tequila chaser. Crumbs spread around the quilt. Bits of chocolate syrup and thick icing got mashed into the sheets. She didn't care. Nothing mattered right now except Planet Oblivia.

The phone rang. Jade ignored it. Through the closed door, she heard Alec leave a message on the machine in the living-room.

'Hi Jade, Alec here. Just wondering how you went today. I was thinking of you.'

He could wait until tomorrow, she decided. Besides, if she picked up the phone now, he'd be here in less than ten minutes. She wanted to be alone. She reached toward the telephone and switched the sound off. At least she wouldn't be able to hear it ringing. A few minutes later, Nick left a message.

'Honey, are you okay? How did it go today? Call when you get home.'

He could wait too, she thought. It was partly his fault she felt like this. He'd helped Alec talk her into making a statement to the police. Now look at her, she was a wreck. Ten minutes later, Herman's tense voice crackled on the machine.

'Are you coming in tonight? Is everything okay? I need you in here.'

'Dammit!' she cursed, her face smeared with chocolate crumbs. She lay on the pillow in a fog of alcohol, trying to forget who and where she was. 'I forgot about work. Ah! To hell with it.' It didn't matter. Herman would either forgive her or sack her.

Just as Jade was drifting away in a drunken stupor, the machine picked up another voice.

'Go away!' she yelled through the door at the answering machine. 'Can't you see I want to be alone?'

She turned up the volume on the stereo to block out the rest of the world. Ten minutes later, Jade was snoring quietly under the roar of her favourite rock music. Smudges of chocolate cake adhered to the side of her face. A dribble of tequila spilled from the open bottle as it toppled onto its side.

30

The curtain billowed in the light breeze coming through the barred window. An owl hooted softly on a nearby tree branch, calling its mate. A ribbon of bright moonlight reached across the floor, stretched toward the bedcovers and gently caressed the sleeping face. Lizzie dozed peacefully, her expression serene, as she dreamed about a summer's day picnic, under the shade of an oak tree, near a cool stream. Down the street, a restless dog barked.

Lizzie stirred and opened her eyes. At first, she felt disorientated. She looked around, wondering where she was. Aside from the bureau and the bed, there was no other furniture; no lamps, no clocks, no pictures on the wall. A stab of fear shot through Lizzie. Startled, she sat up in bed, gazing around the dimly lit room.

'Where am I?' she asked the walls, hoping she wasn't back in the black room.

She turned her head to look for the familiar bathroom door, but it wasn't there. As her eyes adjusted to the low light, she took in her surroundings. She recognised the room as the spare bedroom. Though it was less cluttered than usual, this was the room her mother used as a storage space for the excess furniture that didn't fit anywhere else in the house.

Lizzie looked down at the quilt on the bed. It was the hand-stitched one that had been her grandmother's. As her finger traced around the petals on one of the large sunflowers, she noticed how the moonlight altered the colours in the room and cloaked the plaster walls in a salmon-coloured tinge.

The bureau had also belonged to her grandmother. Nan had bequeathed the beloved antique to Lizzie's mother in her will. All the drawers were missing. As she became more aware of her surroundings, Lizzie wondered why she wasn't in her own bed.

Then, she recalled Alec bringing her home. She remembered the tremors and the visions, the withdrawal from the drug she'd been given. The nightmare of the black room seemed far away now. It hardly seemed real.

'I'm at home,' she told herself, gently rubbing one of the sunflowers. She relaxed.

It felt good to be home. Lizzie felt much better, a little hungry, but okay. She wondered how long she'd been sleeping. Her pyjamas were clean. They smelled fresh. But there was a strange smell in the room; a sickly sweet odour that wasn't pleasant, but wasn't unpleasant either. Curious, Lizzie got out of bed and padded over to the bureau. She noticed the floor was sticky under her bare feet. There wasn't a lamp she could switch on for more light. She tried the switch on the wall. Nothing. Looking up, she saw the empty socket in the ceiling. The moon would have to be her lamp, she decided. She reached out and put her hand in the empty drawer space. It wasn't an apparition, she decided. The bureau was really empty. She inspected the insides of the cupboard. The doors had been removed. The shelves were bare.

'Mother Hubbard,' she chuckled to herself, remembering the old nursery rhyme.

Lizzie realised she was hungry. And, she wanted to go to the toilet. She walked over to the door and tried the handle. It wouldn't open. She rattled the door. It was locked. Why would I lock myself inside? she wondered, standing back to look at the door.

'Mum?' she called out. Lizzie had no sense of time. She could see it was dark, but didn't realise it was the wee hours of the morning. 'Mum?'

Lizzie listened for sounds in the house outside her door. She waited a couple of minutes and called again. She heard footsteps running toward the door.

'Mum?' repeated Lizzie as the door flew open.

Donna looked dishevelled. She was exhausted. The past two weeks had been more traumatic than she'd expected. Lizzie had screamed and howled, shrieking day and night. She'd banged against the walls, floor, and door, and torn shreds of skin off her own body. She'd turned the bed upside down and broken the glass in the window. At one point, when Lizzie had freaked out, Donna had wrestled her to the ground to untangle Lizzie's hands from her hair. She'd called her youngest sister in to help tie Lizzie to the bed and keep watch while she cleaned up some of the foul mess. Changing the sheets on the bed every day became an exercise in wary patience. The long days and nights had been torture. She'd forgotten how destructive heroin addicts could be when they couldn't get their fix. Between coping with her daughter's withdrawal, manhandling the violent havoc it had wreaked on her life, and dealing with her own feelings of rage, Donna didn't get much sleep. When she'd crawled into bed that night, she was almost at the end of her emotional tether.

'What's up, honey? Are you okay?' Donna asked, every sense on high alert.

She inspected her daughter for signs of trouble. She was ready to flip the teenager to the floor again if that's what was needed. She hadn't trained in taekwondo for the last five years and become a black-belt for nothing. While she'd been careful not to hurt her fist-flailing daughter, she'd also had to concentrate on protecting herself.

'Yeah, Mum. I'm fine,' Lizzie answered, sounding like her old self. 'I just need to go to the toilet. And I'm hungry. Is there any food in the house?'

Donna put her arms around Lizzie and pulled the girl toward her. She recognised the signs of recovery and welcomed them with relief. She put her hand on Lizzie's head and gently pressed it into her shoulder. Lizzie let her mother cuddle her. She put her arms around Donna's waist and hugged her back. Donna cried silently. Hot tears trickled down her cheeks, into her daughter's hair.

'Oh, my baby,' Donna whispered hoarsely, barely able to speak. 'Welcome back. How do you feel? Are you alright?'

'I'm okay, Mum. I feel good,' Lizzie replied, standing upright to face her mother. 'Why am I in the spare room?'

'Steph's been staying in your room and it was easier to put you in the spare,' Donna said, smiling with tired, red eyes. 'And I didn't want to mess up your room while we did this.'

Despite the horrors she'd experienced, Lizzie was now more concerned about her mother. Donna looked terrible. Dark rings made her thin face look like a living version of Edvard Munch's Scream painting. Her eyes were deep pools reflecting pain and sorrow. Her face was still wet from crying. Lines of worry etched her normally smooth skin. Her hair was lank. She'd aged a decade. She looked like she needed to sleep for a month. Lizzie cupped Donna's face in her hands, trembling slightly. She kissed her cheek.

'You look so tired,' Lizzie said, feeling guilty that she was the cause of her mother's grief.

'I'm fine, honey. Whatever gets us through,' Donna reassured her. 'It looks like the worst bit is over. And it is almost three in the morning.'

Lizzie took Donna's hand and squeezed it. 'I love you, Mum. You're the best.'

'I love you too, baby. I've missed you so much. We'll get through this. I'm right beside you. We'll do it together,' she promised her daughter resolutely, as she pulled her close again.

'What's going on?' asked Stephanie, stumbling sleepily out of Lizzie's bedroom. 'Is everyone okay?'

'Hi, Aunt Steph,' Lizzie said. 'What are you doing here?' A look passed between Donna and Stephanie. Lizzie frowned, not sure what the unspoken conspiracy was about, but then her physical need took over. 'Oh. I have to pee really badly.' She scuttled down the hall toward the toilet.

When Lizzie returned, the sisters were in the kitchen, huddled together, whispering secretively to each other. They'd finally agreed not to tell Lizzie about Stephanie's old drug addiction, even though Steph thought it might help the girl come to terms with what had happened. They'd also decided there was no point in telling Lizzie that Steph was there to help Donna restrain her throughout the most violent episodes. There had been an ongoing debate about how much the teenager needed to know. The pair stopped talking when Lizzie walked into the room. She didn't notice. She felt light-headed and quickly sat on a stool at the breakfast bar.

'What do you want to eat, darling?' asked Donna, thinking she might heat up some of the pea and ham soup she'd made especially for Lizzie. A lot of it had ended up on the walls and floor of the spare room, leaving green splats all over the place. During the harrowing cold-turkey treatment, Lizzie hadn't eaten much at all; a little chocolate, a baked potato, a can of ginger soda, some popcorn.

'Something tasty,' answered Lizzie, not sure what she wanted.

'How about I make you some bacon and eggs?' suggested Stephanie, then added, 'low fat, of course,' after Donna glared at her.

'With baked beans and grilled tomatoes and mushrooms?' asked Lizzie, her mouth watering. She felt like she could eat a horse and chase the rider.

'Sure thing, kiddo,' chortled Stephanie, taking bacon rashers and eggs from the fridge.

She turned on the stove and grabbed a frying pan from the drawer. Humming as she trimmed the fat off the bacon, Stephanie began to prepare the first decent meal Lizzie had eaten in weeks.

'I'll make coffee, shall I?' suggested Donna, filling up the kettle.

'It's too late for coffee. We'll be awake all night. How about hot chocolate instead?' Stephanie said, pointing at the clock on the stove.

'Yum,' replied Lizzie. 'I want hot chocolate too. With marshmallows.'

'Good idea,' agreed Donna, and got out the milk.

At four-forty-five in the morning, just as the sky turned grey, the three of them headed back to bed, stuffed to bursting with poached eggs and grilled bacon, and steaming mugs of frothy hot chocolate.

'Can I sleep with you, Mum? The spare room smells funny,' said Lizzie as she kissed and hugged her aunt goodnight.

'Sure, baby,' Donna replied, extending an arm for her daughter to walk into the embrace. 'Come here.'

They walked down the hall together, with Stephanie close behind. They climbed into bed and Lizzie snuggled next to her mother, with one arm wrapped around her belly. After weeks of uncertainty, she finally felt safe.

'Are you okay, Mum?' she asked as she began to drift off to sleep again.

'Yes, baby,' Donna mumbled, turning to plant a kiss on Lizzie's forehead. 'I'm alright. Just a little tired, that's all.'

'I'm sorry, Mum,' Lizzie said, squeezing her arm slightly around Donna's middle. 'I'm sorry I caused you so much pain.'

A lump leapt into Donna's throat, choking her. She swallowed it down, forcing her tears away. For a moment, she couldn't speak. Then, reaching deep into her stores of inner strength, she managed to utter a few words. 'It's not your fault, darling,' she whispered, fighting the surge of emotion threatening to overcome her. 'None of it is your fault.' She kissed her daughter again. 'Now go to sleep. We have a long hard fight ahead of us. It's not over yet. Not by a long shot.'

31

'So? What've we got so far?' asked Alec, sitting opposite Orlando Grimshaw.

He leaned back in his chair with his feet up on Grimshaw's desk. Half a dozen takeaway containers were stacked to one side, chopsticks sticking out of one of the boxes. Alec patted his full belly. Since he'd given up drinking, Alec had been eating as if each meal would be his last. He'd gained a few kilos in the last month or so, but it looked good on him. His colleagues often commented lately on how well he looked.

Grimshaw heaved his paunch over the top of his trousers and sat back, sighing with contentment. He loved to feast on a good Chinese takeaway when he had to work late. His usually roly-poly wife had taken to the horrific habit of preparing salads for dinner in an effort for them both to shed some weight. She had succeeded beautifully, and was looking terrific. Grimshaw, however, had fallen off the wagon so many times that his diet was bruised beyond repair. Even the threat of type-two diabetes couldn't deter him from a tasty meat pie at lunchtime.

'Well,' answered Grimshaw, wiping his mouth. He shuffled through the sheaf of papers on his desk. 'We've got Katherine Green's original statement. It wasn't necessary to get another one. There's Jade Randall's statement …'

Alec had found that difficult to read. Since the night he'd almost driven into a tree, and then found Jade prostrate on her bedroom floor, they had become close friends. They had developed an unspoken mutual agreement of trust and respect. As the detective absorbed the details of her statement, his heart had broken. He'd wept as he read line after line, page after page, of the horrific sexual abuse to which Carl Rutherford had subjected her when she was a child. That night,

Alec had gone home tempted to climb into a whisky bottle and stay there for a week. Resisting the urge had been tough, but now his friends needed him more than he needed a bottle. This thought kept him sober. He hadn't seen Jade since then. At first, he'd wanted to race over to her house and hug her, reassure her, tell her everything would be okay, but he'd controlled his desire to comfort her. Instead, he felt he could best help if he remained as professional as possible for the time being.

'And …?' coaxed Alec, wishing Grimshaw would shuffle faster.

'There's the taped interview of Rutherford from when Katherine Green first made her complaint.'

They'd been lucky to find the tape. The one they'd requisitioned from Central had been blank. Suspicious, Alec had pilfered all the tapes from Detective Allen Worth's desk while he was out, leaving the covers, and replacing the cassettes with blanks. Alec had listened to hours of obsolete interviews before he'd found the right one. Then, he'd had Jamie dust it for prints. There'd only been his and Worth's.

In the interview, Rutherford had denied everything, laughed at the accusations, and insisted the police couldn't possibly take seriously the words of a heroin-addicted streetwalker. He'd suggested the girl simply wanted more money to feed her habit. It was merely a feeble attempt at extortion, he'd explained convincingly. The detective interviewing Rutherford had practically promised the suave businessman that this little "inconvenient" problem would quickly disappear. Rutherford had blatantly suggested the detective would soon be reaping the generous rewards of his wise decision.

After hearing the tape, Alec came to a conclusion about his own investigation. He would tell only those who needed to know what he was doing. So far, only Debra, Grimshaw, Jamie, Ryland, and himself were in the loop. He'd discussed his fears and suspicions about Worth with Debra, presented her with the physical evidence, and added that there was no way of telling how many of his colleagues would be prepared to warn Rutherford about the investigation. Despite champing at the bit to investigate this newfound corruption in her own office, she'd agreed to keep a lid on things for now.

'What do you think of Worth?' Alec asked Grimshaw quietly, even though there was no one else in the duty room at this time of day. He was confident he could trust the older detective.

'Smelly as a week-old cadaver,' Grimshaw replied. 'He's going to have to answer some hard questions after this. The Crime and Misconduct Commission will be on him like a ton of bricks.'

'Yeah,' mumbled Alec, glad he'd never been the unfortunate subject of a career-numbing CMC investigation. He'd come close once, but the matter had been dropped.

'We've also got all of Jamie's test results,' said Grimshaw, getting back to the matter at hand. He flipped through a thick wad of papers that were clipped together. 'Hair … Fibres … DNA … Skin cells … Semen.' He listed the headings as he scanned the pages, stopping on the last page. 'In Jamie's conclusion, he basically says that he can place the two of them in the same place, with a high probability they were there at the same time.' Alec closed his eyes and listened as Grimshaw outlined Jamie's conclusions. 'He believes that sexual activity took place between Rutherford and Elizabeth Lawrence. And he recommends a search of the premises to collect fibre samples and any other evidence that would indicate Miss Lawrence had been in the apartment. He also wants to conduct fresh DNA tests on Rutherford, based on his belief that some of the evidence has been tampered with.'

'He's good, isn't he?' smiled Alec, opening his eyes.

'Yup,' agreed Grimshaw. He liked Jamie, but didn't understand a word the man said. 'We need a statement from Elizabeth Lawrence.'

'I'll get on that in the morning. Her mother called today to say she was doing well. I said I'd go and see them tomorrow.' Alec had plans to guide Lizzie toward Debra so she could make a formal statement. He also had the name of a counsellor for the teenager to see. 'They've had a bit of a rough time of it.'

'That was to be expected,' replied Grimshaw, shuddering at the thought of having to detox his own thirteen-year-old son from heroin. He couldn't bring himself to think of everything else Elizabeth might have been through. That poor little girl, he thought sadly.

'This is what I want to do now,' began Alec, sharing his plans for the next step of the investigation. 'We get the search warrant. And a warrant to test Rutherford again. I can probably have that organised for Friday morning. We'll need to keep this under wraps until it happens. I'm not trusting anyone at the moment.' Grimshaw nodded. He felt the same way. Alec spoke quickly, wanting his ideas on the table for discussion before the older detective could interrupt. 'I want to take Jamie with me to search the apartment. I think you should go to Rutherford's office and pick him up for questioning and to conduct the tests. At the same time, I want someone talking to the personal assistant-slash-secretary. She'll probably know everything there is to know about his activities and movements.' Alec paused for breath and continued. 'We'll need to find a couple of people who won't leak the information to back us up. And we shouldn't tell anyone anything until the morning we're ready to go and get him. What do you think?'

'I think,' pondered Grimshaw, nodding, 'that sounds like a plan.'

32

As the bedsprings groaned to a halt, Julia collapsed onto Tom's chest.

'You are amazing,' she panted, gulping mouthfuls of air. Her skin glistened as sweat dribbled from her forehead and ran down her cheeks. It trickled in thin lines between her breasts, gradually reaching her belly button, and continued in a tiny rivulet into her pubic hair.

'You're not bad yourself,' Tom replied, catching his breath after their sexual marathon. He was considering giving up his gym membership. He got ten times more aerobic exercise at work than in the workout room.

Julia climbed off his slick body and settled herself alongside him, nestling her head in the curve of his arm, with her leg across his hip. She ran her fingers through the soft hair on his chest, twirling the curls with her fingernails. Carl had been away for two days, and wouldn't be home for another three. She was making the most of the opportunity.

'I know you don't want to talk about your husband ... ,' began Tom, looking down at her smiling face, 'But I have a question.'

'Another one?' she chivvied. 'Always asking questions, aren't you?'

'It's just ... it's about something I saw—something I thought you should know about,' said Tom, not sure she'd care what her husband did away from home. It was probably none of his business, but Tom's gut told him to tell her. There was no one else he could tell, not without putting his neck on the line. He felt a moral responsibility. After they'd discussed it, he'd decide what to do next.

'What did you see, baby?' she breathed in a child's playful voice, leaning up on her elbow to look at him. She smiled wickedly, and bent to kiss his nipple.

'Well, I was at The Mosh Pit the other night, with some of the guys. You know it. It used to be the Blue Mango. It was closed down, but opened up again on the weekend. Anyway, we were hanging out at the bar, and I saw him there.'

'At The Mosh Pit?' asked Julia, amused that her husband would even dream of going to a place like that. 'Wasn't that the place all the teenyboppers used to go?'

'That's the one, and they still do. The place was full of them …'

'Oh, really? What were you doing there?' she teased, biting his nipple lightly.

'It wasn't my choice. A mate wanted to have a few drinks for his birthday. He decided we'd all go there. Anyway, let me tell you the rest,' he said, wondering how she'd react.

'Of course, baby,' she crooned, nibbling her way down his belly. She was ready for round two.

'I saw Carl at the bar,' he continued, ignoring his body's reaction to her expert ministrations, 'buying a drink for a kid. A young girl. She wouldn't have been any more than fourteen or fifteen.' Julia's finger stopped tracing the outline of his bellybutton. She looked up from between his legs. 'The strange part is, Julia, that he was wearing a blond wig and had some of that fake tan crap on his face. He wore the most hideous shirt I've ever seen; some kind of Hawaiian get-up. I recognised him straight away. If I hadn't been so stunned, I'd have laughed.'

'What else did you see?' Julia asked. He had her attention. She shifted up the bed until she lay beside him. 'Was he with anyone else?'

'He gave the drink to the girl. They went into the crowd,' he said, recalling the incident with clarity. 'I watched them for a bit. He held her glass. She was dancing. Giggling and laughing. You know how they are.'

Julia grunted. She didn't spend much time around teenage girls now that Robert had left home, but she remembered his string of twittering air-head girlfriends with distaste.

'Yeah, like freaking parrots,' she said scornfully.

'So, I saw him giving her the drink, trying to get her to finish it. At first, I thought it was because he didn't want to hold it, then she just collapsed.'

'What?' said Julia, sitting up and crossing her legs.

Tom sat up too. 'Julia, I think he spiked her drink. I can't prove it, but I'm pretty certain. The kid fell in a heap on the floor. Quick as a flash, he picked her up and carried her out. I followed him, but by the time I got through the crowd and outside, he'd driven off.'

'He put drugs in her drink?' Julia repeated. She couldn't believe it. She'd always suspected Carl was a closet homosexual. She'd never thought for a moment that he'd dress in a wig and strange clothes, go to a rock bar, spike someone's drink—a teenage girl at that—and do … do what? she wondered, her imagination running wild.

As she tried to get her head around this new information, Tom said, 'Julia, there's really only one reason you'd slip a teenage girl drugs without them knowing it.'

33

Buildings whizzed by in a blur of earthy colours and oblong shapes. As the car slowed to take the corners, leafy trees and green shrubs planted along the side of the road filled the window. They drove through a handful of suburbs. Kids skateboarded on the footpaths outside their homes. Men watered lawns. Women walked dogs. Children played in yards. Lizzie didn't see any of it. Her mind's eye was far away. As Donna transported her daughter to the police station, Lizzie transported herself to a time that seemed so long ago, when her innocence was still fresh and intact.

When he'd visited a few days previously, Alec had briefly outlined investigation to Donna, including the results of Jamie's tests to date, as well as the fact that he had located two other witnesses who were prepared to testify. Donna didn't need to be asked twice. It was only for her daughter's sake that she hadn't already hunted down the sick creep who had taken Lizzie, put his testicles in a vice, then slowly cut his throat.

'You okay, honey?' Donna asked as she parked the car.

Lizzie reluctantly dragged herself back to the present. She looked across at her mother, her mind still drifting, her expression blank.

'Huh?'

'C'mon, darling. Let's go and meet Debra, the lovely policewoman that Detective Stonewall told us about.'

Lizzie trailed behind as Donna walked briskly out of the car park. It had been bad enough telling her mother the details of what had happened; now she had to tell it all over again to a complete stranger. A part of her still believed it had been her fault. She was terrified that, at some point, she was going to get into trouble for all of this. Even after the advice of her mother, Alec, and the sexual assault counsellor to whom Donna had taken her, Lizzie was still not convinced that she had done nothing to feel guilty about. Donna waited patiently for her daughter to catch up and wrapped her arm around the frightened girl's shoulders.

'Can't we just go home?' whined Lizzie. 'I'm really tired.'

'No, babe,' Donna said, kissing the top of Lizzie's head, 'We're gonna go and have a talk to Debra. The police want you to make a statement. I think that's a great idea. I really believe it will help you go through the healing process. It will also help put the monster who did this to you in jail, where he won't be able to hurt anyone else. You want that too, don't you?'

Lizzie thought about the man who'd forced her to call him Daddy while he had raped her repeatedly, and made her do all those disgusting things to him, for about a month. She remembered those first few days, before the heroin, when she'd been determined to get out of that horrid black room. An image of the bathroom flickered in her memory. She recalled collecting all the little samples—hair, semen, soap—and putting them in the jacket. At the time, she'd been determined to get those things to the police somehow. By some strange miracle, they had made it into a police laboratory. Alec had told her how a forensic scientist had been thrilled at her meticulousness. He'd said she'd provided enough evidence to get a search warrant for the apartment. It might even be enough to make an arrest, maybe two.

Lizzie let the thoughts and memories float in her mind for a while, flinching from time to time at the violence of them. She remembered meeting Lenny and shuddered. Then, there were those other men. Her mother was right. She needed to get this stuff out of her head. The nightmares wouldn't stop until she did. Lizzie was frightened; she wasn't sure if she could do it, but she would make the statement for her mother, she decided, because Donna believed in it so strongly.

Before Lizzie knew it, Donna was shaking hands with Debra Lazarowitz.

'Hey, Lizzie, I'm pleased to finally meet you.' Debra smiled and extended her hand. 'We could use another scientist around here. Are you up for it?'

Lizzie shook the proffered hand limply and mumbled unintelligibly.

'She's a little nervous,' explained Donna.

'Not surprisingly,' answered Debra. 'This is scary stuff. But, I promise I'll try to make it as smooth as I can. Okay?' Lizzie nodded, silent. Donna squeezed her hand. 'Let's go upstairs and find a quite place to talk, shall we?'

In the stark interview room upstairs, after Debra had flicked her switches and dispensed with the formalities, Lizzie told the detective what Carl Rutherford had done to her. In fits and starts, with Donna rubbing her back and passing tissues frequently, Lizzie sobbed out the words that would become her statement.

Debra asked questions, gently probing and pulling more detail from the still-reluctant teenager. Donna said nothing. She sat, almost numb, listening to her daughter repeat the unspeakable details of her abduction, her confinement, how she had been drugged and raped, then sold on to a pimp, and drugged and raped again. After an hour, the girl was overwrought.

'Let's take a break,' suggested Debra. 'Do you like pizza, Lizzie? What say I order us some pizza and lemonade? We can hang out and talk about other things for a while before we start again.'

'That's a wonderful idea,' said Donna, grateful for the chance to pull herself together. She was extremely proud of Lizzie and said so. 'You've been so strong. I know it's hard, darling, but it will be worth it.' As she uttered gentle words of support and encouragement to her daughter, the whirling fireball of rage grew in her gut.

'Talking about it makes me feel dirty,' admitted Lizzie, once Debra had left the room. 'I feel like one of those dirty women that were on the street.'

'You're not dirty, honey. He is,' Donna said, her teeth clenched, 'You are innocent, pure, clean. None of this is your fault. You haven't done anything wrong.'

'What about the fake ID? And going to the Blue Mango?' Lizzie countered, sure she would cop a hiding for those crimes of teenage stupidity. At the very least, she expected a long stern lecture.

'Babe,' sighed Donna, 'I was thirteen when I got my first fake ID and went out drinking. I ended up in a biker's bar with my best friend, Jo, and her sister, Sue. I've never been so scared in my life.' She chuckled at the almost forgotten memory. 'There were some big, hairy men, covered from head to toe in tattoos sitting around tables with their pints of beer in front of them. They glared evilly over the huge glass mugs, growling and snarling through their beards.' Donna made a face. Lizzie giggled. 'When we ran out, terrified we'd be murdered, they roared with laughter. We could hear them halfway down the block.' She pressed her forehead up against Lizzie's, holding the girl's sad face in her cupped palms. 'Honey, it's part of being a teenager; pushing the limits, breaking the rules, finding out who you are, how far you can go, doing stupid stuff.'

'Really?' asked Lizzie, a glimmer of hope in her heart.

She'd never heard much about her mother's teenage antics before, only the rare tidbits Stephanie blurted out at inappropriate moments. None had been quite so revealing as this. Lizzie was intrigued by her new-look mother, and interested in learning more about her life. Her mum was a lot cooler than she'd given her credit for.

'Yeah, really. Look, I'm not going to punish you for wanting to have fun. Not all rules are made to be broken, you know that. My mother had the same rules, and it's taken me a long time to learn that most of these rules are designed to protect our children.' Donna smiled wryly. 'I want you to know that I don't blame you in any way for what happened, honey. You didn't ask for any of this. Please understand it's not your fault.'

Lizzie nodded, looking thoughtful. 'Okay,' she said, still not sure who should carry the blame.

After nibbling at the edges of a slice of pizza, Lizzie continued telling Debra about the dreadful things Carl Rutherford had done to her while she'd been kept prisoner in his apartment. Clutching a tissue to wipe her nose, she described the offender in detail, pointing out certain features, and mentioning with enormous embarrassment the mole above his left buttock. She described the apartment, telling Debra about the locks on all the doors, including the secret one in the shower, the wardrobe hidden in the wall and the huge waterbed. After recovering from a fresh outburst of tears, Lizzie told her about the view of the bookshop and the little street café she could see from the dark, narrow window. She remembered her promise to herself, and the regrets she'd felt about her mother. She recalled her fury when he'd insisted she call him Daddy, soiling the memory of her own beloved father.

Holding Donna's hand in a near-death grip, Lizzie explained the heroin injections, and how she'd quickly become addicted to the drug. She described how she'd felt after that first hit; as if she'd escaped the pain, the agony of what was happening to her. The feeling of freedom had been so strong that she'd wanted more. Eventually, she got to a point where she would have done anything to get it.

'I'm sorry, Mum.' Lizzie broke down and wailed into her mother's shoulder.

'It's okay, baby,' Donna croaked, clutching her daughter, stroking her hair, unable to fight against the force of her own grief, 'it's not your fault. Shhh. It's not your fault.'

When Lizzie recovered her wits from the pile of her shattered emotions, she described Lenny, and told the policewoman about the places he had taken her after they'd left the apartment. Finally, she related how Alec and another detective had scooped her off the street and taken her home.

Lizzie was exhausted. It had been harrowing. Her face was pale. Eyes red and swollen. Hands shaking. Her voice had become a gravelly rasp. Donna was a tangle of jangled nerves. Despite the urge to shut her eyes and ears to escape the horror, she'd forced herself to hear every word. By the end of the narration, her heart ached.

'Well done, Lizzie, you've done a marvellous job,' Debra told the crying girl, aware she'd spend yet another night howling into her pillow. She'd probably go to the pub and get drunk first. 'I think that will do for today.'

34

'Sit down here, please,' requested Grimshaw, pointing to a chair.

Carl said nothing while he scraped the metal seat back loudly. He sat down and pulled himself forward, resting his arms on the table.

'We're going to tape this interview, Mister Rutherford,' explained Detective Sonia Hunter. 'If you could please state your name, age, current address, and occupation for the record.'

Carl reeled off the information. He was furious with the police for humiliating him at his office. They'd taken Sarah off to ask her some questions before he'd had a chance to talk to her. She'd tell them the truth. That's what he was worried about. The truth could get him in trouble. He could hardly blame Sarah, she wasn't to know. He could only hope for the best, but it didn't stop his blood boiling when the police had dragged him out of his office in handcuffs. Worth would never have done that. They'd had a discreet meeting, followed the correct police procedure, organised the results to their liking and went their separate ways. Where was Worth now? Carl wondered, refusing to look at the two detectives sitting on either side of the table.

'Do you know Elizabeth Claire Lawrence?' asked Grimshaw, eager to get started.

Rutherford shook his head. His eyes betrayed nothing. His body was still. He knew that the wrong body language could give him away, so he was careful about how he looked and moved. He checked the way his arms were resting against the table, hands clasped together, fingers interlocked. He sat with his knees together, feet planted flat on the floor.

'Could you please answer verbally for the benefit of the audiotape?' said Sonia, her voice crisp and businesslike.

'No,' answered Carl. 'I don't know anyone called Elizabeth Lawrence.'

'Are you sure,' asked Grimshaw, giving him an opportunity to tell the truth, 'that you don't know anyone by the name of Elizabeth Lawrence? Because she claims you approached her at the Blue Mango, drugged her, abducted her, and raped her repeatedly while you held her against her will, then introduced her to heroin, and finally sold her to a pimp.'

Rutherford snorted with contempt. 'That's absurd.'

Grimshaw continued, ignoring his suspect's irritating smugness. 'I will ask you one last time, Mister Rutherford. Do you know Elizabeth Lawrence?'

'No,' he stated impatiently, 'I do not.'

Grimshaw found him boring and predictable. 'Right,' he went on, 'let's continue, shall we? Do you know a Katherine Ellen Green?'

Rutherford shifted in his seat. He crossed his feet at the ankles. His fingers grasped each other more tightly, until the knuckles turned white.

'No,' he answered.

'Once again, Mister Rutherford, I'm giving you the opportunity to answer the question truthfully. Do you know anyone called Katherine Green?'

'Are you suggesting I'm not telling the truth?' Carl bristled, eyes narrowed.

'Just answer the question please, Mister Rutherford,' interjected Sonia. She'd disliked him on sight. And now, in close proximity, her hackles rose. She sensed his predatory nature, and sat back in her chair to put some distance between herself and the suspect.

'No,' answered Carl. 'I don't know any Katherine Green.'

'So, you did not spike her drink with Rohypnol, abduct her, rape her repeatedly, force her to perform sexual acts on you, get her hooked on heroin and release her into the hands of well-known pimp, Lenny Morris?'

Rutherford grunted unintelligibly. His clasped hands thumped the table twice before he realised his body was subconsciously betraying him. He stopped moving and sat up straight, setting his feet flat on the floor again

'Could you please speak up for the tape,' repeated Sonia.

'No, I don't know anyone named Katherine Green. What you're saying is ludicrous. I've already talked to Detective Worth about this.'

'Yes,' said Grimshaw, tossing up whether or not to tell him Allen Worth was currently under investigation by the CMC and didn't look like he would come out the other end in one piece. 'Okay, there are a few more questions I want to get through before we take you down to the lab.'

'You're wasting your time,' snarled Rutherford. 'And mine.'

'Possibly,' said Grimshaw, 'but I have a job to do here and the sooner you answer all the questions honestly and concisely, to the best of your ability, the sooner we'll be able to get back to what we were doing before.'

'Fine,' said Rutherford, thumping the table lightly. 'Shoot.'

I'd love to, thought Grimshaw with dark humour, but I'd probably lose my job, and a scumbag like you isn't worth the cost of the bullet. 'Do you know a woman by the name of Ruby Lee Smithers?'

'No, I do not,' Carl answered curtly.

Grimshaw let that pass. He didn't expect Rutherford would know Ruby Lee in her current incarnation. She'd been a godsend. He and Alec were still amazed at their unexpected find. It was extremely rare that a witness just popped out of the woodwork, but the irrepressible Ms Smithers had shown up exactly at the right time.

'Do you know anyone called Jade Anna Randall?'

Carl flinched. He hadn't heard that name in over ten years. His eyes widened. What did that little witch have to do with this? he wondered.

'No, I don't know anyone called Jade Randall,' he answered, aware it was only a slight technicality. He hoped he could get away with it.

'What about Juanita Anna Randall?' asked the detective, not leaving any wiggle room.

For the first time, Carl looked Grimshaw in the eye. It was clear the detective knew about his connection to Jade. It would do him no good to lie about it.

'She's my niece,' he replied, surrendering. 'My wife and I raised her after her parents died.'

'Aha,' bellowed Grimshaw, 'Now there's something we can talk about.' He grinned at Sonia, who wasn't clear where her colleague was going. She hadn't been told much, and would have to learn about the case as she went.

'When was the last time you saw her?'

'Must be ten years or so,' Carl answered, unconcerned by questions about his troublesome niece.

'She left home when?'

'She was about sixteen when she ran away. Caused all kinds of trouble and then disappeared. My wife was very distressed at the time.'

Yes, Grimshaw thought, so distressed she didn't even bother to report the teenage girl missing.

'Always up to some shenanigans that kid,' Carl added. 'Can't count the number of times I had to bail her out.'

'What did she call you, Mister Rutherford?'

'What do you mean?'

'Did she call you Uncle Carl? Or something else.'

'Well, she called me "Daddy" from the beginning. I guess she thought I was her father. Called Julia "Mum" too. We never dissuaded her otherwise. Little tyke didn't have anyone else,' said Carl, adding, 'She learned we weren't her real parents when she was about ten. Our son, Robert, told her. Meddlesome little bugger. He'd found some papers in a drawer. Kid was upset; inconsolable. That's when we told her about her parents. She called us "Aunt" and "Uncle" after that.'

'Technically, Miss Randall is not actually your niece, is she?' probed Grimshaw, eager to get his teeth into this juicy subject.

'What do you mean?' asked Carl, not sure what the detective meant.

'During the course of our investigation,' explained Grimshaw, grasping the rare opportunity to skite. 'We've learned that when Maria and Steve Randall died, Mister Randall hadn't yet legally adopted Juanita. That was Jade's name before she changed it, wasn't it?'

'Juanita is my niece. I've known her as Juanita since she was an infant. The name Jade isn't familiar to me,' lied Carl. He thought about what the detective had said about the adoption. That story was news to him.

'So, where was I? Oh, yes; the parents. Now, Steve wasn't Miss Randall's biological father, was he?'

'As far as I knew, he was,' stated Carl, 'I've never had any reason to believe otherwise.' He decided to ask Julia about it later, when the right moment arose.

'Well, Jade's biological father is someone else other than Steve Randall,' reiterated Grimshaw, 'which means that his sister, Juliana Randall, or Rutherford as she is now—I assume she is known as Julia—is not Jade's biological aunt.'

'She isn't?' Carl was surprised by this revelation.

Had Julia known this? he wondered. Why would she bring up a child that wasn't part of her family? She'd never even suggested the orphaned girl wasn't a relative. Neither had Julia's father. It didn't make sense.

'No, she isn't. So,' Grimshaw continued, enjoying himself immensely. He loved a game of cat and mouse. 'So, when you abused Juanita, you weren't raping your niece at all—'

'What the …?' Rutherford exploded.

He leapt to his feet, knocking the chair over. It clattered to the floor. His face turned crimson. Eyes blazed like ice crystals. Fists clenched, jaw working, he stood fast on the painted cement.

'Sit down, Rutherford,' ordered Grimshaw, feeling a great deal of satisfaction.

A flash of hostility hung thickly in the air. Grimshaw glared at Rutherford, his eyes coruscating with barely contained fury. Rutherford glowered back, his lip curled with contempt, and then he remembered where he was. He retrieved his chair and sat down.

'I'd like to call my lawyer,' Carl stated, aware of the sensation that he was sinking fast.

'Sure, but before you do, there's something else I'd just like to clear up,' said Grimshaw. 'When Elizabeth Lawrence made her statement, she gave us the address of the apartment where she was being held. This information was backed up by Katherine Green's statement. You should know that our officers are conducting a search there as we speak.'

Uncertainty flickered in Rutherford's eyes before he hung his head.

'You'd better call your wife right after you call your lawyer,' added Grimshaw, as happy as a cat with a freshly caught mouse between its teeth. 'You're going to be late for dinner.'

35

'A prominent local businessman was arrested at his offices today. Police are conducting an investigation into allegations of child sexual abuse and sex trafficking. The man is said to be a leader in the construction industry and has myriad awards to his name ...' the newsreader read off autocue.

Jade's ears pricked. She opened her eyes. She'd been napping, not taking any notice of the television prattling in the background. It took a moment for her to register what was being said.

'... a police spokesperson has confirmed charges will be laid later today,' continued the broadcaster. 'Four witnesses have come forward ... allegedly victims of the accused ...'

Jade sat up and stared at the television. Just as she opened her mouth to speak, the phone rang. She went to the bureau to answer it.

'Hello?'

'Jade? Alec. I've got some good news for you.'

'You took your time, I just watched it on Channel Four,' she said, still stunned. Nick stirred on the sofa. Jade's roused him awake.

'What? Oh, hell! Already? Someone must have leaked it. I wanted to tell you myself. He's been charged, Jade. Two minutes ago. Grimshaw and Hunter just made it official.'

Jade couldn't believe her ears. Without warning, a painful stopper blocked her throat, choking her. It expanded suddenly, and shot a burning trail through her gut. No words would come. She couldn't breathe. Her heart fluttered, missing a beat. It threatened to stop. Her eyes leaked, a few drips at first, then a cascade. Clutching the receiver, she slid down the wall into a heap on the floor. Alec heard a dull thud.

'Jade? Are you okay? I'll be right over.' Alec hung up, cursing himself for not telling her in person. He wouldn't make that mistake again.

'Jade?' Nick asked, leaping off the sofa. 'What's wrong?'

Jade sat crumpled in a heap on the floor. She sobbed into her knees, pressing the phone into her shins. Nick untangled the receiver from her fingers and put it to his ear. Hearing nothing but the beeps of disconnection, he put it back on its cradle. He knelt down in front of Jade, not sure what to do. She was prone to outbursts of crying lately. He still hadn't figured out how to deal with her when she fell apart. She'd warned him that this process would be hard on them both, but he didn't feel as if he was coping as well as he should.

'Oh, Nick!' she wailed, reaching out for him. 'I don't believe it.'

'What happened? Who was that on the phone?' He manoeuvred his body around so he could hold her comfortably. Last time she'd hit the floor like this, Nick had got a terrible cramp in his thigh. Stroking her hair, he settled her head on his shoulder as she sobbed.

'It was Alec,' she gasped eventually.

'Alec?' he asked, his arms wrapped tightly around her shoulders. 'What did he say?'

'Oh! Nick! He's been charged!'

Nick was confused. Alec had been charged? With what? It didn't seem possible. Alec was one of the good guys. Nick wasn't thinking straight. His brain wasn't its best the first hour after he'd woken up.

'Who's been charged?' he asked, feeling completely fuddled.

'Carl Rutherford. He's been charged,' she repeated.

'Honey, that's bloody brilliant! It's good news! We have to celebrate!' Nick laughed, delighted and relieved nothing bad had happened. 'How wonderful!' Jade nodded, but her shoulders continued heaving. Still trying to understand her overwhelming emotions, Nick held Jade until she pulled herself together.

'Nick?' she sniffled, wiping her face with her hands.

He passed her some tissues. 'Yeah?'

'Can you go and get a mud-cake?' Jade blew her nose.

'Mud-cake?' Nick's eyebrows danced on his forehead.

'Yep. I need mud-cake. From the bakery on the corner,' Jade explained, adamant that it be exactly the one she liked best. 'The same one you got last time.'

'Sure, honey. I can do that for you.' He patted her arm, happy to comply. 'Do you want anything else?'

Jade leaned over and opened the liquor cabinet. There was an empty space. She vaguely recalled making that spot vacant. 'Tequila,' she said.

'Tequila?' Nick repeated, confused, wondering how these two things went together. Yuk, he thought, and screwed his nose up.

'Yeah. Tequila,' she said again, wondering if he'd become deaf in his sleep. 'Get the golden coloured one in the square bottle. It's the best. I can't remember the brand.'

'You want chocolate cake and tequila?' he asked, grinning stupidly.

'Yes, please,' she snuffled, still mopping her face and neck. She didn't see his bemused smirk as he rose to go out the door.

While Nick was out, Jade had a shower. She pulled on clean clothes and brushed her hair. By the time she'd finished, she'd given up trying to control her tears. She let them come, and was still weeping when Nick returned with her order.

'Look what I found in the street,' he said, letting Alec in.

Nick had met Alec at the bottom of the stairs. He'd filled in the detective on the scene he'd left as he departed on his mercy mission to stock up on comfort food. Alec had been unable to talk Nick out of buying the tequila, but insisted on getting some real food into Jade before she was permitted to start her self-destructive binge. Nick was happy to make a diversion to Toi's Thai Takeaway. They ordered vegetarian for Jade and a few meat and seafood dishes for themselves.

Armed with several boxes of spicy food, an extra-large mud-cake, two bottles of soda, a bottle of Mexican rotgut, and a six-pack of lager, Nick and Alec had headed back to Jade's apartment.

'Hey, Alec,' Jade said as they came inside. 'What's up?'

'You scared me, dropping the phone like that. Are you alright?' Alec asked, bending to kiss her cheek.

'Yeah, I'm okay.' Her tears had stopped, but her voice wavered slightly.

Nick went to the kitchen to get bowls and chopsticks. He opened the containers and dished out the food, then popped the lid off one of the beers and put the rest in the fridge. He poured a glass of coke for Alec, and decided Jade could have coke too. He delivered a bowl to Jade, and handed her the drink before heading back to the kitchen to get Alec's dinner and drink. She looked at the Thai curry and rice, and then at the glass of cola and smiled. He's funny, she thought, but didn't say anything. Nick flicked off the television, put on a Vivaldi CD, and settled beside her with his plate, placing the beer on the floor beside him. They ate in silence for a few minutes.

'You guys are great,' said Jade through a mouthful of chilli-drenched broccoli. Toi's Vegetarian Red Curry was her favourite dish. 'Thank you. I love you both.'

Nick leaned over and kissed her cheek, pleased that she felt better. He'd been worried about her, but she seemed okay now. The anticipated binge of booze and chocolate cake seemed much farther away. He was relieved.

'Getting Thai food was a stroke of genius. Thanks, Alec,' Nick said, nodding approval. Digging the chopsticks back into his bowl, he picked up a piece of chili-soaked chicken.

Alec's heart leapt in his chest. For a blink of a moment, he felt pain in his heart. No one had expressed endearment to him for so long. He could barely recall the last time he'd heard 'I love you' from someone he cared about. His ex-wife used to say it all the time, but it had been a lie. She'd savaged him with her caustic love, and then left him for dead. He'd almost forgotten how those three little words could hurt and heal, and still mean nothing all at the same time. Like he always did, Alec put a brave face on it, and beamed at Jade and Nick, knowing they'd never see the misery behind his mask.

'What did you expect?' he said, a cheeky grin spreading across his face. 'I'm not just a pretty face, you know.'

Jade chuckled. Nick grinned back. Alec adored Jade, even as wounded as she was, and he thought Nick was fabulous. He'd had to admit that the two of them were great together. He'd never had friends quite like these generous, honest, open people. Jamie and Ryland were gradually becoming his friends too, but he never saw them outside of work. Despite all Jade and Nick had been through, he mused, they'd been able to forgive and move on. Nick especially. Alec admired the man's resolve; he'd known since day dot who his soul-mate was, and he'd simply bided his time until she came around. Their commitment to each other amazed him. It pained Alec that he constantly felt lonely, even in good company, but there seemed no way to prevent his agony, unless he wanted to crawl back into a bottle. Determined to win his own internal battle, Alec ignored the sharp pangs of loneliness squeezing his heart.

Over ice-cream and mud-cake, Alec became the consummate professional, and explained to Jade and Nick what would happen next. Rutherford would have to appear in court. An application for bail would be made.

'He'll probably get bail,' Alec said, preparing Jade for what was to come, 'since the infamous legal beagle, Richard Gregson, is his lawyer, but it won't be cheap.'

He explained Rutherford would have to make a plea. 'I expect he'll plead "Not Guilty",' he said, 'and there will be at least one committal hearing, maybe two, in front of the magistrate before the trial.'

'It's going to be a long process, isn't it?' asked Nick, wondering how Jade would hold up over the coming months.

'Yes,' agreed Alec. 'Expect it to take about a year. Maybe longer.'

'A year?' breathed Jade, not sure if she could manage to stay sane that long without some kind of positive result.

Nick patted her leg. She knew he'd be behind her all the way. And so would Alec. Jade couldn't wait to tell David about the arrest. She was confident he'd be pleased at the news. He'd been extremely supportive so far. And she still had her fortnightly appointments with Margo, who had turned out to be an angel in disguise. Then, there were the other girls, three of them now. She wondered about them; who they were, how they were coping.

Alec went on, cutting into her thoughts, as he outlined the basic procedure for them. Gregson would probably try to have the four complainants separated, into four trials, he explained. The barrister would be aware that, individually, each witness may not hold a lot of weight at trial.

'You shouldn't worry,' he reassured her.

The prosecution was piecing together the similar fact evidence, he said, of which there was quite a lot, and would base their argument for a single trial on that. The Justice Department anticipated there would only be one trial, regardless of what straws the defence plucked at. Until the judge was ready to hear her evidence, and the evidence of the other witnesses, Jade didn't have to go to court.

'Any questions?' Alec asked them both.

Silent, Jade shook her head, which was buzzing with a million questions. She didn't feel ready to ask them yet. She didn't know if she was ready for the answers either.

'Only a million or two,' said Nick, 'but I'll figure out what they are and ask them as we go.'

The dishes washed, and the kitchen cleaned up, Jade said goodbye to Alec. She kissed his cheek and thanked him for everything he'd done.

He was heading home to get some much needed shut-eye. On his descent to the street, he hoped she wouldn't go on another bender. He'd learned the hard way that alcohol was no way to cope with all the trauma life had thrown at him. Was still learning.

Nick left soon afterwards, glad that Jade had regained some of her usual alacrity. He was confident she wouldn't resort to another drinking binge. He kissed her passionately at the door, wishing he could stay, but she pushed him out onto the landing with a light giggle.

'I want to be alone for a while,' she said, becoming serious for a moment. 'Just to get my head around all this.'

Jade shut the door behind him and leaned against it with her eyes closed for a minute or so. The day had been overwhelming. There was so much to take in. One step at a time, she thought, just like Margo had advised. Despite all the well-meaning advice, Jade still felt the rumblings of another emotional eruption. She flicked off all the lights and went into the kitchen, pulled the rest of the mud-cake out of the fridge, then located the tequila Nick had left on the bench.

'You,' she said in a sultry voice, pointing at the bottle, 'come with me, baby ...'

36

Lizzie, on another planet, gazed out the window, her morose thoughts jumbled as Mister Jenkins' monotone voice droned on about Portuguese explorer, Vasco da Gama, and the European spice traders of the fifteenth century. Students yawned and doodled in notebooks, giggled behind hands, and passed messages to each other. A spitball game was taking place in the back row. John Jenkins pretended not to notice. He continued with his history lesson, letting his class decide whether or not they would pass the coming exam.

Well, he thought with mild indifference, his eye on Lizzie as she stared vacantly into space, the ones who don't sit up and take notice simply won't make the grade.

'I don't want to go to school, Mum,' Lizzie had whined that morning, intent on sabotaging her mother's efforts to get their lives back to normal as quickly as possible.

'Lizzie, baby, I know it will be tough. But I think it's the best thing for both of us right now. School for you. Work for me. I wouldn't say it if I didn't believe it. Can't you just trust me on this?' Donna had pleaded, almost at her wits end.

Over the past weeks, since making her police statement, Lizzie had retreated, escaping inwards, gradually becoming a shell of her former self. She sat in her room for days at a time, doing nothing, speaking to no one. Much of the time, she didn't even come out to eat. Donna had to drag her around to get her out of the house. To the cinema, to the shopping mall, to the therapist. When she was free, Stephanie would come over and try out various activities to bring Lizzie back. They sorted out the photo albums, rearranged the bookcase, and planted azaleas on the front border. For her part, Lizzie looked on while Steph chirruped and chirped, making a show of being enthusiastic about each task, consulting Lizzie from time to time.

'What do you think we should do with all your old books?' asked Stephanie, thinking to put them in a box and donate them to charity.

Indifferent, Lizzie sighed. She glanced uninterestedly at the pile of tattered volumes she'd been reading since she was four, and shrugged. She couldn't have cared less if Aunt Stephanie made a bonfire of them in the backyard and danced naked around it, chanting wiccan spells and magical quatrains.

Finally, drained from the effort of exaggerated cheerfulness, Steph would give in, and leave Lizzie alone.

'She needs to get back to her routine,' Steph suggested to Donna one night.

'I think you're right,' Donna agreed, and set about making the arrangements.

Even Alec had been unable to elicit a response when he'd come to inform them officially of Rutherford's arrest, and explain the charges that had been laid the previous day. The late afternoon sun had shone through the living-room window, giving Lizzie a fuzzy halo. The girl had sat unmoving on the sofa, still in her school uniform, legs tucked underneath her, eyes vacant, face blank, as he sat on the chair opposite and told her the news. Donna was ecstatic. Stephanie elated. Lizzie sat like a statue, dumb, numb.

'Wonderful!' Donna said, beaming. 'That's wonderful news. Did you hear that, baby? You're going to get the justice you deserve. That nasty sleazeball is going to rot in hell.'

'You see, Lizzie,' added Stephanie, 'Everything is going to be okay.' She turned to Alec. 'Thanks, Detective Stonewall. Thank you so much for everything you've done.'

'Please, call me Alec,' he said, uncomfortable with the formality, then began to outline for them what to expect over the coming months.

As the detective spoke, Lizzie closed her eyes, trying to hold back tears. A lone thought traipsed slowly through the desert of her mind; I wish I were dead.

37

Katie wore her baseball cap perched backwards at a rakish angle. She wore an oversized Metallica t-shirt and a pair of baggy, faded red jeans. Her face appeared serene. She wore light makeup; a little lipstick and blusher. Alec almost didn't recognise her when he walked into the music store. He ducked into one of the aisles and flicked through titles, looking up occasionally to see if she was free to talk to him. Katie smiled at the teenager she served as he paid for his CDs. She flirted with him a little. He was about her age. Popping his purchases into a recycled paper bag, she wished him a good afternoon and thanked him for shopping at Musical Madness. The young man beamed as he left the store, happy with his new music, and chuffed she had winked at him. It was the third time he'd been in that week.

'Hey!' she called, when she spotted Alec rummaging through a selection of digitally remastered Creedence Clearwater Revival CDs. 'It's great to see you.'

'Hi Katie,' he greeted her. 'Looks like you've sorted your life out fairly well.'

'Yeah. I'm doing okay,' she smiled and nodded. She pointed at the CD he was holding. 'Are you here to buy old people's music or did you have something to tell me?'

Alec chuckled. He liked her directness. She had a positive attitude, and a fighting spirit that he'd admired from the moment they'd agreed to do the hard yards together. Katie had followed his instructions to the letter. She went to daily NA meetings, she saw her counsellor once a week, and she'd found a job in the music store that occupied four days of her week. In keeping with his part of their deal, Alec stayed sober. The rest of Katie's time was spent in meditation, yoga, and helping her father around the yard. This week, they were rebuilding the dilapidated shelves along the wall of his workshop. She'd had to work at it, but her father was gradually thawing out. She had the odd bad day, opting to spend teary afternoons in bed with a book to escape depression, but it passed quickly when her optimism kicked in again.

'How long till you knock off?' asked Alec.

He intended to give her a ride home so he could include her parents in the latest developments. Alec wasn't certain how she'd react, and was afraid she might freak out on him if he said anything in the shop.

'Oh, about now,' Katie said, looking at her watch.

'Great. I'll give you a ride home,' Alec suggested. 'We can talk on the way.'

'Sure,' Katie agreed, grabbing her bag from behind the counter. 'See you Friday,' she said to the older saleslady, waving as she strode out the door.

Alec had become a friend along the road, first by sending her to hell, and then by bringing her back, and promising to stay by her side. He'd helped her accomplish things she hadn't known she was capable of, including detox and rehab. While her mother was still an emotional time-bomb, Katie was managing to keep herself together most of the time. Alec had given her some tips on how to accept her mother's fragile state, and not allow it to drive her mad. She'd also had to initiate the reconciliation with her father. Gerard was reluctant, and Katie had almost given up in despair. Alec told her that patience would be the key to restoring her relationship with her father. She was still working on it, but he'd been right on both counts. Her counsellor had reinforced his advice. Talking to Alec, the man behind the detective, helped her feel sane.

'How's the job?' Alec asked, trying to stretch out the small talk for the five-minute ride to her house.

'Oh,' she sighed, 'it's okay. Musical Madness is not exactly a mecca for intellectuals, but it keeps me out of trouble, and the pay isn't too bad.' She stretched her legs and leaned her head back. 'And some really cute guys come in from time to time too,' she added cheekily.

'Oh,' he teased, 'like the handsome stud who just left? You had him all goggle-eyed.'

'Oh, please! Give me some credit for taste!' she chided, laughing.

'What about your father? How's that going?' Alec probed, as hopeful as she was that the old man would come around soon.

'He's hard work,' Katie conceded, wondering again if she was wasting her time.

Although, she was glad she'd suggested replacing the rotten shelving. Working side by side with her father had helped a lot. Gerard didn't talk much when he worked. Showing him she was back, she was still the Katie he knew, and she wasn't going anywhere, were the points she was trying to make at the moment.

'I thought he might be difficult,' conceded Alec, 'but you're okay with it, aren't you? We talked about how tough it was going to be.'

'Yep,' she replied, then told him about the building project.

Alec was pleased she was making an effort. In the end, he thought, if the old man didn't thaw out, it would be his loss. As they pulled into the driveway, Katie punched him lightly on the arm. He turned to look at her smiling face. She narrowed her eyes and frowned, pulling a face.

'What?' he said, feigning innocence, hands up in surrender.

'You haven't told me what we were going to talk about,' she pouted comically.

'Let's go inside. Your parents will want to hear this too,' he said, nodding toward the house.

He wiped his shoes on the doormat and followed her inside. Katie kicked her sneakers off and tossed them near the front door. She hung her hat on the coat-rack and bounced into the house. Alec was amazed by her transformation. It had only been a few months since he'd hauled her off the streets and tossed her into rehab. She was a new person. It delighted and surprised him.

He hoped Lizzie would eventually make a similar recovery. He knew Jade would get through okay, she was a tough cookie. And then there was Ruby. Ruby Lee Smithers. She'd breezed in out of the blue and blown him away. She'd been through a lot with Carl, a long time ago, and her timing in coming forward could not have been better if Alec had planned it himself. Ruby was a fighter if ever he'd seen one.

'I'm home!' yelled Katie, 'Mum? Dad? Where are you? Alec is here!'

Amanda came out of the kitchen wiping her hands on a damp apron. She called out to her husband, and Gerard appeared from down the hall. He'd been in the study, trying to balance the cheque book before dinner.

'Welcome, Detective Stonewall,' boomed Gerard, marching into the living-room with his hand outstretched. He nodded at Katie, grunted a short greeting, and walked over to Alec.

'Hi. Just Alec will do, Mister Green,' he said. 'No need to be formal.'

'In that case, you'll call me Gerard, and my wife, Amanda,' he responded, clearly unaccustomed to calling officials of any description by their first name.

'Good,' said Alec, pleased that was sorted. 'I have something I want to tell you all. And I've kept Katie in suspense long enough.'

'Alec gave me a lift home,' Katie butted in, overly eager to share every minute of her daily experiences with her parents so that they could learn to trust her again.

Amanda appreciated this running commentary on her daughter's life. She found it soothing. She was still dealing with the horror of what Katie had been through, and it comforted her immensely to know where her daughter was and what she was doing. Gerard felt differently. He could have lived happily without knowing how many times Katie smiled each day, learning about every mundane thing she'd seen on her walk to work, and hearing about when she was getting her period. He was still extremely angry. Katie thought he was mad at her, and considered his rage justified. But, Gerard had admitted to himself recently, he was actually furious with himself.

'What is it?' asked Amanda, eager to hear what Alec had to say.

He told them about Rutherford's arrest the day before, and listed the various charges. Before he'd finished speaking Amanda burst into tears. Katie held her mother as she cried. Her own relief was riddled with guilt and fear. Gerard sat stone-faced, his jaw working, teeth clenched, lips pursed tightly. He said nothing, but when Alec caught his eye, he nodded once. Alec saw the mixture of pain and gratitude in the man's eyes, and didn't comment. When the women settled down, Alec repeated the rest of his spiel about the immediate future for the third time. He answered their questions, and handed out helpful advice.

'I think we should celebrate,' said Katie, quickly recovering her composure. 'Mum, you can open that bottle of champagne in the fridge!'

Amanda looked at Gerard in alarm. That nasty word 'addiction' ripped through her mind. She was afraid that a single drink would undo all Katie's hard work. It had been such an agonising battle for all three of them. 'I don't know …' she began.

Katie cut her off. 'C'mon Mum, for you and Dad. I'll have juice.'

'I think,' rumbled Gerard, 'that a glass of bubbly is a sterling idea.'

Katie beamed, and clapped her hands, nodding at her mother with wide happy eyes. Her father's approval was a big step in the right direction. It meant a lot. Amanda gave in to the moment and nodded her consent.

'Not for me, thanks,' interjected Alec, knowing one drink would be his downfall. 'I'll have to toast you with juice too.'

Katie gave him a knowing wink, and ran out to the kitchen to get the bottles and some glasses. She poured apple juice into wine glasses for Alec and herself. Gerard opened the champagne, careful not to knock the lights out again. He'd done that by accident on their twenty-fifth wedding anniversary. He filled two glasses with the fizzy liquid, handed one to his wife, and raised his in a toast.

'Here's to you, Alec,' he said solemnly, 'for restoring our lives.'

'Please stay for dinner, Alec,' invited Amanda. 'There's more than enough food for all of us. I made chicken lasagne with pesto topping.'

Alec thought about his empty, lonely flat. He pondered the constant urge to run down to the bottle-shop and drown his sorrows. The sleepless nights. The lack of stimulating company. The endless boredom of the same four walls. The perpetual ache of loneliness which was amplified tenfold at night. The instant noodles he often ate because he couldn't be bothered preparing real food. He sipped his apple juice, appreciative of Katie's sensitivity.

He grinned brilliantly at Amanda, and replied, 'Thanks, I'd love to.'

38

Mick Jagger pouted and pranced, marching up and down the stage, gyrating his hips, his trademark lips pressed up against the microphone, as he sang at the top of his lungs. Ruby joined in, singing out of tune as loud as she could. She wiggled her shoulders and tapped her toes, flicking her hair from side to side as she bounced her head to the beat. From time to time, she paused in her task and looked up at the television. Tap, tap, tap, echoed the glass-topped table as the sharp edge of plastic crushed the crystalline blow into fine powder. Using her expired credit card, she expertly arranged the small pile of white dust into two short lines.

'This,' she told Mick, 'will start me up, doll!'

Ruby took the centre from a plastic pen and put the end in her left nostril. She leaned down to the first line and sniffed hard, running the pen casing along the tabletop. The white powder quickly disappeared from the glass surface, flying up the thin shaft into Ruby's nose, where it was quickly absorbed into her bloodstream.

'Oh! Yes!' she shouted, revelling in the hot rush of euphoria.

When she looked up, a musician she didn't recognise had taken over from Mick. It was one of those so-called modern music videos she loathed. All doof doof and no bloody sense. Ruby touched the mute button on the remote control and let the blessed silence roll over her. If it wasn't rock and roll, she didn't want to know about it. Ruby inserted the end of the pen into her right nostril. Just as she leaned toward the table, the doorbell rang.

'Damn!' she cursed, sitting straight up with the pen sticking out of her nose.

She scanned the room for something to scrape the line of cocaine into. The little plastic wrapper it came in had vanished. Then, she spied the thick magazine. She opened a centre page and placed the periodical carefully over the powder. She hit the off button on the remote control. Satisfied her drug of choice was out of sight, and that she wouldn't have to arrange it again, she wiped her nose with a thumb and forefinger, let the forgotten pen fall to the floor, and then opened the door.

'Good morning, Ms Smithers, can I have a word?' Alec asked, taking in her bedraggled appearance.

Ruby wore her long, frizzy hair loose. She resembled one of Medusa's long-lost cousins. Snakes of dark hair framed her wide oval face, curling around her neck, looping around each other, and dipping seductively down her back. The ends were split and dry. The remains of ancient henna applications streaked towards the tips. A fuzzy halo of tangled stragglers danced around the outside layer of her thick hair. She had on a man's frayed shirt, much too large for her stick-insect frame, with a well-worn tie-died tank top underneath, and paint-stained track-pants with a large hole on the hip. No shoes. No underwear. No makeup. The diamond stud in her nose gleamed.

Ruby's azure eyes pierced Alec's as she stood gaping at him through the doorway. Holy hell, she thought, her mind spinning wildly, and clamped her mouth firmly shut. Her pupils were dilated. Shining blue rings, black in the centre, looking slightly glazed, devoured the handsome detective.

'Hello, gorgeous!' she greeted enthusiastically, instantly recovering from the shock of finding a scrumptious policeman at her door while she was halfway through snorting her wake-up buzz. 'Come in, come in. Sit down. Would you like some coffee?'

'Yeah, that would be great. Thanks,' he replied, ignoring her casual flirtatiousness as she grazed lazily on his features with her sexy bedroom eyes, a sensual smirk on her full lips. He stepped through the doorway and walked into the cavernous living-room, eyes widening at the sight of her massive music library.

'Why don't you choose some music, and I'll go put the kettle on?' suggested Ruby, hoping to distract him for a moment.

Alec walked over to Ruby's impressive collection of records. He was interested in learning her musical tastes. There were more than three thousand CDs, mini-discs, DVDs, and audio cassettes lining the shelves, roughly arranged in alphabetical order. He bent to read some of the labels, his back to her. Silently, Ruby slunk over to the table, picked up the magazine, and wiped the line into the open pages with the side of her hand.

'Phew,' she mumbled under her breath, 'that was close.' Then, so he could hear her, 'Back in a tick.'

She closed the magazine and tucked it under her arm, picked up the pen casing and its innards, and took them into the kitchen. Flicking the kettle on, she made clattering noises with the cups, the sugar bowl and the milk jug with one hand, and scraped bits of powder off the side of her other palm onto the glossy page. Working fast, she flicked the line into the centre of the fold she'd made in the middle of the page, quickly snorted it into her right nostril, then licked the rest of the powder from her hand. It was slightly sweet.

'Hmm, cut with sugar,' she whispered to herself as her tongue went numb.

Now, she was ready to make coffee for her unexpected visitor.

At the same time as Ruby spooned freshly ground Mocha Harar into the glass filter jug, Alec opened her favourite cassette case. He raised one eyebrow, looked over his shoulder to see if she was there, and quietly pushed the cover closed.

The tape was gone. In its place was Ruby's stash of first grade Afghan?Black, pressed into the shape of a tape and wrapped in a thin layer of cling film. Emboldened by the clinking noises in the kitchen, Alec opened the plastic case again, lifted one corner of the cling wrap and sniffed. He recognised the pungent smell of the soft, sticky hash from a drug bust he'd been part of a few years ago. He grinned, resealed the package, and returned the cassette cover to the shelf.

'Very interesting,' Alec mumbled, chuckling at her cleverness, wondering when and where she'd bought the high grade hash.

There was a good two, maybe three ounces there, he deduced, possibly more, probably worth a few grand at that quality. Enough to bust her for possession in any case, he figured. Disinclined to put one of his best witnesses away, Alec put the thought out of his mind. He wouldn't say a thing about her secret stash of Mazar-i-Sharif's finest export. He chose a Pink Floyd CD, Dark Side of the Moon, and put it on. Sarcastically, he considered it appropriate. He turned the volume low so they could hear each other speak. Alec settled himself on the sofa and waited for Ruby. When he noticed a couple of white powdery spots on the table, he smiled and shook his head. She was bloody incorrigible, he thought, grinning inwardly.

Ruby came out of the kitchen carrying a large wooden tray. She'd cut a few slices of fruit cake and put them on a plate. Cups, sugar, milk, spoons and the coffee jug sat to one side. She plopped the tray on the table in the living-room and sat down.

'Sorry it took so long, kettle's on the blink,' she explained, slowly pushing the spiralled plunger to the bottom of the jug. 'Milk? Sugar?'

Coffee served, Ruby sat back and sipped from her mug. She appraised Alec over the rim, and speculated on the reasons for his visit. The day she'd gone to the police station to talk to someone, she'd liked him immediately. He'd been walking past the busy front desk, on his way out the door when she'd decided he looked reasonably trustworthy. After chatting with her for a few minutes, he'd taken her upstairs and introduced her to Debra, filling the Senior Sergeant in on the essential details. A few hours later, both women had emerged from the interview room. Ruby came out sniffing, a tissue pressed to her mouth, her eyes red and puffy. Debra had gently reassured the overwrought woman that she'd do her best, that justice would be done, and then returned to her office after asking Alec to see her out.

'You okay?' he'd asked, once again feeling sharp stabs of guilt and weighty responsibility for making all these poor women so miserable.

He'd never seen so many tears in his life. He felt guilty that they had all cried so much, and that he had contributed to their suffering. Then, he felt guilty for feeling guilty. Get it together, he'd admonished himself, you're only doing your job.

'Yeah, I'm okay,' she'd answered, gathering the tattered shreds of herself together. 'Jeez, I needed to do that. It's been simmering away for ages. Don't mind me. I cry all the time. It's like getting the pipes cleaned out. How about that for brilliant timing, huh? Just when I was beginning to lose hope of redemption.' Ruby babbled animatedly. 'Debra said you're the boss on this case, and if I needed anything I should call you.' Can I call if I need an orgasm, she thought wickedly, her expression deadpan, or a gorgeous body to rub up against?

Alec nodded and smiled. 'That's right. I'll walk you out, if you like,' he'd offered, taking to her instantly. She was like an older version of Jade, with more balls, a happier disposition, a much bigger mouth, and an irrepressible aura. He admired her courage.

'Thanks. You're a doll,' she'd said, 'Debra is wonderful too. Supportive and sympathetic. I liked her. But,' Ruby lowered her voice to a barely audible whisper, 'she needs to get laid something fierce.'

Alec had burst out laughing and led Ruby toward the front door. 'I'll let you know the minute anything happens,' he'd promised, handing her his card.

Now he was here in her apartment, checking out the scope and variety of her narcotic habits and wondering how she'd accumulated such a magnificent library of rock music. Alec sipped the freshly brewed coffee for a moment, enjoying the rich chocolaty taste, and then turned to give her the news. For some inexplicable reason, his brain changed gear without telling his mouth.

'Do a lot of drugs, do you?' he asked, instantly mortified that the wrong words had made it into the atmosphere where they couldn't be retracted.

Ruby giggled. Cocaine made her feel ten feet tall and bullet-proof. She put her coffee cup on the table and sat to face the detective squarely. Smiling broadly, she patted his leg. 'Are you busting me for drugs, or did you want to tell me something?'

'I'm not going to bust you,' he assured her, but decided it was definitely a subject they needed to address, 'but I do want to talk to you about drugs.' First, he told her about Rutherford, and filled her in on what to expect over the next few months. Ruby listened intently, without comment. 'If you are going to go through with this, Ruby, I need you to be straight.' He felt more comfortable using her first name. She didn't object.

'I'm straight,' she said, picking up her mug.

'No you're not,' he countered, wiping his finger across the edge of the table. The tiny spot of powder on his fingertip tasted sweet. 'You were doing cocaine right before I walked in the door, and you have enough Afghan Black in the cassette rack to be charged with possession.'

Ruby gasped. Her eyes flew open. She didn't believe he'd discovered all this in the last five minutes. 'Have you been watching me?' she asked angrily.

'No, it was just a fluke,' he admitted. 'I opened the Creedence tape, and found your impressive stash.' Ruby sat up and stared at him. 'Don't worry, it's still there.' He pointed to the cassette on the bottom shelf and shrugged. 'I'm a big fan,' he explained. 'Creedence are one of my favourites. And then, I sat here to wait for you and noticed the powder in the crack between the glass and the frame.'

'Okay, so I'm not straight,' Ruby sneered, frowning, pouting, ice-blue eyes flashing. 'What are you going to do about it?'

'Right now, nothing,' he told her. 'But the other three girls have worked really hard to get themselves straight, and off drugs, and it would be a terrible shame if you were to let the whole side down.'

She sighed and lowered her eyes. A twinge of shame flickered through her. She couldn't let the team down, even if she hadn't met them yet. But, she thought, I feel so good. How can I go through this if I'm not out of it?

'Ruby,' Alec continued, sensing her distress, 'you still have a while. It's going to be a few months before you have to testify. But, when the time comes, I want you clean, straight, and with your head together, got it? The defence can blow you out of the water with drug use, and we don't want that to happen. We have to be clean, all of us. Can you do that?'

'Okay,' Ruby nodded, unsure if she could make this promise. 'I can do that.' It was a huge ask. She didn't trust her level of commitment.

'If you're hooked and need help to detox, I can help. I've already been through this with the three other girls, including drying myself out,' he confessed, 'and we're all going to be counting on you to be a hundred per cent credible in the witness box.'

'I've been taking drugs a long time, Alec,' she said, unsure how she'd survive without her indispensable crutch. She wasn't an addict, but she enjoyed using drugs. 'They kill … the pain … and everything else.'

'I know,' he whispered, sympathetic, able to empathise. He knew how it was. He missed his liquid life-support. Then, an idea struck him. 'Ruby, let's focus on the hard stuff. The cocaine and any other hard drugs you take. Get rid of them. Stop taking them. Those are the ones that will get us in trouble. In the meantime, a bit of top-notch pot probably isn't going to hurt.'

Ruby was listening. She could do compromise much better than she could do cold turkey. Besides, cannibis is not a drug, she told herself.

'Ah, hell,' he said, throwing caution to the wind, 'half the justice department smokes dope, anyway. So, on that note, why don't you roll a joint? Then, we'll discuss ways to tackle the future.'

'Are you serious?' Ruby shouted, stoked.

'Yeah,' he grinned, 'go for it.'

'Oh, doll, I could kiss you!' she grinned back madly, and put her coffee down.

'You're gonna need a few friends to help you get rid of a block that size before the trial,' he joked, vaguely wondering how much of it she would smoke in the next three months or so.

'I could always sell it,' she suggested playfully, heading for the tape deck.

'I'll pretend I didn't hear that,' he laughed, and settled back on the sofa. He watched as she took a long toke, and declined when she offered him the joint.

Alec hadn't spent a leisurely Saturday morning for over five years. Thanks to these incredible women, all survivors of horrific abuse, his life was now worth living, and he was content to leave his own fate in destiny's hands.

39

'The Crown versus Carl Robert Rutherford,' announced the court clerk. She shuffled some papers and then looked around the empty courtroom. Due to the nature of the crime, and the age of some of the witnesses, the judge had decided on a closed court.

'Please state your appearances for the record,' requested Judge Samuel Leonard.

The chief prosecutor stood, resplendent in wig and gown. 'Ellen Johnson and Stephen Frederick for the Prosecution, Your Honour,' announced Stephen in a clear baritone voice that echoed throughout the cavernous room.

'Thank you,' responded Judge, tapping the document on his bench.

'Thank you,' repeated Stephen, acknowledging the judge with a nod before he sat down.

Gregson adjusted his wig and then stood to answer that same question. 'Richard Gregson and Gareth Thompson for Mister Rutherford, who is present in the court, Your Honour,' he stated in a gravelly voice thick with decades of nicotine abuse.

'Thank you,' said the judge, appraising the legal teams over the top of his half-lens spectacles. He mumbled an instruction to the clerk.

'Would the accused please stand. State your full name for the record,' requested the clerk.

Carl got to his feet, feeling numb, still in a state of shock. Since his arrest the previous day, he'd had almost no sleep, and had been in continuous consultation with his legal defence team. 'Carl Robert Rutherford,' he replied after clearing his throat.

'How old are you?' the clerk asked.

Judge Leonard scribbled notes on a pad in front of him. Gregson shuffled through a pile of papers. Stephen whispered in Ellen's ear. She nodded and made a note on her legal pad.

'Fifty-four,' replied Carl, his voice flat.

'How far did you go in school?'

'I have a Bachelor of Architecture, a Graduate Diploma in Business Management and an Honours Degree in Electrical Engineering.'

Bored with the mundane questions of the young clerk, Carl tapped a pen on the hand rail as he answered, and studied the inverted sawtooth pattern on the polished floorboards rather than address the clerk directly.

'What is your current occupation?' continued the clerk, unruffled. Defendants of all different backgrounds, came through this room, she was accustomed to belligerence from reluctant defendants.

'I'm the managing director of Rutherford and Rutherford Construction Industries,' he said, then added in a boastful tone, 'and I'm also a board member of several other prominent building companies …'

'Are you presently on probation or parole for any offences other than the charges we are hearing today?' interjected the judge, ignoring Carl's smarmy, gloating attitude.

'No, Your Honour,' Carl answered, wondering why the judge had taken over.

'Have you ever been treated for any mental illness or addiction to drugs of any kind?' Judge Leonard continued.

'No, Your Honour,' Carl lied, confidently.

No one knew about the struggle he'd had with cocaine in his late twenties. Besides, it was so long ago and, technically, he hadn't been treated in the official sense of the word. He'd given himself the cold turkey treatment while hidden away at his beach house during the same summer that his first wife, Claire, had died of lung cancer. His friends and colleagues had believed he'd been on extended leave because he was grieving. He'd never informed them otherwise.

'Are you presently under the influence of any drug, medication or alcoholic beverage of any kind?' asked the Judge, not looking up from his notebook.

'No, Your Honour,' said Carl smiling. He found the question inexplicably amusing. Judge Leonard wasn't impressed.

'Have you consumed drugs, alcohol or medication in the last twenty-four hours?' droned the Judge, bored with routine questioning. He was thinking about the delicious chicken and cashew salad his wife had prepared him for lunch. She'd doused it with his favourite mustard dressing, and had also wrapped the last piece of blackberry cheesecake and put it in his lunchbox for a special treat.

'I had a glass of wine with dinner last night, Your Honour,' Carl said, half smirking, 'a scotch and soda just before I went to bed, and a couple of paracetamol tablets this morning, for a splitting headache.'

Gareth Thompson chuckled. Judge Leonard grunted impatiently. He had no time for smartalecs. His brain ached, he was hungry, and he could have killed for a cup of coffee. He fancied cappuccino with his dessert, which he was considering eating before he ate the salad.

The judge glared at the defence team with a malevolent eye as he went on. 'Mister Rutherford, have you received a copy of the indictments pending against you, that is, the written charges made against you in this case and in the case filed in the Magistrates Court; and have you fully discussed those charges and the case in general with Mister?Gregson and Mister Thompson as your counsel?'

'Yes, I have, Your Honour.'

'Okay, good. Thank you,' Judge Leonard said, addressing Gregson, 'I have received a written memorandum of pleas which the Court understands represent the pleas of the defendant; is that correct?'

'That is correct, Your Honour,' Gregson replied, leaping to his feet.

The judge turned to Rutherford again, who had been deciding if he should sit or remain standing. 'Are you entering these pleas voluntarily because it is what you want to do?'

'Yes, Your Honour,' he said, straightening up.

'Has anyone made promises or assurances of any kind in an effort to induce you to enter any different pleas to the charges in this case?'

'No, Your Honour.'

'Has anyone attempted in any way to force or threaten you to plead differently in this case?' Judge Leonard raced through the questions, hoping none of the lawyers would find any reason to comment.

'No, Your Honour.'

'Do you understand that the offences to which you are offering these pleas are serious offences which may result in a Supreme Court trial?'

'Yes, Your Honour.'

'Mister Rutherford, you have been charged with two counts of maintaining a sexual relationship with a child under seventeen, sixteen counts of rape, two counts of deprivation of liberty, two counts of administering a stupefying drug with intent to commit rape, and three counts of supplying dangerous drugs. For the record, how do you plea to the charges laid against you before this court?'

'Not guilty on all counts, Your Honour,' replied Carl, squaring his shoulders.

'Sit down please, Mister Rutherford,' said the judge, leafing through a sheaf of papers. Just a few more minutes, he thought with satisfaction.

'I'd like to submit ...' called Gregson, standing quickly.

'In a moment, Mister Gregson,' said Judge Leonard, waving a hand in dismissal. 'Has an application for bail been made?'

'The Crown objects to the bail application, Your Honour,' Stephen said, unfolding his lanky frame to stand gracefully. 'Mister Rutherford has unlimited funds at his disposal, and is considered a high flight risk. Considering the seriousness and extent of the charges he is facing, the Crown is concerned he will leave the country. Accordingly, we respectfully request the court orders the defendant to remain in remand for the duration of the trial.'

'That's absurd,' countered Gregson, spitting the words out. 'My client is currently running a family business. He has an excellent standing in the community and has a reputation—'

'Regardless of his reputation, Mister Gregson,' cut in Judge Leonard, 'these are extremely serious charges. The accused will surrender his passport and report to Central Police Station on a daily basis. If he fails to comply with the orders of this court, he will quickly find himself in remand. Bail is set at one million dollars.'

While Judge Leonard hashed out the details of the committal hearing date with Richard Gregson and Stephen Frederick, Tom

Hancock sat in his car across the street from the municipal courts. A few minutes later, when Rutherford emerged from the courthouse, huddled head to head with his lawyers, Tom tried to figure out how he would describe the incredible results of the snooping Julia had asked him to do.

40

Jade saw him as soon as she stepped out of the health food store. Wearing a dark suit, he looked like an autumn leaf in springtime, stark against the bohemian surrounds of the avant-garde shopping district. She gasped in fright, her heart beating fast. Her fingers fluttered in panic as they flew to her mouth. Dark, round sunglasses, a relic from the seventies, hid her face.

'Hell!' she cursed, wondering how long he'd been following her.

He was across the street, leaning on a light post, trying to look casual as he lit a cigarette.

He looks like a character from a Bogart film, she thought fleetingly as she pulled her wide-brimmed hat down, almost over her nose. She turned left, hurrying down the street with her head down, her bag strap slung across her chest, the bulky contents bumping gently against her hip. He watched her leave the shop, adjust her hat and stride down the sidewalk toward the park.

'Hello, my little darling,' he sneered under his breath, tossing the cigarette into the gutter. 'It's time for you to come home.'

Jade forced herself to walk, breathing hard as she neared the arcade. Carl followed her, easily decreasing the distance between them. His long legs carried him as fast as they could without jogging. Frightened, she looked over her shoulder and saw him closing in.

A rush of adrenaline kicked in and she took off at a run. Her bag slipped lower, and was thumping hard against her backside. She turned into the arcade. Jade knew the covered alleyway. When Carl reached the entrance a few seconds later, she was nowhere to be seen.

'Damn,' he mumbled, scanning the darkened lane.

Aside from a dozen or so window-shoppers, and a teenage couple sipping cappuccino in the alfresco café, the place was deserted. In her hiding place, she held her breath, not moving. He walked up the narrow strip, bursting into shop doors as he went, poking his nose around dark corners. Startled customers turned to stare.

'Sorry, wrong shop,' he apologised with a smile, and continued on.

It was as if she'd vanished into thin air. Jade stayed where she was, her arms and legs wrapped around the centre of the circular shirt rack. Then, she saw the long strap of her shoulder bag trailing along the floor. Her heart leapt into her mouth. She'd taken off the cumbersome bag and sat it between her legs, then shoved her hat inside it. He strode toward the next shop, looked inside. No one there except the salesgirl. He inspected the dressing rooms in the little boutique. She held her breath and reached out to pull the strap under her leg, hoping it wouldn't be noticed. He looked over his shoulder, sure he hadn't missed her, and certain she hadn't doubled back. He eyed the line of shops ahead of him.

'Where did you go, you nasty little witch?' he chuckled evilly.

He felt in his pocket for the syringe. It was there, ready for her. She sat still; sure no one had seen her dive headfirst into the shop and scramble under the display of colourful resort-wear. He approached the doorway.

Don't move, she told herself, ignoring the cramp in her calf. Not even a muscle.

Suddenly, she saw his shoes. Her eyes widened. The cramp intensified. Unable to bear the pain, she flexed her toes, thankful she'd worn cloth sneakers. Slowly, silently, she swallowed and took a deep breath. She forced herself to breathe in and out. Her heart pounded in her ears. The shoes stepped forward, coming straight toward her.

'Where are you, little witch?' he whispered, confident he'd find her in one of the shops. 'Did you fly away on your broom?'

He looked around the shop, and saw the assistant talking intently with two customers. No one took any notice of him. The rest of the shop was still. She willed herself to become one of the batik shirts she sat amongst. The shoes turned to go, then paused for a moment.

'Have you seen a red-head in a green cap?' he asked the assistant.

'No,' she answered curtly, annoyed at being interrupted in the middle of her brilliant sales pitch, and turned back to her customers.

Jade shut her eyes and pretended she was a length of brightly coloured fabric. If I can't see him, she thought illogically, then he can't see me. She put her forehead gently against the cold steel centre of the clothing rack and prayed her mobile phone wouldn't ring.

He stalked across the carpeted floor and glanced behind the counter, thinking she might have crouched there to conceal herself. Satisfied she wasn't in the shop, Carl headed to the next one, furious she'd outwitted him. He'd planned to knock her out and take her home. There was a disused basement under the greenhouse he could keep her in until he decided what to do next.

'Sneaky little witch,' he muttered under his breath as he headed up the arcade to search the other shops.

41

David threw the canvas bag holding his scant belongings over his shoulder and walked to the waiting car. At last, he was a free man. Jade smiled from behind the steering wheel, and waved as he emerged from the grey concrete archway.

It had taken some effort, but his second application for early release had been successful. Finally, the parole board had been convinced that David Rivers was not a danger to society. He'd behaved in prison and had an impeccable work record. They'd agreed to release him six months early and strongly urged him to meet his parole conditions if he didn't want to find himself back behind bars. David had solemnly promised to behave. Prison life wasn't up his alley.

'Hi there, stranger,' called Jade.

'Hey, how are you?' David answered with a wide grin. He climbed in the passenger side and shut the door.

'We're moving,' Jade said. 'There've been some unexpected developments.'

Jade had visited David in prison whenever she could. She filled him in on the case and told him about herself and her life, asked him about his life, and learned about her mother, the love of David's life. They'd hugged and shared their grief over her death, laughed together over the tales David told of his illicit adventures with Maria, and agonised over the lovesick couple's foiled plans to elope.

'We should've run away the day before,' David had lamented.

He vividly recalled the crimson fury on Maria's father's face and the sinking feeling of dread as he'd stared down the twin barrells of the loaded shotgun, when Mister Devereaux had discovered them together behind the chook shed, trying to make good their escape.

Over a short period, Jade and David had become as thick as thieves. Surprising everyone, the cactus had transformed into a sunflower.

Both Nick and Alec had been stunned at how quickly she'd let her guard down and allowed her newfound father into her normally barricaded heart. David was equally shocked at how quickly his effervescent daughter had melted the cast iron bindings on his own.

'Moving? What happened?' David was surprised.

When they'd last spoken, three days earlier, she hadn't mentioned moving. From what Jade had told him he knew she adored her little apartment in the bustling artists' village. During one of her visits she'd described in detail the comfortable little haven she'd put together, her carefully designed escape from the world. When she'd offered him a bed on the couch in her tiny flat he'd felt honoured to be invited to share her sacred domain.

'Rutherford followed me on Monday,' she explained. 'I barely got away, had to hide in a shop. Alec has organised an Apprehended Violence Order, but I don't think that will stop him. Debra is trying to get him put in the remand centre.'

David narrowed his eyes and clenched his jaws. He was pretty sure the parole board wouldn't even try to understand if he found and killed his daughter's abuser, but that didn't stop him thinking about the numerous ways he could do it. To begin, he'd slowly torture the paedophile. Castration came to mind …

At the t-junction, Jade turned right and drove away from town.

'Where are we going?' David asked, making an effort not to sound as furious as he felt.

'Nick's cabin on the beach,' Jade replied, smiling. She sensed his anger and wanted to dispel it. She wanted his first day out of prison to be easy. 'It's okay, David. I'm not giving up my place. I just don't want to be there right now. Besides, the cabin is huge. It has four bedrooms and sleeps a dozen in a fix. We'll be more comfortable there. And it's not too far out of town.'

'How do you know Rutherford won't come looking for you on the beach?' he asked, wondering how much protection she would need until the trial. He was prepared to do whatever it took to keep her safe, regardless of the consequences. As much as he'd hated prison, he'd go back in a flash for Jade.

'I don't,' she answered truthfully, 'but I'm pretty sure he doesn't know about Nick. Or Alec. Or you.'

Jade explained that she was confident that Carl followed her only once, tailing her to the shops from outside her building. She'd been alone, on foot, and hadn't returned to the flat afterwards. She'd waited in the middle of the circle of batik shirts for over an hour. When she was sure Carl had gone, she dialled Nick's number and whispered her distress, adding her suspicions about the recent strange phone calls she'd been receiving lately. On his way over, Nick called Alec and filled him in. Immediately, Alec rang Ellen Johnson who went to find Stephen. Alec informed Debra of the latest drama, and then rang Donna, Gerard and Ruby warning them all to be on the alert.

Twice Nick ambled slowly through the arcade, pretending to be window shopping, checking that the coast was well and truly clear before slipping into the resort-wear shop to rescue his terrified girlfriend. By the time Jade was safe in Nick's apartment, Judge Leonard was having a brief conversation with Stephen Frederick. Soon afterwards, Richard Gregson was summoned to the judge's chambers. At the same time, Alec drove to Jade's apartment with Ryland. They were going to set up a few hidden surveillance cameras and divert Jade's phone through one of the expert hacker's home computers.

'So, we're going into hiding,' David said, thinking it wasn't such a bad idea.

He could use some time to get used to the scary wide spaces around him. Four years of prison had almost erased his sense of independence. It would be good to learn to fend for himself again in a quiet environment. A beach would be perfect, he thought. He'd been a little concerned about being unleashed on the city, totally unprepared for whatever he might find.

'What about your job?' David asked.

'I talked to Herman this morning,' Jade explained. 'He's very supportive, David. But he needs someone there and I can't do it right now. So, I quit.'

'What about money?' he asked. 'Do you have enough?'

'Not really,' Jade admitted, shrugging her shoulders. 'An old friend of Nick's is going to throw some freelance copy editing work my way which will help. He's bringing a laptop with him tonight.'

'Well,' David said, his mood lightening. He felt more relaxed as she drove toward the ocean. 'Life on the beach can't be too bad.'

'I reckon it'll be fun,' said Jade. She was looking forward to getting to know her father better without stern-faced prison guards peering over her shoulder every second. Visits in the bland grey room had sometimes been difficult. 'Do you like fishing?'

'Love it,' he laughed. He couldn't remember the last time he'd caught a fish.

'Good,' she chuckled, 'then you can teach me. I'm hopeless.'

42

Fear clutched at Katie's heart. For a moment, she couldn't breathe. Torn between her uncontrollable desire to flee, and her desperate need to remain anonymous, she froze. She was grateful to Alec for his timely warning. She'd half expected Carl to come after her. It was the nature of the beast, she'd figured. Now, here at Musical Madness, he was standing right in front of her.

'Excuse me,' Carl said, approaching the counter with his trademark wolfish smile, designed to charm all who experienced it. 'Does Katie Green work here?'

Katie was relieved he didn't recognise her. She'd shaved her head, added five earrings to each ear, stuck a small silver stud through her bottom lip, pressed a fake tattoo onto her shoulder and strapped her chest in an elastic bandage to flatten it. Blue denim overalls gave her figure the shapelessness of a gangly teenage boy. The backward baseball cap helped. Thick kohl around her eyes and dark foundation makeup only added to her mystique, giving her a distinctively strange appearance. Katie took a deep breath, reminded herself not to look into his eyes, and lowered her tone, adding a slight foreign accent to complete her disguise.

'No. She go. Las' week. Work supermarket, I tink.' Not looking up, she continued pricing the pile of CDs on the counter with the sticker gun.

'Do you know which supermarket?' Carl asked pleasantly, hoping the odd-looking shop boy would know where she'd gone. Surreptitiously, he patted the syringe of tranquiliser in his pocket.

'No. She go. Las' week,' Katie repeated, shaking her head, not looking up. She turned away to put the stack of CDs on the shelf.

Her back to him, she closed her eyes, held her breath and wished as hard as she could that he'd leave. She arranged the CDs in alphabetical order, stretching the seconds out. When she heard his footsteps retreating, she dared to look over her shoulder. As Carl vanished into the street, she fainted.

'Katie?' Gerard whispered a few minutes later, 'Katie? Wake up, sweetheart. Dad's here now.'

When Katie had hit the deck, Henrietta Gordon had called Gerard straight away. Then, she'd put the small pillow from her office chair under Katie's head and waited for him to show up. Henny didn't know that much about the girl, except that she was hard-working and reliable, and didn't cost her much in wages. Katie's father had come in the previous afternoon, when Katie wasn't working. He'd left instructions that if anything happened to his daughter, Henny was to call him immediately. Henny had thought it odd, but didn't comment. Katie's horrendous new look had been far more startling, but she'd accepted it with good grace. The girl was a workhorse, efficient, friendly, and knowledgeable about music. Who cared what she looked like, Henny figured.

'Katie?' repeated Gerard, gently patting his daughter's pale cheeks. He looked at Henny over his shoulder. 'Could you get her a glass of water, please?'

Katie opened her eyes and saw her father. She burst into tears. He pulled her into his arms. She buried her face in his chest and cried.

'He was here, Dad,' she snuffled into his shoulder. 'He was here asking for me. I was so scared.'

Henny stood nearby with a glass of water in her hand, watching Katie cry on her father's freshly ironed shirt. She was confused. 'Asking for who?' she demanded. She'd seen the older man come in, but didn't take any notice when he said a few words and then walked out. Lots of people did that.

'Never mind, Missus Gordon. I'm taking her home now. I'm really sorry, but I don't think Katie will be able to work here any longer.'

'But …' she stammered, not sure she'd heard right. She placed the glass of water on the counter.

'I'm sorry, really I am,' Gerard insisted, 'but it's impossible for her to come again.'

'Dad, I'll be okay …' began Katie, feeling better now that she was securely wrapped in her father's arms. 'I like it here.'

'No sweetheart,' he said, feeling like a mongrel for being forced to disappoint her after all her efforts to reclaim her life. She'd been doing so well, too. It wasn't fair. 'It's not worth it. He might come back. We'll figure something out when we get home. I promise. We'll get through this somehow.'

Katie saw the sincerity in his eyes. He's back, she thought, seeing his love for her on his face. She nodded silently, accepting the decision he was making for her. As much as she hated it, she knew he was right. She'd have to find something else to do. Staying sane was her biggest challenge, but for now, she was thrilled her father had come back to her.

'I don't have enough cash on the premises to pay her right now,' squawked Henny, suddenly coming to her senses. Maybe, she thought shrewdly, the girl would vanish and forget about the money. She made a few calculations in her head.

'That's okay,' smiled Gerard, already on to the wily old lady. 'I'll be around late tomorrow afternoon to pick up her pay.' He helped Katie from the floor and put his arm around her waist, squeezing her into his side. 'See you then, Missus Gordon.'

As they left the store, Katie hugged her father tight. 'I love you so much, Dad,' she whispered.

'I love you too, sweetheart,' he replied, and kissed the top of her head, his heart full of love and terror.

43

Sarah leapt out of her chair and ran around the desk. 'You can't go in there,' she shouted, her severe features puckered with fury as she chased Alec through the office.

Alec ignored her. He went to the carved wooden doors. He yanked them open and let them bang shut as he marched into the room.

'I'm sorry, Mister Rutherford, he just …' Sarah tried to explain, stopping short when Alec shot her a fiery look.

Carl, momentarily startled, looked up from the blueprints spread across his desk. The man he was conferring with frowned at the sudden interruption. Alec marched over to Carl's desk, walked around to the side, and stopped within face-slapping distance.

'This is for you,' snarled Alec, and thrust a folded document into Carl's hand.

Carl glanced at the papers in his hand, scanned the title page of the AVO, and then looked back up at Alec in disbelief. His associate snorted and grumbled his discontent at being disturbed during an important meeting.

'What?' Carl snorted.

Alec cut him off. 'And if you, or anyone even remotely associated with you ever comes within ten kilometres of any of those women again, I'll personally escort you to the prison and turn the key myself. It will be up to you to pray that the gun I'll be carrying doesn't accidentally go off into the back of your head. Is that clear?'

'I don't know what you mean …' blustered Carl indignantly, putting on a show for his colleague, who was now very interested in this curious exchange. Eyebrows raised, the visiting executive listened intently for any juicy gossip he could convey back to his offices.

Rutherford had already explained to the members of the board that the entire kerfuffle was a weak conspiracy by a group of drug-addicted prostitutes to extort money from him, something that had been tried before as they all knew. He assured them that the matter would be cleared up quickly. Unfortunately, he'd explained, someone had leaked information to the press.

'Police are following all the necessary procedures and I have my lawyers working around the clock,' he assured the doddering group of sympathetic old men. Rutherford was thankful for the closed court ruling.

The board members had frowned upon his apparent frequent use of cheap streetwalkers, especially considering the unmatched beauty of his wife, but conceded that it was not a crime, nor should any action be taken. A few of the members, with far less attractive wives, were guilty of similar activities in the not so distant past. The board didn't connect the sensational news items of sexual abuse they had recently seen on television to Rutherford's latest misfortune. The papers were rife with allegations and reports of sex abuse every day; the offenders almost always anonymous. The board was willing to concede that this latest scandal was a minor issue that had simply got out of control. Carl was warned to keep his nose clean, to stay out of the public eye, and ordered to keep the board immediately informed of any further developments. Delighted at this result, Carl had agreed, confident he would only have to tell them what they wanted to hear.

'If you like, I'll outline the charges against you once again just to clarify the stance the police department has taken in light of the allegations of sex—' Alec began, also making a show for the benefit of Carl's curious colleague.

'That won't be necessary,' interjected Carl, his ruffled feathers settling. It was vital to put a good face on the situation. He didn't want gossip spreading. 'Can we speak privately for a moment?' He pushed his chair back and stood up.

Alec stepped backwards. 'No. I have nothing further to say and I don't want to waste any more time here,' spat the detective, his face a mask of disgust, as he stalked out of the office. Sarah stood aghast, staring at his disappearing back, shocked that anyone would dare speak to her highly-esteemed boss like that.

In the lift, Alec wondered if Rutherford would dare to call the Senior Sergeant and try to get him cited for misconduct. He didn't care. Debra might rap his knuckles at best. On his way back to the duty room, Alec made one quick stop.

Later that night, as Carl emerged from his office block and walked to the car park, a tall figure dressed in black, a balaclava over his face, waited in the darkness. The masked assailant crept up behind Carl as he opened his car door. He grabbed the businessman around the neck, and held a knife to his throat.

'If you so much as drive down any one those girls' streets ever again, I'll slice your throat from ear to ear, and toss your rotten carcass in the river' Herman warned, before he vanished into the night.

44

'The whole process scares the hell out of me,' admitted Jade, who normally didn't scare easily.

She had tackled the last decade of her life clad in spiky, impenetrable defences, but Rutherford had given her a fright. Since the day he'd followed her, she'd taken steps to protect herself and, looking on the positive side, had also seen it as a kind of wake-up call. This was the real deal. It was happening. She was part of it.

'What scares you the most?' asked Margo, probing deeper.

She'd been impressed with Jade's progress through therapy. They'd hashed out some important issues. Anger was one of Jade's troubles. The pent-up rage that she'd kept inside for so many years, simmering and bubbling to the point of eruption until she'd almost blown off her own head to escape, had ultimately torn open the whole can of worms and landed her in Margo's office as a patient. Anger was Margo's speciality, and she welcomed the challenge Jade had presented to her.

'Everything,' said Jade evasively. She wasn't sure she could pinpoint it and she felt overwhelmed talking about. Now, she wished she'd never mentioned her fear. Once she got her teeth into something, thought Jade, Margo was so damned persistent.

'Okay,' conceded Margo, aware she'd get nowhere if she didn't take the lead, 'let's write a list of all the scary things. Then, we'll have a look at them and see where we are.'

'List?' repeated Jade, wondering if there was enough paper in the world to write down all the things that she was afraid of lately.

Afraid of her own shadow, she even made David go outside first thing every morning, just to make sure Carl hadn't discovered her whereabouts during the night. She wore large floppy hats and big sunglasses, disguising herself in long sleeved shirts and flowing skirts when she walked on the beach. If somebody walked behind her for more than the length of a block, she ran blindly down the beach, dialling David at home to come and rescue her.

'Please come and get me,' she'd pleaded, close to tears after a strange man had followed her for more than five blocks along the shorefront. 'I ran past the house in case he saw where I lived. I'm at the end of the cove, on the rocks.'

Sudden noises had her jumping through the ceiling. Once, in the middle of a sleepless night, she'd been at the fridge when a cockroach scuttled over her foot. Her screams had awakened David in a state of panic, and had the neighbours looking over the fence to see if she was okay. Humiliated, she'd asked Nick to call the pest control company. Cocooned from the outside world, Jade had devoured the editing work Nick's friend Mel had sent over, and she constantly begged him for more to keep her mind busy. Pleased with the quality of her work, he complied. When she wasn't working, Jade spent time learning about the world on the internet. News was something she'd avoided in the past, but now she couldn't get enough of international events.

Margo grinned. She'd begun to enjoy her sessions with Jade. 'Sure, now, what have we got? There are the big scary ones like stepping into the unknown, going to court, facing the accused, talking about the details of the abuse at the committal hearing, and then again in front of a jury when the trial begins.'

Margo verbally counted the fears she and Jade had been talking about. As she spoke, she noted each item on a blank page in her notebook with an asterisk next to it. 'Then, we've got the day-to-day scary stuff; fear of rejection, fear of love, fear of losing the people you've learned to love and trust, fear of being seen to be human.'

'When you say it like that, it sounds silly,' mumbled Jade, ashamed of being scared of so many trivial things.

'It's not silly at all, Jade,' reassured Margo. 'There's a lot going on at the moment that you've never had to deal with before. Some are within your control. Some aren't. It's normal to be afraid.' She smiled. 'What I want to do with you is tackle each of them one by one.'

Jade nodded, appreciating Margo's forthright comments. 'Okay.'

'Let's look at the list, and tell me what you're afraid of right now.'

Jade and Margo went over the list of fears, adding a few more as they talked about the coming court battle and the role Jade would play. As she went through the healing process with Margo, Jade felt more confident that coming forward and making a statement had been the right thing to do. It had been difficult describing events to Debra, and then there'd been the agonising wait to see if anything would come of it. She'd read so many times how paedophiles escaped because there was not enough evidence. That was scary too. But, this time she'd had backup.

Jade was curious about the other three women. 'Les Goily Goils,' as Alec jokingly called the four of them. Suddenly Jade sat up, slapping her palms loudly on the table, inspired by an unexpected thought. She startled Margo.

'Margo, do you think it's a good idea if I meet the other three women?'

'Hmm,' Margo replied, frowning as she thought about it. 'It would depend on them. Would you like to meet them?'

'I think so,' said Jade, her mind working quickly. 'I think it might be good for me. And maybe for them too.' On the other hand, she thought, being in a roomful of miserable abuse victims might be extremely depressing. She wouldn't know if she didn't try.

Margo smiled. She agreed. But it would depend on how the others felt about meeting Jade. Preparing her client for the worst, she doled out solid advice.

'Jade, first up you'll need to talk to Alec about it. From what I hear, he seems to have developed good relationships with all of them.'

Jade nodded. Over the past few months, Alec had amazed her. Since he'd stopped drinking, he was a new man altogether. He'd really got involved in this case. Maybe too involved. 'Why don't you ask him to broach the subject with each of the women, see if they're interested in meeting you, and maybe each other. If they agree, then do it. And yes, I do think it's a good idea. But if they object, then you'll have to let it go.'

'I'll ask him,' Jade replied, thinking she would call Alec the minute she left the psych's office. 'Now,' she said, tapping the notebook Margo had placed on the table, 'back to my fears. The thing that scares me the most, more than anything else, is having to tell complete strangers what he did to me.'

'Good,' Margo said, beaming.

Jade was pleased she'd nailed it. 'It's the most horrific thing, having to say those things. When Debra took my statement, I was a wreck for days afterwards. I'm not sure I can do it again.'

Jade had been embarrassed when she told Margo she'd retreated to her bed with a mud-cake and a bottle of tequila after seeing Debra, and again after the news of Rutherford's arrest and subsequent charges. Margo had laughed, and suggested there were much worse ways to console oneself after a disturbing experience. Comforted, Jade had relaxed and begun to trust Margo.

Trust was something she'd always had a hard time with. Between her intensive hour-long sessions with Margo, getting to know David, falling in love with Nick again, and allowing Alec to become her friend, Jade's defences were lower than they'd ever been. A couple of times she'd pondered the wisdom of letting all these people in. But the positive feelings she'd been experiencing lately told her it was the right thing to do for her own wellbeing. Even so, Jade was terrified that if any of them hurt her during the course of this life-changing trauma, she'd never be able to trust anyone again. Even more frightening, she wasn't sure she could trust herself not to flee in panic.

'Okay, we'll go over it together,' suggested Margo, adding a few words of warning. 'This won't be easy, Jade, but I think it will help. Next time you come in bring your statement. I'll make a copy and we can read through it. We'll do it slowly over a few sessions. I have to warn you that it will be quite traumatic, but I can teach you how to manage so that when you finally get into the courtroom, you'll be able to talk about it without falling to bits.'

Jade sighed deeply, reassured by the practical advice and the offer of tangible help. It was the best thing about Margo; her no-nonsense, feet-on-the-floor attitude toward treating her patients. The last time Jade had sought therapy, she'd just turned eighteen, and the spaced-out quack had told her to blow up a handful of balloons, draw the faces of all the people who had ever hurt her on them, scream at them how she felt about what they had done, and then stick pins in them. This action was meant to represent the banishment of all her problems from her troubled mind. Disappointed and disillusioned with what mad mind-menders had to offer, Jade had avoided therapists until now.

'Okay, I will,' said Jade, making a mental note to get her statement out of her drawer. She scanned the other items on the list and saw one that had been bothering her. 'There's something else here. Is it possible to go and see the courtroom before the committal hearing next month? I've never been in a courtroom before and the whole idea of it is a bit scary.'

Jade wanted to walk around the room, see it, smell it, get the feel of it, and make herself comfortable in it. She wanted to sit in the witness stand and take in the room, inspect it from all angles. She wanted to sit in the prosecutor's chair and see what he'd see when he was asking her questions. She thought that seeing the layout of the room, and the proximity in which they'd all be sitting, might give her some new perspective on her ability to give her evidence competently. Jade also thought it might give her confidence a boost if she wasn't worrying about who or what would be in the courtroom. She hoped Margo didn't think she was a fool who worried about every little thing.

Margo nodded approval. She had a friend in the justice department who could easily arrange that. 'That's a brilliant idea, Jade. Just tell me when you'd like to go. I'll be happy to organise it for you.'

45

Her fingers strained to keep their grip on the creaking bed-head as she arched her spine, thrusting her body backwards to meet his. Manicured fingernails dug into the decomposing wood. She didn't notice the worn spring digging into her right knee. He could no longer hear the screeching wooden frame over her vociferous pleasure. She threw her head back and howled, insane with lust. He braced his knees, tightened his cute butt, and pumped even harder.

'Oh, yes! Oh, yes! Don't stop!' Julia growled, throwing her bottom backwards, almost winding him with the force of her passion.

'Uhuh. Uhuh,' Tom panted, his hips slamming into her taut buttocks, his sweaty hands gripping her narrow waist, his quadriceps burning, straining with the effort.

Their slick bodies sucked and slurped at each other, slapping and sliding, tickling and teasing, each grabbing what it needed from the other until a powerful mutual climax overtook them.

'Aaaargh!' yelled Tom, agony and euphoria simultaneously ripping through his loins.

'Yeeeees!' shrieked Julia, the depth of her orgasm sending pulses of pleasure to every nerve ending in her lithe body until she finally ground to a halt.

Their sweat mingled and joined the trickle of juices running down their legs. Tom sat back slowly on his haunches, pulling Julia with him, staying inside her as he ran his hands over her breasts. She threw her hands above her head, revelling in the amplified sensations, and leaned her head back on his shoulder.

'Hmm,' she muttered, her body still zinging.

Turning to kiss his neck, she wrapped her arms behind his head. He kissed her mouth, exploring it with his tongue, sucking at her lips. She bounced lightly on his lap, and slid off, turning to kiss him back.

'You are the man!' applauded Julia, lying back on the mattress. 'But we have to get a new bed! This one is terrible.'

Tom laughed. He'd suggested it months ago. Julia had told him there was nothing wrong with it, insisting the collapsing wreck of a bed was raw and passionate.

'It epitomises our relationship,' she'd giggled.

Tom settled beside her, wrapping an arm around her shoulders. She snuggled into his neck. They lay quietly for a few moments, inhaling each other, catching their breath. Julia twirled a finger through his thick chest hair. He played with a stray lock that had escaped her carefully coifed bun, curling it through his fingers.

'You'll have to redo it,' he chuckled breathlessly, pulling at her hair.

Tom had returned from the courthouse earlier and immediately sought Julia out. She'd been inside arranging table flowers for the dinner party Carl was giving for his colleagues that evening. She'd been peeved at first. He'd been absent for almost a week, and then he expected her to be ready for an onslaught of dreary businessmen and their equally dull wives within a few hours. But Julia had rallied, and thumbed through her phone book.

'Casper? I have an emergency …' she'd told the manager of Ghostworkers.

Within two hours, the house was a hive of activity. Cooks shouted at waitresses in the vast kitchen. Uniformed maids ran around polishing cutlery and ironing linen tablecloths. Waiters set tables, organised the bar and chilled the wine. On short notice, Julia had hired a team of ten catering and cleaning staff for the evening. They raced around frantically, organising her social life, while Julia pottered about, casually checking preparations, discussing details with the head chef, issuing the occasional order and letting the chaos rumble around her. She left all the stress to the catering team; they were professionals, paid to be highly strung.

After asking the head waiter where the lady of the house could be located, Tom was sent from the kitchen. He made a pretence of enquiring which flowers Madame wanted cut for the guest rooms, in the event her guests got too drunk and needed to stay. As soon as she'd seen him, she led him out to the greenhouse, where they were supposed to be choosing fresh blooms.

'Don't speak,' she'd ordered, covering his mouth with her palm when he shut the door behind her. 'Not yet.' She'd leapt into his arms, and wound her legs around his body. 'Just screw me stupid.'

Immediately, he'd carried her down to the basement, thrown her on the bed, and complied with her wishes. She was, after all, the boss, he conceded, and he didn't wish to displease her. She had about an hour in which she wouldn't be missed. Now, serviced and sated, her leisure time was beginning to run out.

'What time is it?' Julia asked Tom.

He reached over to find his watch. 'Quarter to five,' he answered, wondering how long they'd been under the greenhouse.

'Right. I have about fifteen minutes left,' she grinned. 'Now, tell me what you found. I've been busting to know.'

'Well, I could have told you before …' Tom smirked.

She put a finger to his lips. 'Every minute counts. Just tell me.'

'Okay,' he said, and got down to business.

Tom explained how, on Thursday, he'd followed Carl from his office to an apartment building across town. He'd seen Carl go inside, and then watched him come out about half an hour later.

Tom had noted the address on a bit of paper, so reached down to the floor to retrieve it from his trouser pocket, and handed it to Julia. She took it without comment, and looked at the street name. Something about it seemed vaguely familiar, but she couldn't remember what.

'Was he with anyone?' she asked.

'Not when he went in or when he came out,' said Tom. 'But while he was in there, some sleazy looking guy in a long coat went into the building.'

'He could have been from any one of the apartments,' remarked Julia.

'Could have been,' agreed Tom. 'I'm just telling you what I saw when I was there. Wait, I haven't got to the best bits yet.'

Tom related how, on the following Monday, he'd tailed Rutherford from his office to a restaurant and back to his office, and hung around outside for a while. Just when he was getting ready to die of boredom, the police had shown up.

'Less than ten minutes later,' he told her, 'Carl came out in handcuffs. The cops shoved him in the back of an unmarked police car and drove him away.'

'What? He was arrested?' Julia sat up straight. She was gobsmacked.

'Yeah,' chuckled Tom. 'I couldn't believe it. Interesting development. So, of course, I followed him to the police station to see if I could find out anything.'

'Why didn't you tell me about all this straight away?' Julia admonished, frowning and pouting.

'I wanted to bring you a whole picture, not just a small part,' he explained, figuring it made more sense to find out what was going on before Julia began brewing up some sensational story that would get them both into trouble.

'And …?' Julia asked, dying to know what Carl had been up to.

'I'm not really sure,' admitted Tom. 'They were in the copshop for several hours. Then, around nine, he left with two other guys. I'd seen them go in earlier so I assumed they were his lawyers.'

Tom had become bolder after a whole afternoon of sitting around observing Carl's increasingly interesting activities, and had got out of the car to follow the trio on foot. He'd pulled his hat down over his ears, shoved his hands in his pockets and ambled along behind the three men, blending in with everyone else on the busy street.

'They talked about going to court at ten this morning. One of the lawyers mentioned charges of sex abuse,' he added. The street had been noisy, he explained, so he hadn't heard very much. 'So, today I went along to see what was going on. The court was closed. No one allowed inside except legal eagles. I sat on the bench outside the courtroom for a while. Carl was in a waiting room all morning, with the two lawyers. Then, just after lunch, a bailiff came out and took him inside. I went downstairs then, and asked at the desk if Rutherford was in court that day. They wouldn't tell me anything, so I went back to my car to wait. After half an hour or so, Carl came out with the lawyers again. And that's all I know so far.'

'Hmm,' mumbled Julia, curious about this turn of events. 'How very interesting. I wonder if he was caught with that girl you told me about.'

Tom admitted he didn't know, but whatever it was, he said, it looked as if Carl was in deep trouble.

Julia smiled. 'Good,' she stated. 'I hope he is in so deep that nothing will save him. That will make him easier to divorce.'

Tom was surprised. She'd never talked about divorce before. 'You're going to divorce him?' he asked, wondering what she had up her sleeve.

'I've been thinking about it for quite a while,' she explained. 'But our pre-nup has made it complicated. If he's in trouble, if he's done something seriously bad, the pre-nup will be null and void. For now, I'll just wait and see what happens.'

'And then what, after you divorce him?' Tom asked, curious.

'Oh,' she laughed, 'I haven't thought past that bit.'

She lay back on the mattress, resting another moment before she had to plunge back into the drudgery of domestic affairs.

'It's almost five,' announced Tom, aware she liked to stick to deadlines.

'Really?' she answered, rolling onto her side. She licked his nipple, and ran her tongue down his belly. She nibbled at his flat stomach, her fingers lightly tickling his balls. Her body slid down the bed. She nestled between his legs, grinning wickedly as she bowed her head. 'In that case, I still have another minute to do this …'

'You,' gasped Tom, running his hands through her hair, 'are wicked.'

46

Lenny Morris stared vacantly across the harbour. He leaned against the pylon, his mind and body as still as the water in the bay. Eager yachtsmen motored out to sea, hoping the wind would pick up. Recreational fishermen puttered past, in search of good currents and a better catch. Somewhere in the distance, the ferry carried passengers across the bay.

Nearby, a couple of kids threw fishing lines off the pier, hoping to take a few snapper home for lunch. Lenny sat with his trademark black coat wrapped tightly around his body, his hands tucked under the opposite armpits. His long legs stretched out, the right knee bent slightly. The light breeze tickled stray curls across his forehead. Lenny gazed blankly at the horizon, oblivious to his surroundings.

He'd been to The Mosh Pit the previous night to meet Daddy-O. It was an unscheduled meeting, out of character for the secretive man who supplied him with girls. Lenny never knew who the girls were, or where they'd come from. All of them were heroin addicts. He assumed Daddy-O found them on the street and promised them a better life. Lenny figured the slick, middle-aged man had a taste of them before he sold them, the same as Lenny always did, sampling their wares before he paid a princely sum and took them away. Most of the time, Lenny quadrupled his investment by hiring the teenage girls out to anyone with the money to pay for their favours.

Daddy-O had called out of the blue the previous day. Usually there were procedures to follow, certain times to call, code words to use. This time had been different.

'I want to discuss a new business opportunity. A special deal, big money. Mosh Pit at seven,' Daddy-O had ordered before hanging up.

Near the appointed time, Lenny had headed into the pub. He'd walked into the crowded bar, keeping his eyes peeled for the man.

He was a little early, and Daddy-O hadn't arrived yet. Lenny ordered a beer, and sat at the bar, appraising the talent while he waited. A couple of cute backpackers rubbed elbows and chatted nearby. They both wore tiny denim cutoffs and revealing midriff tops, displaying yards of soft tanned skin. He winked at one of them. She giggled in reply.

'He's very cute,' she told her friend.

Lenny salivated, imagining the possibilities, but didn't approach. He'd finished three beers by the time he realised Daddy-O was forty minutes late. He shrugged, got another beer, half-watched a game of pool going on nearby, and figured it wasn't his night to get rich.

'May as well enjoy myself while I'm here,' he muttered, watching the barely dressed Scandinavians writhe as they bopped to the music.

Halfway through Lenny's next beer, Daddy-O appeared at his shoulder. 'Let's go and talk somewhere quieter,' said the businessman.

He didn't apologise for keeping Lenny waiting. Unaccustomed to good manners, Lenny accepted that. He downed his beer and, after blowing a kiss toward the giggling Swedish girls, followed the man outside, through an alley into a nearby car park. Daddy-O approached a waiting car and opened the back door. Lenny climbed in, eager to talk business.

'So, what were you thinking?' asked Lenny as Daddy-O climbed in beside him.

'Take it easy, sport,' laughed Daddy-O. 'We have all night.'

'Sure,' apologised Lenny. 'Sorry. It's just that, ya know, opportunities like this don't come up too often.'

Daddy-O's driver, Marco, pulled out of the side street onto the top end of Martin Street.

'I understand,' nodded Daddy-O patiently. 'Would you like a drink?'

'Um … sure,' replied Lenny, feeling fuzzy from four beers. 'Why not?'

'I only have scotch,' stated Daddy-O, taking a small silver flask from a compartment in the centre console between the front seats.

They cruised down toward Ellison Boulevard, and then turned down Rogers Street.

Daddy-O poured a couple of man-sized slugs of Chivas Regal into two glasses he'd taken from a pocket in the back of the seat. Lenny took a glass from Daddy-O's fingers.

'Bottoms up,' toasted Daddy-O, sipping his drink.

'Here's to that, mate,' agreed Lenny, tossing the eighteen-year-old scotch down his throat.

The dark car slid past trendy cafés, restaurants and wine bars, then headed up to King George Road, before turning into Baker Street. As the smooth malt whisky warmed the back of his throat, Lenny watched people on the streets, walking, dining, drinking.

'So, how's business?' asked Daddy-O, pouring another generous nip into each glass. He swirled the amber liquid around the bottom of his glass before taking a sip.

'Good. Yeah. Good. Got me some hard-working girls,' Lenny answered, wondering when they would get to the deal.

'Heard you had a run in with the police recently,' probed Daddy-O.

'Yeah, 'twas nothin' really. I didn't tell 'em nothin'. I told 'em I got nothin' ta say,' he said, grinning, stumbling over words in his eagerness to impress, hoping Daddy-O believed him. Nervously, he rubbed the rim of his tumbler, and then swallowed a large mouthful of scotch. The police had asked him a lot of strange questions about the rich man.

Marco drove aimlessly around the inner-city suburb, going nowhere in particular, just as he'd been asked. The boss would say when he was ready to go somewhere.

'Good,' replied Daddy-O. He leaned back in the seat and sipped his scotch. 'I'm pleased. Now, let's discuss our new joint business venture.'

The two men began to talk, exchanging ideas. Daddy-O led the conversation. Lenny listened, gazing at the lights on the harbour. A few minutes later, his whole world turned fuzzy.

Now, he leaned against the round cement pole, staring out over Hendersons Bay as another busy day began in the city centre. He would sit there for hours, gazing blankly towards the horizon, until someone noticed him, or the tide claimed him. Lenny wasn't breathing.

His heart had stopped. His skin was cold. His dead eyes didn't see the yachts, or the fishermen, or the ferry. He didn't hear the kids.

When he was found, the coroner would probably declare he'd taken too many drugs, including Rohypnol, ecstasy, and crack cocaine, Lenny Morris's predictable death the result of a drug overdose.

47

A fat spliff rested in the ashtray. A thin swirl of aromatic smoke rose into the air above it. A bottle of beer, half full, sat on the glass tabletop. A deck of tarot cards was spread out on the floor, ten of them arranged in a Celtic cross. Hypnotic relaxation music drifted from the stereo, whispering to the walls, caressing the corners. A pair of incense sticks burned on the shelf above the television, filling the room with the heady perfume of dragon-blood resin. A cluster of candles arranged around an art-deco candelabrum burned brightly from their position on a corner table.

Ruby looked at the two centre cards first, which represented the present, and held them to her chest. She rose from her cross-legged position on the floor and began to twirl in circles, balancing on her toes, in time to a rhythm only she could hear. She closed her eyes and spun, throwing her head back. Her hair fanned out behind her as she circled. The cards spoke to her of her current issues. She listened intently as her body moved, accepting the visions that came to her, until the Magician and the Seven of Wands became silent five minutes later.

'Yes,' she sighed, clearly understanding which path she needed to take, what she had to do, and who she had to see.

Ruby stopped twirling, and returned the cards to their position in the centre of the cross. She reached over and picked up the joint from the ashtray. Inhaling deeply, Ruby studied the rest of the layout. Just as she reached for the Fool, the influence card, the doorbell rang.

'Dammit!'

She hated being disturbed during a reading. It put her off. She marched over and flung the door open, prepared to tell whoever it was to take a flying leap off a cliff. Then, she saw Alec, a pizza box in his hand, standing at the door.

'I'm inviting myself for dinner,' he told her cheerfully. 'There's something I want to talk to you about.'

Hostile thoughts instantly forgotten, Ruby smiled beatifically. 'Come in, doll. What do you want to drink?' she asked, letting him in and closing the door before heading to the kitchen.

'I brought some coke,' he told her, used to supplying his own soft drink.

'Good,' she stated. 'I don't have any of that. But I can get you some ice.'

He sat on the sofa and gazed around the candlelit room. He wondered what the strange looking cards were all about, and chuckled lightly about the ever-present spliff on Ruby's coffee table. Ruby dooby doo, he thought, amused at his little quip. 'Am I interrupting something?' he shouted in the direction of the kitchen.

'Nothing important,' she called out, tossing ice cubes into a glass.

Alec moved the ashtray to one side of the table, and repositioned the beer. He considered taking a quick toke on the joint, but then decided against it. He was already walking on the edge. Instead, he opened the pizza box and tucked the napkins underneath.

'I hope you like supreme,' he said as she sat opposite him and put the tumbler of ice on the table. 'I wasn't sure what to get and then figured I'd get the whole lot and hope for the best.'

Ruby laughed. 'You did great. I'll eat anything that isn't moving.'

Alec poured coke over the ice, while Ruby grabbed a slice of pizza. They ate in silence for a few minutes, enjoying each other's company. Alec liked Ruby. A resilient fringe-dweller, she was great fun. She often regaled him with tales that made him laugh until he cried. She liked him too, thought he was gorgeous, and found his job fascinating. Alec wasn't sure where he stood with her. Aside from giving evidence at the committal hearing, and then the trial, he'd pretty much finished his job. Ruby was no longer his 'case' but they had become friends along the way. Grimshaw had warned him about skating on thin ice, so he'd tried to maintain a professional attitude. Ruby had quickly pooh-poohed that. She'd penetrated the detective's mask, and saw the man behind the badge. So far, they'd only hung out as friends, but

Alec was attracted to Ruby and he was sure the feeling was mutual. He didn't want to jeopardise the trial, and so maintained a respectful distance. It would be a relief when it was over.

'I have a question,' said Alec, wondering how Ruby would feel about his proposal. He put his pizza slice down and tried to look serious.

'Go ahead,' she prompted, her mouth full of olives, cheese and pepperoni, the dooby in her left hand. She took a sip of beer, had a toke on the joint, and stuffed the pizza crust through her lips.

As she chewed, Alec chortled at her unorthodox eating habits. He'd never known anyone who could eat like a pig and still somehow manage to look like a lady.

'One of the complainants has suggested meeting everyone,' he began. 'She's a bit afraid of ending up in a morose group of potential suicides, but I told her there's little danger of that. I wondered if you'd like to meet her.'

Ruby chewed and thought. She took another toke, then finished her beer. Burping loudly, she grabbed another slice of pizza and bit into it. Alec sipped his coke, and picked up his pizza. He took a bite and waited for Ruby to reply. A few minutes later, Ruby went to the kitchen to get another beer. She popped the cap and came back to the table.

'What's her name?' Ruby asked, looking into Alec's eyes.

'Jade,' he answered, returning her gaze.

'No freaking way!' she exploded, slapping the slice of pizza down on the table. 'Are you serious?' Ruby stood up.

'What's wrong?' asked Alec. He instantly regretted upsetting her.

'Jade?' Ruby shrieked, eyes wide with disbelief, her hands on either side of her head. 'She was in my reading tonight.' Ruby calmed herself so she could explain this fascinating revelation to Alec. 'I'd just started when you showed up. She's in my destiny. Red hair. Green eyes. Sadness. Grief. And yet, she has this inner strength no one yet knows about.'

Alec was aghast. 'How do you know that?'

'Alec, she's part of my destiny,' Ruby stated matter-of-factly. 'We are inexplicably entwined. Yes, of course I want to meet her.'

Ruby sat down and took a large mouthful of her beer. Then, she inhaled deeply on the joint and bit into her pizza again. Alec was bemused. Sometimes in Ruby's company, he didn't know what to think. Or say. Or do.

He'd talked to Jade at length about how meeting the other complainants might not be a smart idea. He'd warned her that, if they did agree, under no circumstances would they be allowed to discuss evidence, hers or theirs. She'd taken this on board, and assented to his terms. She'd also understood that it might be upsetting, but told him she wanted to give it a shot.

'What have I got to lose?' she'd reasoned. 'If we get to know each other, maybe we can support each other through this.'

Alec had agreed to talk to them, beginning with Ruby. He was glad it hadn't been a mistake. Ruby's eyes widened again. Alec could see her brain ticking over.

'What?' he asked.

'Do you think she's busy now?' asked Ruby 'Why don't you call and ask her over?' She was eager to meet the girl who'd been in her head when she'd been twirling around the living-room.

'Now?' repeated Alec, certain Jade was not expecting to hear from him this soon.

'Sure, why not?' she replied. 'This woman is ready, Alec. She's ready to meet her destiny. Jade should come over now.'

Alec couldn't explain why he believed her. It was completely illogical. If he'd tried explaining it to anyone besides Jade they'd have laughed at him. But, despite his misgivings, somehow he knew Ruby was right. Nodding, he dialled her number on his mobile phone.

'She's bringing Nick,' he reported to Ruby after signing off. 'But David is tired. He's going to bed early. You'll meet him some other time.'

'David!' Ruby breathed. 'He was with her in my vision.'

She closed her eyes and recalled the vivid pictures she'd seen in the brief tarot reading. 'He's experienced great loss, pain, and fear. He was imprisoned in his anger for a long time.' Alec shook his head, unable to believe the depth of her perception. He was profoundly impressed.

Her passion only served to make her more attractive. Ruby went on, not conscious of the effect she was having on Alec. She talked about David and Jade as if she'd known them all their lives. Alec listened to her musical voice, entranced by her insight. He watched her face as she spoke, her animated expressions, the flutterings of her fingers, and instantly fell head over heels in love.

'There is a magnificent love,' Ruby told him, 'an unbreakable connection between them. She is his past and his future. He is her future. Wow,' she concluded, smiling. 'What a beautiful thing.'

'Wow,' he said, blown away by her vision, and by her. Somehow, he felt he'd known this incredible woman forever. 'That's amazing.'

Alec fought the urge to leap over the table and kiss her. He wanted to hold her in his arms. He wanted to wake up next to her every day for the rest of his life. He wanted her to want him like that, too. Struggling to remain composed, Alec intertwined his fingers under the table, locking them together. He didn't trust himself to move in case his body betrayed him and he gave in to his desire.

'I wasn't meant to do the whole reading,' Ruby muttered, oblivious to Alec's inward battle. As he fought with his conscience, debating professional ethics and moral responsibility, she shrugged her shoulders and smiled happily. 'That's why you're here.' Ruby cocked her head to one side. 'It was meant to be. It's destiny, Alec. Destiny. You can't fight it.'

'I believe you,' he said, laughing to cover his myriad emotions. 'Have you had enough pizza?'

Ruby nodded absently. She'd zoned out and was floating about on her own planet. He left her to fly on her magical carpet of inward reflection, flipped the lid on the takeaway box and took it to the kitchen. The simple task helped to settle the overwhelming feelings rushing through his body. It was frightening and exhilarating at the same time. He hadn't felt like this in years.

Not since … not since her, he thought, unable to utter his ex-wife's name, nor allow it to be spoken aloud inside his head.

Alec returned to the living-room and grabbed his empty glass off the table. Ruby sat with her eyes closed, a smile on her face. He went back to the kitchen to refill his drink. He cracked the top off another beer for Ruby and went out again, feeling calm and in control. One step at a time, he told himself. The court case was the main priority and then there was the rest of his life after that. He could wait, he reassured himself. Ruby wasn't going anywhere soon.

As he came out, she was waiting for him in the doorway, her hands on either side of the frame, blocking the exit. She beamed at him. Holding a soda in one hand and a beer in the other, he stopped dead.

'And you, Alec Stonewall,' Ruby whispered throatily, 'are my destiny.'

She leaned over and kissed his mouth. He almost dropped the drinks. She eased the tumbler from his hand and stepped into his embrace. Neither of them spoke. He put the beer on the counter and held her in his arms, kissing her as if he thought she would fly away forever. She put the glass down and ran her chilled hand up his back. A surge of passion rippled through Alec's body, taking his breath away. Ruby pressed him against the wall, holding his face in her hands. Fingers tangled in her hair, he pulled her against him. She mashed her lips into his, and thrust her tongue deep inside his mouth. His tongue found hers. They intertwined and danced to a wild tribal beat, the ancient rhythm rocking them both. Ruby's knees felt weak. She groaned her pleasure. Her desire for him roared through her limbs, out of control. She wanted him inside her. Not just now, but forever; physically, emotionally, spiritually. Alec held her tightly, mumbling his love into her mouth. Their bodies became one. Alec couldn't remember feeling happier. Ruby felt as if she'd finally come home from a long, lonely journey.

Just as Ruby pulled Alec's shirt over his head, the doorbell rang. 'Holy Leaping Bananas!' she cursed. 'I forgot they were coming.'

Reluctantly, she broke the embrace. Alec kissed her one last time and tugged his shirt on. He retreated to the kitchen. Ruby patted her hot cheeks, still feverish with unsatisfied ardour. She smoothed her skirt, straightened her hair, and opened the door.

'Hi,' said Jade, 'You must be Ruby. I'm Jade. This is Nick.'

'Welcome! Welcome!' Ruby gushed, her face slightly flushed. She kissed Jade's cheek. 'Come on in, doll. Alec is refreshing our drinks.

It's so great to meet you at last. I've heard some wonderful things,' Ruby shook Nick's hand and showed them to the sofa.

The joint had gone out, and the CD had stopped. The incense sticks were on the verge of death. Jade saw the dooby and winked at Nick. On the way over, she'd told him she had a feeling that Ruby would be super-cool. She handed the six-pack she'd been carrying to Nick and settled herself amongst the scattering of soft cushions. Nick was about to sit down but stopped when he spied the rows of CDs on the opposite wall. Ruby, who never missed an opportunity to show off her music collection, tapped Nick's shoulder.

'I'll chuck these in the fridge. You choose some music,' she suggested, taking the beers from his hand and heading out to the kitchen where Alec was still hiding, collecting his wits.

'I'll open those,' he said, taking the six-pack from Ruby.

'Thanks,' she replied, then planted a kiss on his nose and returned to the living-room.

Alec brought out the three beers; the fingers of his right hand looped around the necks, the glass in his other hand. He placed his coke on the table.

'Hi, Jade. Glad you could make it,' he said casually, bending to kiss her cheek. He handed her a beer and stood up. 'Good to see you, Nick. Impressive isn't it?' He indicated the music library and gave Nick the second bottle. Nick whistled, awed at the collection. His mind boggled at the choices.

Ruby took the third beer from Alec's fingers and winked. 'Thanks.'

Jade glimpsed the electric charge that passed between them and smiled. 'So, what have you two been up to?' she asked, wondering about the nature of the relationship between the cop and the witness.

'Nothing,' they replied simultaneously, then laughed.

'As you can see, Ruby was doing a tarot reading when I arrived,' Alec explained. 'And she was just telling me about how she saw you and David in her reading. It was extremely intense. I was stunned, and also impressed. But she can tell you more about it.'

'You see, Jade ...' began Ruby, settling into the cushions to explain her interpretation of the reading. The two women put their heads together and got into a long, meaningful discussion. After a few minutes, Ruby lit up the joint and handed it to Jade. 'And so ...' she went on, while Jade inhaled, and listened, fascinated. 'That's how I realised that David played a crucial part ...'

Alec and Nick studied the labels on the shelves in front of them, content to let Jade and Ruby get acquainted. They mumbled comments back and forth, remarking on groups, singers or songs that they liked. After some time, Nick chose an Enigma CD, and handed it to Alec to put on. Then, making sure it wasn't too loud, they retreated to the kitchen to have a proper matey chat without disturbing Ruby and Jade.

48

The house was quiet in the late autumn afternoon. A fresh breeze ruffled the curtains. A trail of black ants marched to and fro across the living-room floor, exchanging morsels of gossip as they passed, carrying crumbs of toast back to their nest in the window. In the kitchen, a retro-funk clock Donna had bought in a garage sale whispered in time with the heartbeat of the cosy home.

Lizzie prowled from room to room, still in her pyjamas, bored, lost. She felt as if she were wallowing in a deep hole, unable to climb out. Her mind played tricks; it fogged up and blanked out. Wave after wave of depression crashed over her, forcing her to the rocky bottom. Drowned in misery, the glum teenage girl wasn't coping with day-to-day life. The little things overwhelmed her. She didn't know what homework she was supposed to do. School was a living nightmare. Deciding what to eat for breakfast became a major dilemma. Choosing clothes to wear left Lizzie in tears of rage and confusion. She hated every day. Getting up in the morning was a task she didn't want to tackle. She'd rather loll in bed all day, hiding under the covers. Almost daily, she burst into tears while her mother made her lunch. Often, Lizzie begged Donna to let her stay home from school.

'Please, Mum,' Lizzie wailed, tears coursing down her cheeks, her eyes red, her face puffy from another night of crying into her pillow. 'Please, I can't stand it today. I just want to sleep.'

On the worst days, her mother gave in. Lizzie seemed disconsolate, and Donna was at her wits end. She missed her bright, bubbly daughter desperately, and didn't know how to bring her back from the abyss. Lizzie hated therapy, and rebelled against the counsellor. She refused to take the Zoloft she'd been prescribed and wouldn't practise her relaxation exercises at home. She didn't feel like going shopping, lost her interest in clothes and makeup, never went to the cinema any more, and wasn't interested in her friends. She didn't want to go out, even with Donna. Lately, except for school, she never left the house. More and more, she retreated to her room. Her memory was terrible. She forgot the simplest things, and drove Donna nuts. Most of the time, Lizzie couldn't even remember what day it was, or how long she had felt like death warmed up.

'Lizzie, please make an effort,' pleaded Donna.

In reply, Lizzie sulked, and stayed in bed for days at a time.

Late for work again that day, Donna had given up arguing and left Lizzie at home. Ambling around the house, Lizzie sighed loudly and shuffled into the kitchen, her arms flopping loosely at her sides. The lack of energy had kept her in bed all day, and now, hungry, she got up to look for food. Pouting, she heaved the fridge open. The shelves were packed with fruit and vegetables, cold meat, bread, milk, eggs and even a carton of chocolate custard.

Lizzie gazed at the contents and grunted. 'Boring.'

Nothing took her fancy. Cupboard doors opened and slammed shut as Lizzie searched the kitchen. Even though Donna had shopped the day before, Lizzie couldn't find anything she wanted to eat.

Perhaps, she thought petulantly, I should just go back to bed.

On her way, Lizzie went to the bathroom. She sat on the toilet for a long time, staring vacantly at the fish on the shower curtain. Lizzie felt a deep desire to sleep. She wanted to go to sleep and never wake up. Barely able to drag herself off the seat, she wondered if Donna still had any of those pills the doctor had given her. They had helped her mother sleep just after her father died. Lizzie wiped herself and rose. She hauled her pyjama pants up, flushed the toilet, and opened the bathroom cabinet.

Vitamins. Headache pills. Toothpaste. Soap. Lizzie rummaged through the cupboard, tossing bottles and packages in the basin as she took them from the shelves and inspected the labels. Evening Primrose. Paracetamol. The cupboard was almost empty when Lizzie spied the little brown glass jar. It had her mother's name on it. She read the label. Valium. She took the cap off and looked inside. There were about forty pills left in the bottle.

'How many should I take?' she wondered aloud, not sure what effect one tablet would have on her.

Her mood lifting slightly, Lizzie took the bottle to her bedroom. She sat on her bed and looked at it for a long time. The longer she stared into the dark glass, the stronger her urge to take the pills became.

'I'll need a drink,' Lizzie said, almost cheerful now.

She felt clear-headed at the sight of the end to all her problems. She went toward the kitchen to get a glass of water and spotted the bottle of vodka in the sideboard in the living-room. Changing tack, she scooped the bottle off the shelf and took it back to her bedroom. She'd been sneaking shots of vodka since she was twelve, when her mother had allowed her a tiny taste of it. Lizzie decided then that it was delicious, and it had become her drink when she went out with her friends.

Delighted that she'd found the solution, Lizzie placed the half-empty bottle on the side of her bed. She opened the bottle of Valium and poured the pills out onto her quilt. Lizzie counted them. Thirty-six. Not sure how many to take, Lizzie put four little yellow pills in her mouth, then took a swig from the vodka and swallowed. The tablets tasted metallic. Lizzie waited a few minutes. Nothing happened. She took two more pills, followed by a vodka chaser. Then, she remembered that she hadn't written a note for her mother. Lizzie wasn't sure what to say to Donna. For a fleeting moment, she felt sad that she would miss her mother, but it passed quickly. Lizzie got a pen and pad off her dresser and tapped the pen on the blank page for a while.

'I'm sorry, Mum,' she wrote, 'but I just can't deal with everything. It's too much sadness. I hope you understand. I love you. Lizzie.'

She returned the pad to the dresser and left the pen on top. The pills hadn't acted yet, and she wasn't feeling anything from the vodka. Lizzie threw four more pills down her throat. She tipped the vodka bottle upside down and tried to skull it. It choked her and she spilled the clear liquid down the front of her pyjamas. She looked down at her wet clothes and decided it didn't matter.

'No one will care,' she whispered, wiping her hand down her front.

Then, getting down to business, Lizzie swallowed twelve more Valium, two at a time, washing them down with mouthfuls of vodka. After fifteen minutes, she began to feel woozy. There was two of everything in her room. Amazed at this intriguing sight, Lizzie gazed at each item, gradually taking in the room. When her eyelids felt heavy, she lay down. She rested her head on her pillow and let the sensations overtake her body. She closed her eyes and began to float, feeling wonderful.

'Yes,' she murmured to herself. 'It's time to go to sleep.'

Fourteen little yellow pills lay scattered on the quilt beside Lizzie's hand as she drifted away. An inch of vodka remained. She'd left the cap off, and the bottle rested in the cradle of her arm as she dozed, her fingers curled around the base, the nails slightly blue. As she sank deeper into the warm black fog, Lizzie's heart slowed. The clock ticked quietly in the kitchen. In the living-room, the trail of ants carried the last crumbs across the floor.

49

Jade left Margo's office, feeling refreshed after the hard but successful session, and headed toward her car, which was parked a few blocks away. She planned to stop by the fish market on the way back to the beach house and pick up some king salmon fillets for dinner. She'd also stop for fresh vegetables from the Italian market. Normally when she came to town, Jade wore a large floppy hat, but the basset hound next door had chewed it up overnight. She'd loudly cursed the errant beast and the apologetic owner promised to replace the broad-brimmed hat. The old one had been well-loved, despite being slightly worn, but Jade had accepted his offer after he'd assured her the dog wouldn't get out again.

Bare-headed, and feeling vulnerable, Jade strolled down the street, enjoying the last warm days before the winter chill set in. She window-shopped a little, wishing she had more money to buy pretty things. She passed a busy sidewalk café, browsed through a bookshop, and strolled across the road toward the car park. As she reached the gutter on the other side, someone tapped her on the shoulder, startling her. She spun around in fright, unable to defend herself. Her hand leapt to her mouth to stifle the scream as she saw him.

'Winny?' Robert asked, calling her by an old nickname. 'Is that you?'

'Robbie,' she admonished, frowning at him, 'don't sneak up on people like that! You scared the life out of me.'

'I'm sorry, Winny. I didn't mean to scare you. I was in the café when you walked past.' He smiled, his dimple prominent. He still looked like the cute little brother, or cousin, she'd had over a decade ago. Now she wasn't sure what he was to her. 'I wasn't sure it was you, Winny. You've changed so much. I had to follow you to be certain. I'm so glad it is. I've missed you. Are you busy?' He smiled eagerly. 'Do you have time now? Can we talk?'

Jade looked up and down the street. She narrowed her eyes and puckered her lips in thought. Trust no one, she told herself. Instinctively, she felt safe with Robert, but she had to be sure.

'Is your father here?' she asked, trying not to sound suspicious.

'My father,' he snorted derisively. 'Since when is he ever around? I've been home a week and have only seen him once. No, I'm alone.'

'Okay,' she breathed, relieved that he wasn't setting her up. Who knew how far Carl would go? 'But stop calling me Winny. I'm not a bloody horse, you know!'

'Sure,' Robert laughed, and escorted Jade back across the street. 'What would you like me to call you?' he asked, happy to call her whatever she liked as long as she didn't run away again before he'd had a chance to talk to her.

'My name is Jade,' she informed him. 'It has been for over ten years.'

He'd never called Jade anything other than Winny; his lisping toddler-talk pronunciation of Juanita, a name she'd accepted until she'd run away from home.

'Sure, Jade,' he consented, the unfamiliar name sounding odd on his tongue.

'Thank you,' she smiled, realising she was happy to see him. 'I assume you're still Robbie? Or do you need to introduce yourself to me again?'

Robbie Rutherford had been in the café, reading the papers, sipping latte, people-watching, while he waited for the tailor down the street to finish off his new suit. When Jade had ambled past, he couldn't believe his eyes. Every nerve ending in his body said he had to follow the woman. He was glad that he had.

'Let's sit over here,' Robbie suggested, leading Jade toward the table he'd abruptly abandoned moments before.

He pulled a chair out for her with an elegant flourish. She sat, impressed with his impeccable manners. He took the seat opposite and smiled broadly. A relieved waiter swanned over to take their order, pleased the good-looking young man hadn't absconded without paying the bill as he'd first assumed. After a brief consultation with

Jade, Robbie ordered more coffee and they settled in to catch up on the last ten years.

He told her about being sent away to boarding school soon after she left. He'd despised it, and was angry at Jade more than a year for making his life miserable. As he got older, he realised it had been his mother's decision, and that his absent father had agreed to her request. Carl Rutherford had very little to do with his son, preferring to leave that up to the boy's mother. Julia was happy to have her son at home for holidays and the long lazy summers. Robbie talked about his girlfriends and the parties they'd had in the huge house.

'The year I bought the drum kit was about the last straw for Mum, though,' he chuckled, recalling how she'd made the gardener soundproof the basement so she couldn't hear him banging away while she pruned roses in the greenhouse above.

He regaled her with hilarious tales about his love trysts in the basement, seducing a string of bimbos on a pile of hessian sacks, or stealing a bottle of bourbon for his friends to get smashed on. In the secluded room, no one could hear their shrieks of laughter.

At university, Robbie told her, he realised what freedom his parents had afforded him. They'd funded his world-travel during the breaks, and bought him an apartment near the campus. He was also appreciative of the quality education he'd gained along the way. But, he confided, almost every day for the last decade, he'd wondered where his beloved Winny had gone. And why.

'Why did you run away?' Robbie asked, after telling Jade how her disappearance had broken his heart. When, as a ten-year-old boy, he'd discovered some adoption papers in one of his mother's drawers, he'd teased her mercilessly. He'd regretted being so terribly mean to her for so long, and had thought it was his fault she'd gone. Since that day, he'd known Jade wasn't his biological sister, but all his life, she'd been the only sister he'd ever had.

'Oh, Robbie,' she began, almost in tears. 'I don't even know where to start. It's such a long and terrible story.'

'I have all day,' he declared, throwing his hands in the air. 'I've told you everything there is to know about me, leaving out some of the more sordid details, of course.' He grinned cheekily. There are some things you just don't tell your sister, he thought. 'Now, Sis, I want to know what you've been doing. And,' he lowered his voice, 'I want you to tell me why you ran away like that.'

Jade sipped her coffee and thought about the enormity of what he was asking her to do. She wasn't sure he could handle the truth, and she had no way of knowing how he would react. She appraised him over the rim of her cup. He was extremely handsome, with a lovely face and a huge friendly smile. He looked like his mother. Soft-spoken, well-mannered, with a gentle nature, he was the antithesis of his father. Thankfully.

'I don't know if I can,' admitted Jade, terror gripping her gut.

'Jade,' he coaxed, smiling. 'How bad could it be?'

'Oh, you have no idea,' she replied, still not sure if she could tell him the gory story of her life, the long list of traumatic events taking place under the same roof where he grew up. Often in the same basement where he'd had so much fun.

'Jade,' he contended, palms upward and outstretched across the table. 'Not a day has gone by when I haven't thought of you, and hoped you were okay. I prayed and prayed that you'd come home so I could tell you how sorry I was for teasing you.' Jade reached out and placed her palms on top of his. He held her hands, pretending not to notice the tears escaping from the corners of her eyes. 'My biggest regret in life is finding those awful papers in Mum's drawer.'

'Robbie,' Jade sniffed, fighting the urge to cry. 'It wasn't your fault.'

'I know that now,' granted Robbie, lowering his voice. 'But I don't know the truth.'

Jade dabbed at her eyes with a tissue, forcing herself to breathe through the lump building in her throat. As she inhaled deeply, taking in positive energy as Ruby had shown her, and exhaling loudly, expelling the negative, Jade decided it was time Robbie knew the truth. She nodded, bracing herself, and gathered shreds of courage. Realising she'd need a little more time to pull herself together, she chose to take a little assertive stalling action before she'd be fearless enough to open her heart.

'Okay,' she conceded, feeling it was the right thing to do, 'I'll tell you. But I want to go somewhere quieter, more private.' She didn't feel courageous at all.

'Done!' he assented, and threw money on the table to pay for the coffee, leaving a tip for the waiter, who winked at Robbie as they left.

Chortling at the frisky waiter, Robbie linked his arm through Jade's and they ambled toward the nearby park. It was a vast garden with paths looping and winding through the trees, over bridges, and eventually circumnavigating the man-made lake in the middle. As they stepped through the gate, Jade clenched her teeth and swallowed hard. It was now or never, she told herself. Everything she and Margo had been working on was about to come to fruition.

'Robbie,' she began, barely audible. She tightened her grip on his arm, 'I don't really know how to say all this without hurting you. It's not a pleasant story.' She focused on the path ahead. 'I don't even know if you'll believe me.'

'Try me,' he said, squeezing her hand to reassure her.

As they strolled arm in arm, Jade told Robbie her story. Starting at the beginning, she stumbled tearfully over the first few phrases. He stopped dead in his tracks and gaped at her. She was terrified he didn't believe a word of it. After a moment, Robbie gathered her in his arms and let her sob. When she recovered, he asked her to continue. He said little, was numb from shock, horrified at what she had been through. He stopped her narration occasionally to ask a question, and listened intently to everything she said. Withholding the explicit details, she explained how the abuse had begun, while his mother was carrying him, and continued until she was a teenager, only stopping because she'd run away. Robbie wept as she talked about the life she'd had to live on the streets after she'd fled.

'I'm so sorry,' he cried. 'Oh, Winny, I'm so sorry.'

'It isn't your fault,' she told him, her tears mingling with his as they stood cheek to cheek.

Jade spoke for over an hour, bringing him up to date on what was happening. She told him about Alec and Nick and David, filling in the blanks as Robbie requested more details.

'So, technically,' he reasoned, thinking through the complications. 'You're not even my cousin.'

Jade nodded, wondering how this would affect him.

'It doesn't matter. You'll always be my sister. I don't care what anyone says.'

Jade was relieved. She'd always considered him her brother, regardless of the blood connection. She told Robbie about the other three women, and how she'd already met the adorable madness that was Ruby. As she repeated the terrible news Alec had told her about Lizzie the day before, Jade burst into tears.

'She was very lucky,' Jade sniffled. 'Her mother found her just in time.' Robbie frowned at this tragic news, and rubbed his sister's back to show his support. 'Ruby and I are planning to visit her in hospital. It will be a strange first meeting.' She pulled herself together. 'And Katie, I've yet to meet, too. Alec suggested we have a barbeque and invite the other two families. Ruby loves the idea. He's going to talk to them sometime this week.'

She was pleased Robbie hadn't shrugged her off and run away. That was the reaction she'd been expecting. Instead, he was supportive, understanding. And furious.

It wasn't until Jade stopped speaking that Robbie realised both his jaw and fists were clenched painfully.

'I could kill the prick,' he swore, his rage overtaking his logic.

'We're gonna get him, Robbie,' she told him, confident of victory over the long battle ahead. 'The committal hearing is a month away.'

'Does Mum know about all this?' he asked, wondering how much his father had told her.

'I don't know,' admitted Jade, allowing thoughts of Aunt Julia to pass through her mind for the first time in a decade. 'I haven't seen her since I took off.'

'Well,' announced Robbie, pleased he could take some kind of action, even if it wasn't murder. 'It's time she was filled in, isn't it?'

Robbie made a mental plan of what he would say to his mother when he arrived home for dinner later. It was easy to assume his father would be absent, as usual. Stark realisation hit him between the eyes; his father was a paedophile. Robbie barely knew him, and had lamented that saddening fact for a long time, until this moment. Now, just the thought of his father made him sick to the stomach. Robbie ran over to a nearby bush and vomited into the leaves. Jade rushed to his side and patted the retching young man between the shoulder blades as he emptied the contents of his stomach. Spent, he collapsed on the grass a short distance from the bush. Jade sat beside him, holding his hand.

'Are you okay?' she asked, handing him some tissues from her bag.

'Yeah,' he mumbled, out of breath. 'Sorry. I couldn't stop it.'

'It's okay,' Jade said, sympathetic, 'it's a lot to take in. Here, take this,' she added, handing him a peppermint.

Robbie accepted the sweet. He rallied, regaining his composure quickly. A million thoughts zigzagged through his mind. Emotions bounced around his body, gathering strength as they fed off each other. He felt physically exhausted. Rage burned in his gut. Drawing his legs up, he rested his chin on his knees for a moment, letting the tide of realisation flow over him. Jade sat beside him, silent. After a moment, Robbie wrapped an arm around her shoulders.

'I love you so much,' he whispered, squeezing her lightly. 'Welcome back.'

50

The old frame creaked, and the mattress groaned as Julia landed, sprawling on the bed, her limbs tossed carelessly across the rumpled covers. Her loose hair fanned across her back. She stretched out on her stomach, with her face buried in the pillow. The frail bed rocked as her body shuddered, its legs tapping the floor rhythmically. Animal instincts took over as she abandoned her usually graceful poise. At first, Julia made no sound, her mouth stretched wide in a silent grimace. For a long moment, she stopped breathing, her muscles tense. As the sensation built to a crescendo, she threw her head back and howled, the volume increasing with the intensity of the raw fervour boiling through her.

Julia was alone. She was fully-clothed. She lay diagonally across the bed and bawled. Hot tears of grief, despair, and guilt flowed into the pillow, soaking its thin cotton cover. She could feel nothing except the anguish that dominated every nerve ending. Every part of her ached. Her heart felt as if it were being squeezed by an unseen fist. Her lungs burned, near to bursting. Her mind was a whirl of such profound agony that it could no longer function. Even her fingers hurt as she clawed at the mattress, symbolically digging a hole through which to escape. She lay prostrate for quite some time, weeping and wailing, until Tom opened the door and bounded down the stairs.

'Julia?' he called uncertainly, and raced toward the bed.

Tom had never seen Julia cry. He'd never even seen her unhappy. She was usually such a bundle of giggles; all lust and laughs. Her prone, heaving form shocked him. He wondered what terrible tragedy had happened. He sat on the bed and gathered her into his arms, leaning back against the bed-head. He'd promised himself he wouldn't get emotionally attached, but over the last few months they'd grown close, sharing intimate moments that only lovers who care can share.

They had so much fun together. Tom knew he wasn't in love but, he admitted to himself, he couldn't help liking Julia a great deal.

'Oh, Tom,' she sobbed, a macabre grin twisting her face into a grotesque mask.

She let him pull her into his arms. Curled into a foetal position across his lap, she buried her head in his chest, one arm around his waist, the other thrown over his shoulder. She clung to him, her tightly clenched fists pressed against his back. Instantly protective, Tom wrapped himself around her, enveloping her petite form in his comforting embrace.

'Julia, what's wrong?' he asked, stroking her hair, kissing the top of her head, rocking her to and fro. He gently shushed and shooshed in her ear as she wrestled to contain the force of her savage emotions.

'Oh, Tom,' Julia spluttered, heaving air into her lungs, struggling for control. 'It's horrid. It's too horrid.'

She burst into tears again. Each time she calmed herself, the abhorrent thought burst her resolve. Her suffering moved Tom, awakening a forgotten instinct deep within his core. Julia abandoned herself to her heartache, her stomach tightening with nausea each time the sickening notion penetrated her brain. Tom held her, uttering whispered consolations, until she lay exhausted in his arms.

'Tell me what happened,' he urged gently, his lips caressing her hair.

'Do you have a hankie?' Julia sniffed, ashamed of the sticky mess her outburst had left on the front of his shirt.

He leaned to one side and pulled a grass-stained rag from his pocket. 'This is the best I can do,' he offered, handing it over. 'Are you okay?'

Julia shifted slightly, bringing her hands back toward her chest. She took the cloth and wiped her eyes.

Gosh, she thought, blowing her nose, I must look a wreck.

Mascara streaked her high cheekbones. Her lipstick had vanished. Her face was swollen, eyelids puffy. Her red-rimmed eyes burned. Her throat was raw. She felt wretched.

'You're not going to believe this, Tom,' began Julia, taking a deep breath, bracing herself for another onslaught of torment. 'It's too terrible for words.'

Faltering, her voice cracking, she tearfully repeated what Robbie had just told her about her husband of twenty-four years. Her perturbed son had left her stunned, standing like a wax statue in the middle of the library, and bolted upstairs to his room. Blindly, Julia had run out to the greenhouse in search of solace. The gardener had come down to get fertiliser for the orchids, and heard the keening.

Tom listened, speechless, to her unspeakable words. The colour drained from his face. His mouth went dry. He felt sick. Shocked, he trembled involuntarily. When he'd spotted Carl behaving strangely at The Mosh Pit, he'd suspected something hideously amiss, and had uncovered some dubious, if vague, facts, but he hadn't expected anything like the incredible abomination his lover was describing.

Julia finished her narration and wept quietly in his arms. Dumbfounded, Tom sat unmoving, cradling her limp body, trying to absorb this loathsome revelation.

Some time later, he found his voice. 'I think I should go and talk to the police.'

Silent, Julia nodded. She felt dirty, guilty by association. She closed her eyes and thought of the role she had played in her husband's debauchery. Anger burned in the pit of her stomach. She had married a paedophile. She shivered with revulsion. Deeply remorseful, she promised herself that she would try to make amends, beginning with Robbie.

'I'm so stupid,' she mumbled into Tom's damp shirt. 'I'm so idiotically stupid.'

51

Despite the chilly breeze, it was a glorious day on the beach. A trail of sunlight shimmered across the calm water. Seagulls squawked overhead. In the distance, a group of small children built a sand castle. Their parents sat chatting nearby.

Jade and David walked hand in hand across the white sand, wading in the gentle swell. Heads together as they strolled, they laughed and chatted amicably. As the pair approached the house, Nick watched from the wide verandah, a can of beer in his hand. Alec sat next to him, leaning back in a canvas chair, with his feet on the rail. He sipped his coke, and surveyed the tranquil scene.

'This was a great idea,' Nick commented, nodding toward Jade. 'Right from the start. Look at her. She's a totally different woman.'

'She is,' Alec agreed, smiling into the sun.

He dragged his thoughts away from his dead witness, Lenny Morris, and gazed toward the water. Despite the setback, he was glad things had worked out. It seemed like forever since those miserable nights when Jade had stood on the other side of the grimy bar, frowning glumly as she served her most persistent customer another shot of watered-down bourbon. Alec could barely remember the lost years of lonely drunken binges. The fuzzy-tongued hangovers. The chills. The nausea. The depression. And his aborted attempt to wipe himself off the planet. It was as if they had taken place in a previous life.

'Barbecue's hot!' shouted Gerard from the beach.

He was in seventh heaven with a pile of hot coals, a pair of tongs, and a 'Kiss the Cook' apron. He sipped a can of beer and eagerly snapped the metal teeth of his utensil together. He arranged the coals, settling them evenly so he could cook lunch to perfection. Nick carried the tray of steaks and sliced onions out to the enthusiastic chef.

'How do you like 'em?' Gerard asked, waving his tongs above the barbecue.

Amanda and Donna sat on the bench in front of the long picnic table, chattering happily as Amanda sliced tomatoes into the salad. Donna chopped fruit into a large glass bowl and listened, responding whenever she could get a word in sideways.

Lizzie and Katie were inside, huddled together, as they sorted through the enormous pile of CD's Ruby had brought with her.

'Oh!' enthused Katie, 'this one is amazing.' She thrust her selection into Lizzie's hands. 'They're so cool, and funny too. Powerful vocals, rhythmic guitars, gorgeous harmonies …'

Lizzie cocked her head to read the label; under a different sky— women in docs. 'I've never heard of them,' she said shyly, impressed with Katie's vast knowledge of music.

'Well,' laughed Katie, taking the slim case. 'Let's put it on. You'll love it. Seriously, these chicks rock.'

Lizzie watched Katie as she inserted the CD and pressed play. A centimetre of dark hair stuck out in all directions on the older girl's head. Long, gold earrings dangled to her shoulders. Her face glowed with health. She'd plumped out a little since she'd changed jobs. Now, she worked in an office, filing documents for a real estate agent who was an old friend of Gerard's.

As capricious as ever, Lizzie had recovered from her overdose, although Donna was still recovering from the shock of discovering her daughter half dead. When Jade and Ruby had visited Lizzie in hospital, they'd presented her with a combination of tough love, hard facts, and a little understanding.

'We need you, doll,' Ruby rasped. 'If you check out too soon, we'll be all messed up. We're a team now, baby. All four of us. And we're counting on you not to let the side down. Comprende?'

'Lizzie, honey,' said Jade, holding the girl's hands. 'It's not worth dying over. We can get through this, and we can make a life afterwards. We'll do it together, all of us.' She gazed into Lizzie's sad eyes. 'And if you need me to come around to your house and kick your cute little butt all the way to Antarctica, then just call and I'll be there.'

'Me too,' piped up Ruby, smirking. 'Kicking butt is my speciality.'

Donna had been astonished when Lizzie had giggled uproariously after hearing one of Ruby's crazy travel tales. It was the first time her daughter had laughed in ages. Overwhelmed, Donna made a feeble excuse and rushed outside to bawl her eyes out.

Since then, Lizzie had slowly emerged from her shell.

'I like it,' she told Katie, waggling her head from side to side, and tapping her feet, as vibrant, soulful music blasted from the stereo.

Out on the balcony, Ruby sat on a deckchair behind Alec, stretched out under the late autumn sun in denim cut-offs, purple leggings, and a thick cheesecloth shirt. Her sweater hung over the back of the chair. Hiding behind a novel, she surreptitiously rubbed her toes across Alec's pert backside. When Nick stepped off the verandah with the plate of sliced potatoes, Alec turned and threw her a funny grimace. Ruby raised an eyebrow in mock innocence, and winked slyly with a twinkle of mischief in her eye.

'I dare you to rub up against me in the shower,' she muttered, teasing him mercilessly, knowing she'd be in for a treat at home.

Alec grinned. 'You'll keep,' he whispered, squirming in his seat. 'You are in big trouble.'

'What are you gonna do?' she chuckled, 'arrest me?'

'Oh,' he threatened playfully, 'much worse than that.'

Ruby inconspicuously retracted her foot as Jade marched up the beach with David trailing close behind. Despite Jade's initial suspicions, Alec and Ruby had managed to keep their torrid affair a closely guarded secret, and would until after the trial.

'Don't cook mine,' called David, coming up behind Gerard who was putting steaks on the barbeque. 'Just scare it.'

Gerard turned to face him and raised his eyebrows dramatically. David grinned cheekily. He reached into the esky and grabbed a can. Cracking open the icy lemonade, he laughed at the cook's comical expression.

'He'd actually prefer it if you just branded the cow and put the hot bit on a plate for him,' Jade told Gerard, her nose screwed up in disgust.

'What's wrong with that?' exclaimed David, his hands raised in surrender. 'Cows are vegetarian.'

'Good,' retorted Jade, refusing to rise to his bait. 'I'm going to get the tofu kebabs. Gerard, can you please make sure there's a meat-free corner on the hot plate?'

It was David's turn to screw up his nose. He liked his meat, and would eat just about anything that was thrown at him. Once, in Vietnam, he'd eaten fried waterbugs. After that, he figured, anything was tasty. Jade ate a little fish every so often, but she mostly survived on beans and pulses. David hated tofu, and couldn't stand seaweed. Since they'd been living together, meal times had become an interesting exercise in logistics.

'Sure,' Gerard replied as Jade headed up to the kitchen.

'Can I do something?' called Ruby from her chair. She put her book down and sat up. 'Would you like me to set the table?'

Donna nodded. 'Good idea.'

Ruby busied herself with cutlery and plates. Donna listened while Amanda babbled incessantly as they tossed the freshly made salads, then placed them on the table.

Amanda had been doubtful when Alec had asked Katie if she wanted to meet the other girls. But Gerard had seen an ideal opportunity for his daughter to heal, and access to an extra source of support. He had talked his wife into it. Katie was enthusiastic, but she'd kept silent until her parents had sorted out their feelings.

Lizzie and Katie had taken to each other instantly. Their heads together while they talked about music, movies and clothes, the four and a half years between their ages became meaningless. Katie was thrilled to meet Lizzie, who resembled a little lost bird with broken wings. Empathetic, Katie remembered feeling the same way. Lacking family support, she'd plunged headfirst into a dark, dangerous world.

'You're so lucky your mother is such a strong woman,' said Katie, wishing hers was half as resilient. 'Mine didn't cope at all and I ended up in all kinds of trouble.'

She talked non-stop, while Lizzie listened passively, happy to have a new friend who understood where she was at. Both Lizzie and Katie knew they'd suffered the same horrors, but it was a subject they didn't broach. Instead, Katie focused on positive subjects, and Lizzie made an effort to participate. Donna was thrilled with her progress.

At lunch, Ruby regaled the captive audience with hilarious tales of her travels around the globe. She mimicked the voices of the characters in her stories, adopting their native accents and taking on their wonderful idiosyncrasies. Gesticulating madly as she acted out each part, she spun her outrageous yarns.

'So,' Ruby breathed, grinning wickedly, 'we leave him there, stark naked, in the middle of nowhere, and drive off in his car.'

Fascinated, everyone at the table was mesmerised, entranced by both the animation in her face, and the sheer audacity of the woman. They roared laughing as she brought her third story to its conclusion.

Nick and Alec laughed aloud, while Amanda smiled behind her hand. Donna haw-hawed at the punch line, spluttering potato salad down her shirt. Jade threw her head back and chortled.

'Oh,' gasped Gerard, holding his sides. 'That's the funniest thing I've ever heard.'

Katie and Lizzie tittered quietly until David, who collapsed in hysterics, fell off his chair. Then, they burst into musical peals of giggles, helpless in their mirth. Ruby beamed, pleased she'd hit her mark.

'Ruby, have you been all over the world?' asked Lizzie when she regained control. She was awed by the woman's seemingly endless adventures.

'Yes, I have,' replied Ruby, her tone becoming serious. 'Well, nearly. I've been running away from myself for years, looking for something obscure that I could never quite put my finger on.' She smiled at Lizzie, and stretched her hand across the table. Silently, the girl took it as Ruby gazed into her eyes. 'But I came back recently because I felt I needed to face my demons before I could find whatever it is that's missing.' Lizzie extended her hand behind Donna's back toward Katie, who wound her fingers through Lizzie's.

'I knew it would be a tough battle,' Ruby went on, 'but I'm a stubborn cow and I decided it would be worth the fight.' A tiny tear formed in the corner of Ruby's eye. Only Lizzie noticed it. Katie offered her hand to Jade, who sat opposite her. Jade squeezed Katie's fingers in her palm, and completed the circle by picking up Ruby's other hand. 'I'm really glad I did, because now I've met all you gorgeous people,' Ruby added, squeezing both her hands. Donna reached for Amanda's hand and let a tear roll down her cheek. David closed his eyes and let the flood of emotion rush through him. Nick, Alec, and Gerard nodded silently in contemplation. Ruby continued, 'and now we can kill this monster together.'

Katie nodded, deeply moved, understanding Ruby's need.

Jade sighed, recognising in herself a younger version of the nomadic woman.

Lizzie gazed into Ruby's moist eyes and felt a glimmer of hope. For the first time since Alec had found her on the street, she dared to be optimistic.

52

Nerves jangling, Jade tossed clothes across the bed. When she'd almost emptied her wardrobe, she surveyed the collection of garments.

'I've got nothing to wear,' she complained to Nick, who was dressed and ready to leave.

'What's wrong with this?' he asked, picking up a hanger with a pretty blue woollen skirt and matching long-sleeved shirt.

'Too cheerful,' she grumbled, assessing the tangle of shoes at her feet.

'This?' Nick asked, holding up a slim black pants suit.

'Too glum,' she pouted, not sure what look she was after.

Nick picked up each item, and then put it away as Jade tossed unreasonable criticisms at her entire collection of apparel. Too stern. Too flippant. Too dowdy. Too bright. Too short. Too long. Too old. Wrong colour. Nick was patient, aware she was nervous, and said little as Jade pulled more clothes out of her drawers. Half an hour later, she was still flitting about in her underwear, on edge, and more confused than ever.

'Are you two ready yet?' called David from the hallway.

Nick sighed. If they weren't gone in fifteen minutes, they'd be late. 'Coming,' he called. He could have killed for a cup of coffee. 'Just a minute.'

'Okay, Jade,' Nick declared, asserting himself. He handed her some clothes. 'Put on these black pants. That purple top will go well with them. And this jacket will be fine over the top. Put on those boots too,' he added, pointing to her pile of rejected footwear. 'They'll make you feel strong.'

Jade didn't argue. Incapable of thinking for herself, she obeyed. As she dressed, Nick returned the unwanted clothing to the drawers. He stacked the shoes back on the rack. Choosing a small black bag, Nick threw in her favourite lipstick and a small hairbrush, as well as a lovely mother-of-pearl hair clip he'd given her soon after they'd first met.

Crikey, thought Nick, as he organised his girlfriend, I'd have saved time if I'd just dressed her in the first place, and got that cuppa I'm hanging for.

Finally, Jade was ready to go. She was sitting on the bed, trying to gather her wits, when a blinding panic-attack struck. Her legs jiggled frantically up and down. Her mind went blank. A rush of terror charged through her. She burst into tears, shivering uncontrollably.

'I can't do it,' she wailed, collapsing to the floor. 'I don't remember anything.'

'Shhh,' Nick whispered. He picked her up and sat her on the bed, sitting with his arm around her. Jade's hands flew to her face.

'What's wrong?' David asked, coming into the room.

Nick shrugged, confused. He didn't know what was going on. David sat on the bed and took his daughter into his arms. She wrapped her arms around his neck and sobbed on his shoulder. Filled with terror and self-doubt, Jade wanted to run away screaming, and never come back.

'I'm scared,' howled Jade.

'I know, sweetheart,' David soothed, gently patting her back. 'It's going to be fine. Shhh. I know it's hard but you're so brave and strong. We're with you all the way. Come on now. It's time to go.'

Nick felt helpless; no, worse, useless. A lump caught in his throat. Rage burned through his veins. He shut his eyes and tried to pull himself together, hoping the sick pervert who did this to her would pay for his crimes. With an ache burning in his heart, he watched father and daughter as they rose from the bed. David walked Jade out to the car, handing her a hankie as she climbed into the back seat. Nick followed, bringing her bag. David drove. Nick sat in the back with Jade, holding her hand, as they went to the courthouse. During the twenty-minute ride, the silence was deafening.

'Thanks. I'm okay now,' breathed Jade as she got out of the car.

Stern-faced security guards investigated all the suspicious blips and bleeps as the threesome went through the metal detector at the entrance of the courthouse. Ruby was waiting in the foyer when they arrived. She sat in a hard plastic chair, her back like a ramrod, her legs pressed tightly together, and her hands placed firmly on her knees, elbows straight. Her face was tense, the cheekbones accentuated, and her eyes vacant. She looked as if she were about to explode. When she saw the little group, she instantly leapt to her feet and regained her normal gangling composure.

She hugged Jade and then wrapped her arms around Nick in a greeting hug. 'Hi,' she spluttered. 'I'm so nervous.'

'Me too,' said Jade, near to tears again.

'Shall we go upstairs?' suggested David, eager to get started.

'We can't,' whispered Ruby conspiratorially. 'He's up there, waiting on the bench.'

'Is anyone with him?' asked Jade, wondering if his hideous wife would be there to support him throughout the case.

'No, he's alone,' said Ruby. 'But I saw one of the lawyers.'

The little group chose some free chairs in the corner. They huddled close and talked quietly. A few minutes later, Lizzie and Donna arrived and were greeted with hugs and kisses. They were followed quickly by Gerard, Amanda and Katie, and another teary hug-fest ensued. Feeling more relaxed, happy all their support systems were in place, everyone settled themselves and chatted idly. Alec trailed in last, resplendent in a dark suit.

Ruby whistled. 'Woohoo, you scrub up alright, doncha?'

Everyone agreed, and complimented Alec on his unusually spiffy appearance. Alec beamed. He hadn't felt this good in so long.

Stephen Frederick came down the stairs, his long black gown trailing behind him, and located the group squished in the corner. Stephen hadn't slept all night, labouring until the wee hours preparing his case, and then double-checking everything until dawn. The last week had been a whirl of legal research and witness interviews involving long, complicated explanations articulated in simple layman's terms.

He'd talked to each of the four women separately, gone through their evidence, shown them through the courtroom, and discussed possible underhanded strategies the defence might use against them.

He'd also reassured them that they could ask the judge for a break any time they needed one. Stephen hoped he'd prepared them sufficiently for the committal hearing.

'Now,' he said in his distinctive baritone, 'is everyone ready? We're starting in a few minutes. He's still outside the courtroom, sitting with all his friends,' joked the friendly barrister, lowering his voice to a deep rumble. 'Wait down here about ten minutes, and then come up. The coast will be clear. He'll be inside.'

'Is there a private room where we can wait?' asked David, knowing that the girls would be trouping in and out of the courtroom all day, and so would Carl. 'So the girls don't have to walk past Rutherford when they adjourn and stuff.'

'Of course,' nodded Stephen. 'I'll get the bailiff to show you in a few minutes.' He walked up the stairs again, confident the committal hearing would be a success.

'I'm glad I'm not late,' panted Robbie, striding quickly toward Jade. He kissed her forehead and smiled broadly, taking in all the new faces. 'Hi. I'm Robbie.' He paused a moment before adding, 'Jade's brother.'

A miniature ripple of shock went through the little assembly. Jade had never once mentioned a brother. It was a surprise to all, except Alec. Nick's jaw hit the floor. He'd known Jade over five years and she hadn't ever talked about a sibling. David registered this new information and quickly figured out who Robbie was, in relation to Jade. He was delighted the young man had come to support her.

'Hello, I'm David,' he introduced himself. 'I'm Jade's father.'

Ruby giggled. She'd never met anyone whose father didn't know their brother. It struck her as hilarious and she fell about laughing. Sucking in gulps of air, she managed to explain her mirth between fits of giggles. Lizzie and Katie chuckled. As they recovered, Jade introduced Robbie, omitting the fact that his father was the defendant.

'Different families …' she said, leaving it in the air. One shock was enough for the moment, she decided.

'It's so good to meet you,' said Amanda, shaking Robbie's hand.

Everyone else followed suit, firmly clasping his hand, or hugging and kissing him, welcoming him into their unique little clique.

They went upstairs and a court officer showed them into a large waiting room. Vinyl-covered chairs, in a range of dulled colours, lined the walls, and a laminated table took up the centre of the room. The nicotine-stained walls were bare. Ironically, a sign suggested that smoking would incur a large fine. Apparently, the walls had been there much longer than the sign.

'Ugh!' gasped Ruby, taking in the décor. 'This is the epitome of government-funded interior design. A la blandé.'

Everyone chuckled. Gerard and Amanda settled in one corner, with Katie in the middle. Lizzie and Donna sat nearby. On the other side of the room, Ruby and Jade sat together, surrounded by Alec, David, Nick and Robbie. For the first time since she was four years old, Jade felt like she had a real family. She looked around at all the people who cared about her, and was instantly glad she hadn't checked to see if the gun was properly loaded all those months ago.

Inside five minutes, Lizzie had switched chairs with Amanda, and was sharing a headphone with Katie so they could chat and listen to music. David moved over to sit near Gerard while Amanda and Donna gabbed on about nothing, talking to calm their nerves more than anything else.

Jade's leg began jumping up and down. Nick put his hand on it. It stopped for a few minutes, then began again. Nick gave up. She had a right to be nervous. His nerves were shot, too. He closed his eyes and imagined the whole table covered in steaming mugs of freshly-brewed filter coffee.

Ruby talked quietly to Alec and Robbie for a few minutes. Suddenly, she had a flash panic-attack. Trembling and sweating, she clapped both hands over her mouth.

'Oh, no!' she bawled, 'I knew this would happen.'

Leaping out of her chair, she patted her cheeks with her palms, inhaling deep breaths to calm herself. Her face felt hot. Her heart raced. Her mind went blank. A look of terror crossed her face. Jade stood up and wrapped her arms around her friend. Katie clutched Lizzie's hand, fighting the tears that threatened to overcome her. Amanda and Donna turned to their children, and smiled tightly, projecting dewy-eyed encouragement. Ruby and Jade shed a few tears, whispering comfort into each other's ears before finally resuming their seats. No sooner had Ruby sat down than the bailiff burst in the door.

'Peregrine Prudence Smythe,' he called briskly, glancing around the room.

'There's no one here with that name,' said David, trying to be helpful.

Ruby stood up, her head hung low. 'Yes there is,' she muttered, mortified.

She glowered at the hapless bailiff for letting out one of her deepest, darkest secrets. Spears of contempt shot from her eyes. No one had called her by her birth name since she was almost twenty-one, and the last smart-alec who'd uttered the dreadful moniker, just to tease her, had scored himself a black eye and a bloody nose. The barrister had agreed to address her by her current name. She couldn't believe there had been such a humiliating stuff up.

'Peregrine?' smirked Jade, hiding her giggle behind her hand.

'Prudence?' sniggered Alec, one eyebrow high on his forehead.

'Smythe?' chortled Nick, joining in.

'Oh, piss off!' sneered Ruby, and followed the uniformed man out the door.

As Ruby walked into the courtroom, Carl's jaw dropped open. He hadn't seen her since … He couldn't even remember. There was no mistaking that face, though. It was the same girl, now grown into a beautiful woman. Refusing to look at him, she walked tall and proud toward the front of the room, and took her seat in the witness box.

Aside from Judge Leonard, his clerks and the bailiff, the two barristers, the defendant, and herself, the courtroom was empty. While she affirmed that she would tell the whole truth and nothing but the truth, the bailiff slipped quietly out the door. He returned momentarily with a note for the judge. The judge read the message, contemplated the words for a moment and nodded.

'Yes, the support persons may be present in the court,' he said, gesturing to the bailiff.

Nick, Gerard, Robbie, and David settled themselves on the back seat in the gallery as Stephen went through the few routine questions. When Carl saw his son entering the court in support of the witness, his chest tightened. He felt as if he would have a heart-attack. Ruby was also stunned, for different reasons. She was half terrified of having them hear her evidence, and half thrilled that they cared enough to support her. Gerard winked his encouragement as the prosecution posed his first real question.

'Can you describe for the court, your very first recollection of childhood, Miss Smy— err, Smithers?'

Ruby took a deep breath. She felt in her pocket for her calming stone, a small amethyst that she'd put there the night before. Wrapping her fingers around the little polished rock, she nodded, summonsed her inner-strength, and began to speak.

'Yes,' she said in a clear voice. 'I was about four years old, maybe a little younger.' Ruby's eyes found a small electrical switch on the wall opposite, just above the jury box, and focused on it. 'My parents had taken me with them to his parents' house. They were all close friends, and visited often. This time we went there, and he was there.'

'Pardon me, Miss Smythe … ah, Smithers, who was there?' asked the judge, seeking clarification.

'He was.' She threw a thumb in the direction of the defendant. 'Carl Rutherford,' she spat the name of the man who had stolen her childhood and almost destroyed her life. Judge Leonard made a note on his pad then nodded, so she continued. 'I guess he was about twenty, maybe twenty-one then.' Ruby took the stone from her pocket and held it in her hand. Her heart pounded in her ears. 'He … um … when … after lunch, he took me into the garden to play. Our fathers were smoking cigars and talking, while our mothers washed the dishes. I remember that clearly because that was the day my mother accidentally dropped one of Missus Rutherford's precious Doulton Watteau bowls. Ma was very upset about it.'

'Go on,' boomed Frederick, making a note on his papers.

'We were out the back, playing hide and seek in the garden, when he told me to count to ten, and then come and find him. I could hear him giggling in the bushes. So I walked through a gap in the hedge and he was there. He pulled me down on top of him and started tickling me. By then, I thought he was lots of fun to play with.'

Ruby fought back tears. Her old nemesis, guilt, made a brief comeback. She shoved it back in its box and kept talking.

'I was laughing and then he pulled my dress over my head. It was a hot day and I didn't think it strange. He took his shirt off too. Then, he took the rest of my clothes off. He told me "I've got something to show you" and then took his shorts and underpants off too.'

Ruby swallowed. She glanced at the men at the back of the court. Their faces were stony. Jaws clenched. Robbie looked distressed. Carl leaned forward and peered around the screen, trying to catch her eye and intimidate her. She shut down her peripheral vision, and focused on the switch on the opposite wall.

'Okay,' said Stephen, 'and then what happened?'

'He … um … he kissed me. And he kissed my chest and stomach. He picked me up and rubbed his face into my body, and kissed me on the … err … vagina. I remember thinking that all the kissing felt nice. I didn't feel afraid of him then.' Ruby's voice faltered. 'He lay me on the grass behind the hedge and told me to put my arms and legs out like a star. I thought it was a game,' Ruby's voice cracked, and she sobbed. Instantly, she rallied and pulled herself together.

'Then,' she continued, 'he lay beside me. He told me to touch his penis. I didn't want to. That's when I remember feeling frightened for the first time. He laughed at me and said I was a scaredy cat. He said we were just playing. That it was fun and wouldn't hurt. I believed him because we'd had so much fun until then. He took my hand and put it on his penis.' Ruby took a deep breath.

Stephen nodded and asked, 'What happened next?'

'He … um … told me to touch it, to play with it. He said it was just like a toy. He held my hand against it and stroked himself. He told me we were playing Mummies and Daddies. He said I was the Mummy and he was the Daddy. He wanted me to call him Daddy.'

Robbie shut his eyes. Not sure he could stand much more, he gripped the wooden bench hard. Struggling with his own rage, David squeezed the young man's shoulder. Gerard's face was awash with tears, but he made no sound at all. Nick sat with his eyes shut, his jaw working overtime, his clenched fists trapped between the vice of his knees.

'I told him I already had a Daddy, and he said that I could have as many Daddys as I wanted,' Ruby testified, her voice sounding more and more like it belonged to a frightened little girl. 'He was stroking his penis with my hand on it, and then he started touching me with his other hand. He was kissing me too, on my chest mostly. Then, he put his … um … fingers inside my vagina.' Ruby paused a moment, gathering strength. 'It really hurt, and his fingers felt scratchy.'

Carl coughed, trying to distract Ruby. Empowered by her own presence in the room, she ignored him. Gerard shot him a death-ray look. Bile rose in Robbie's throat. He felt as if he'd vomit. Nick felt sick, too. David's heart broke.

'He rubbed his fingers on my vagina,' Ruby told the court, feeling stronger, 'and then he got to his knees and knelt over me. He held my arms above my head. I said I didn't like this game and told him that I wanted to go home. He said that I was home and that if I didn't do what he said, then he would kill my parents.' Ruby broke down again.

'Would you like a break, Miss Smithers?' Judge Leonard asked, his voice gentle.

'No, thank you,' said Ruby. She wiped her eyes and took a sip from the glass of water the clerk had put near her elbow. 'I'm fine. Okay.' She slapped her cheeks and inhaled deeply. 'I didn't know what that meant. He told me that I'd never see my parents again. That they'd go away and leave me alone forever. I was terrified. I didn't want my parents to go away. Touching and feeling was part of the game, he told me. I was so scared I couldn't move. I started crying, begging him not to send my parents away. He said he wouldn't, but only if I did what he told me.'

Ruby took another mouthful of water. She brought her hands up to rest on the podium. The little rock was hot in her fingers as she rubbed it frantically, trying to calm her racing heart. She again focused on the little switch on the opposite wall.

'He was holding my hands above my head. Kneeling over me and then, he lay on top of me and pushed his penis into my vagina. It hurt so much. I thought it would never stop. I was crying, begging him not to hurt me.' She paused a moment, rallying her courage. 'He pressed down on my mouth with his stomach until I couldn't breathe. He was so big; I was just a little girl, still a baby. I struggled, trying to breathe. Then, after a moment, he laughed and got to his knees again. He picked me up and cuddled me for a while. He said he was sorry he hurt me and that he'd kiss it better. Then, he lay me on the grass, and licked my vagina. It tickled a bit, and felt a bit soft, after all the pain.' Ruby blushed, beginning from her toes. This was the thing that shamed her the most about her life-long ordeal. 'He did that for what felt like a long time.'

'Do you know how long?' asked Stephen.

'No, but I was very frightened, and didn't move. At the same time, he was playing with my nipples. When he stopped, he said we'd go and get some ice-cream. He gave me my little dress and panties to put on. They were inside out and I didn't know how to fix it.' Ruby's voice wavered.

Twice, she inhaled, letting the air out slowly each time. Robbie cried, not making a sound, dabbing at his face with a hankie. David squeezed his eyes shut and wondered how on earth anyone except a heartless cold-blooded monster could even think of hurting a little girl. Gerard felt as if he'd been punched in the stomach. Nick was on the verge of tears, only checking them with his increasing admiration of Ruby.

'He was getting dressed,' Ruby went on, 'when he stopped and said there was one last part of the game. He had his shirt on, but not his pants. He made me lie on my stomach on the grass. It was itchy, so he put my dress underneath. He lay on top of me again,' Ruby sucked air into her lungs sharply. Sobbing, she struggled to get the words out. 'And he rubbed his penis between my buttocks until he had an orgasm.'

'Miss Smithers, would you like a break now?' asked Stephen, proud of her for her brilliant testimony so far. Alas, he thought, most of the other witnesses won't get through today. He made a mental note to keep the next two days free.

'In a minute,' she said, wanting to get this particular incident over and done with. There were hundreds of others, all fairly similar, that took place over the following twelve years, and even beyond, but it was this one she remembered most vividly.

'Miss Smithers, how do you know the defendant had an orgasm?'

'I was only three or four then,' she said, following Stephen's lead. 'So, I didn't know what an orgasm was. But when he was rubbing his penis between my buttocks, he was holding my hips at the same time, and pushing me into the ground. At one point, he squeezed my hips really hard, hurting me. Then, I felt a spurt of hot liquid on my back. I thought he'd thrown something on me. It wasn't until many years later that I realised what he'd done.'

'Uh-huh, so what happened next?' Stephen boomed, content with the clarification they'd discussed a few days earlier.

'He wiped me clean with the tails of his shirt. And then he helped me get dressed. He gave me a big cuddle and said I'd been really good. He was kissing my face, and then he said that he was sorry he'd hurt me, that he didn't mean to do it, and that we were going for ice-cream. When we got to the back door of the house, he said to me, "If you ever tell anyone about our Mummies and Daddies game, your parents will get killed."'

Ruby was upset. She blurted the sentence out, ignoring the tears on her face. 'Then, he held my hand and took me into the house. I'm sure we ate ice-cream, but I don't remember it that well. I was too concerned about never seeing my parents again.' Ruby bawled. 'Can I have a break now?'

'Of course,' said the judge, his ears ringing from the content of her testimony. 'We'll adjourn for ten minutes. The witness may leave the courtroom.'

As the bailiff led Ruby from the room, Robbie looked across at his father, his red-rimmed eyes filled with hatred and contempt. Carl met his gaze, saw the tear-stained face of his only heir, and bowed his head, closing his eyes to shut out the image.

Ruby stumbled into the witness room and fell into Alec's arms, howling. She shuddered involuntarily, as he held her. David came in right behind her, with Gerard hot on his heels. Nick and Robbie followed them in. Jade leapt out of her chair and wrapped her arms around Ruby. Lizzie and Katie joined her. They all cried as they embraced the traumatised woman.

'Ruby,' said David, sniffing. 'You're doing well, sweetheart. You're kicking butt. You really are. You're a bloody champion.'

Ten minutes later, the bailiff was at the door, smiling gently. 'Ruby?' he said, 'They're ready to begin again.'

53

A bottle of golden tequila sat on the table between them, the level dangerously low. Next to it were the remains of a badly mutilated mud-cake, a large porcelain bowl with a couple of Belgian liqueur chocolates left in the bottom, a half-empty packet of Tim Tams, and a plate of sliced limes with the used rinds lining the rim. A wooden salt shaker sat to one side near an ashtray holding the roaches of seven joints. Dragon-blood incense wafted through the candlelit room. Aretha Franklin belted out tunes in the background.

'You know,' Ruby slurred, 'this was a brilliant idea.'

'Yep,' agreed Jade, trying to focus on the woman sitting opposite. 'It's been my favourite cure for stress, depression, and life-changing crises for almost ten years.'

'Better than a Prozac prescription,' giggled Ruby, trying to steady her hand as she set the refilled shot glasses on the table in front of them. She'd long passed the point of being capable of rolling another spliff.

'Men just don't get it,' mused Jade, glad Ruby had understood her tequila-and-chocolate-cake therapy.

A hand-written sign on Ruby's front door declared, 'No Boys Allowed!!!' in thick red ink. Three quarters of the way through the bottle, giggling like schoolgirls, they'd made the crude sign on a sheet of crumpled newspaper, and fastened it with a bit of Bluetac.

Decorum abandoned, Jade licked the web of Ruby's hand, between her thumb and forefinger, and sprinkled salt on the skin. Then, she licked her own hand and did the same. She passed a slice of lime to Ruby, and settled another one between her own finger and thumb.

'Down the hatch,' she said, and licked the scattering of salt.

Ruby licked hers and they threw the fiery liquid down their throats, then sucked the lime dry. Jade screwed up her eyes as the sour juice squished through her teeth. Her mouth became a tight moue, processing the combination of bitter flavours.

'You know,' said Jade, smacking her lips as she mulled over her past loves, after their long conversation about men, 'I had the sweetest boyfriend when I was nineteen. He was gorgeous. Kieran Bryson. A lovely boy. Oh, but so messed up.' She screwed up her face in dismay as she recalled him and his monumental problems. 'And of course, I was a mess too, so we were doomed from the beginning. Honestly Ruby, his family life was psychotic.'

'You do realise,' slurred Ruby, hiccuping drunkenly. 'with this whole family deal … that there is "fun" right in the middle of "dysfunctional" don't you?'

She chortled and lay on her back, feeling extremely pissed. Jade, used to this method of self-annihilation, wasn't quite so drunk, but could no longer make out the individual CDs in Ruby's music library. The whole wall was a blur of colour.

'Come over here, you,' muttered Ruby, sprawled on the floor.

Jade grabbed a chocolate biscuit in each fist and crawled around the table. She collapsed in a heap of giggles at Ruby's side.

'We have to do this first,' ordered Jade, her tongue almost numb. She handed a biscuit to Ruby. Then, she poured two more shots of tequila.

Ruby groaned. 'Oh, no. Again?'

Jade nodded, then hauled her friend into a sitting position and handed her one of the little glasses. Then, Jade bit the opposite corners off her Tim Tam. She dipped one end into the liquid and sucked the alcohol through the centre. When her biscuit got soggy, she stuffed it in her mouth, and threw the remains of the shot in with it. Simultaneously, Ruby did likewise.

She flopped back to the floor and stretched her arms out, still chewing her tequila-soaked Tim Tam. Jade climbed into her embrace. They lay for a long time on the floor, just holding each other. Ruby inhaled the perfume of Jade's sweet-smelling hair. Jade could smell chocolate on Ruby, and a hint of essential oils. Jasmine and sandalwood.

'I love you,' mumbled Ruby, barely coherent and teetering on the brink of unconsciousness.

'I love you too, honey.'

Wrapped around each other, Jade and Ruby drifted off to sleep on the floor. As the night crept along, the incense sticks came to their ashy end, Aretha finished her last song and finally, the candles flickered out, the wicks drowning in their own wax.

After the harrowing committal hearing tensions had run high. For Jade and Ruby, there had also been a thread of relief running throughout. Actually saying the words out loud, getting them on the outside, and in a public place, had been a cathartic experience. They'd both felt empowered, liberated by the process of giving evidence. Lizzie and Katie were still traumatised by having to tell of the horrors they'd been through, in front of a room full of gowned and wigged men. Afterwards, they'd been carted off to intensive counselling sessions by their respective parents. All of them would have to repeat the whole process in another couple of months, in front of a jury. Overall though, everyone involved agreed it was worth the stress.

The news had come that morning that the committal hearing had been a success. There would only be one trial. For that, everyone was thankful and hugely relieved. After Ellen Johnson from the Prosecutor's office had hung up, Jade got on the phone to Ruby, and then called Katie and Lizzie for a quick celebratory chat.

That evening, accompanied by Nick and David, Jade and Ruby had dinner in a lovely harbour-side restaurant. After they had dispensed with coffee, Ruby informed the boys that they'd have to find alternative entertainment. It was girl-talk time, and they weren't invited.

'You can go and do some male-bonding, or whatever it is you blokes do when women aren't looking,' laughed Jade, cheerfully dismissing them.

Happy to oblige, Nick and David raced back to the beach house to watch the end of the semi-final football match. Jade dragged Ruby to the liquor store, then to a late-night supermarket to stock up on supplies before heading back to Ruby's apartment. Soon after arriving, they got stoned enough to laugh uproariously at nothing.

Then, devoured all the chips and peanuts in the house, before starting on the chocolate.

'Ha ha ha!' gasped Jade at yet another of Ruby's hilarious travel tales. 'And he didn't know the guy upstairs was faking?'

'No,' chuckled Ruby, shaking her head. 'Those Saeth Efrecins really are a scream.'

Still chortling, Jade had cracked the tequila and thrown the lid away. 'We'll have to drink a toast to them,' she declared.

Ruby was delighted, and quickly adapted to Jade's way of thinking. 'Certainly,' she giggled, raising her glass. 'And here's to those voracious, villainous Vikings too!'

They spent the night talking about their lives, their dreams, their hopes; skipping over the bits that had hurt the most, and skimming the gory details off the top. Funny stories were often autopsied until uncontrollable laughter brought tears to their eyes and made their stomachs ache. At the same time, anything that was regarded as evidence was off limits.

In between tales, Jade dispensed shots of tequila with salt and lime, and Ruby butchered the mud-cake. By the time they'd drunk half the bottle, Ruby was scooping chocolate cake off the plate with her hands. Jade sucked the rich icing off Ruby's gooey fingertips while the older woman wrestled one-handed with the contrary biscuit packet.

'I'm so glad you're here,' Ruby had slurred in a quiet, contemplative moment.

'Yes,' Jade had agreed. 'I'm glad I'm here, too.'

54

'Why don't you come with me?' invited Robbie, before he had to run upstairs to get dressed. He was going to meet Jade for lunch.

'Oh, she doesn't want to see me,' said Julia, deeply ashamed of the dreadful way she'd treated the poor, distressed girl all those years ago. She'd only just come out of hiding, and still wasn't sure she was ready to face the world, much less have lunch with someone for whose unbearable pain she had been partly responsible.

On returning from the courthouse, Robbie had told his mother about Jade's testimony, repeating some of the details, reliving the hearing once again. Julia had listened, her heart shattering into billions of pieces. Then, she had cried for days, berating herself, torturing her mind, beating herself over the head for her stupidity. When Tom had arrived at work after his day off, he'd related his brief appearance in the witness box. He'd explained that he hadn't hung around the courthouse afterwards, preferring to say what he had to say and then leave. Julia was still inconsolable. Tom had given her some Valium and put her to bed.

Initially, Robbie had been shocked when his mother had confided that she was secretly boffing the gardener, but he'd taken to Tom immediately. They'd talked a lot while Tom waited to be called on the third day of the committal hearing.

'Mum,' said Robbie, putting his coffee cup on the table. 'I think she'd love to see you. Jade really is a great person. And I think it would be worthwhile for you two to get together. The past is gone. Everyone is dealing with the aftermath of it now. The time is ripe for reconciliation. Can't you see that?' He stretched his hands out, pleading with her, hoping she would take what was probably the only opportunity she'd ever get to make amends. After the trial, it might be too late.

'Oh, Robbie. Just the idea of it scares me,' she admitted, running her finger around the rim of her empty cup.

'Well, you're not alone there. Everyone is scared right now,' Robbie told her, briefly outlining some of the traumas Carl's victims and their families had experienced over the last few months. 'Mum, please come,' he cajoled.

Julia looked at her son. It still amazed her that somehow, in the short time between giving birth to him and now, he'd suddenly grown up. He was a lovely man, the complete opposite of his father. Julia shut her eyes and shuddered. She'd banned Carl from the house, and wouldn't speak to him on the phone. He'd written a note, but she'd torn it up, unopened and unread. She didn't want to know. Her lawyers were negotiating a divorce, but had suggested she wait to finalise it until after the trial. She'd agreed, knowing that a guilty verdict would leave her with everything.

Robbie looked at her with his big, pleading puppy eyes which, even at twenty-one, still melted her heart. She decided he was right. Only good could come of it.

'Okay,' she agreed, 'I'll come.'

'Oh, Mum, you're the best!' exclaimed Robbie, and leapt up to hug her. As he wrapped his arms around his mother, her heart ached. She wished she really were the best. Until now, she'd never even reached the mediocre mark.

'What should I wear?' Julia asked, pulling back. She smiled and shrugged. 'Is this a formal or casual meeting?'

'Jade's perpetually casual; just wear jeans and a sweater,' he laughed, wondering what chic designer planet his immaculately dressed mother orbited. Come to think of it, he'd never seen his mother dressed casually. 'Do you even own a pair of blue denim jeans?' he joked.

'Of course,' she replied, feigning indignation and grinning, 'I have a lovely new pair of True Religion hipsters that I just worship, and a gorgeous Jean Paul Gaultier pullover that I was going to give to charity, but I'll wear it today instead, with a long Micheal Kors leather jacket over the top.' Julia gesticulated comically, expertly mimicking one of her campest friends, who was a fashion consultant. 'Only if that meets with your approval, of course.' Robbie rolled his eyes and smiled. 'Or maybe I'll wear the short Ralph Lauren …'

An hour later, Robbie drove his casually designer-dressed mother to the restaurant where he was meeting Jade. He hadn't told his sister of the slight change of plan, and wondered how she'd react. He drove slowly, and took his time finding a place to park so that they would arrive a few minutes late. That way, he reasoned, Jade wouldn't be able to easily escape if she didn't like the idea. It would give him time to introduce his new-attitude mother, and convince Jade that talking to her was a good idea.

As he predicted, Jade was waiting at a table in the back corner. She was alone, sitting with her face buried in the menu. Robbie strode over, with Julia in tow, and bent to kiss Jade's cheek.

'Hi, Sis,' he said, blocking her exit out of the retro-themed booth.

'Hi, Robbie,' she said, putting the menu down and offering her cheek to accept the kiss. She didn't see Julia for a moment, but then a long leather coat caught her eye and she looked past her brother. 'Oh,' she gasped, frozen in shock.

'I believe you two already know each other,' said Robbie nonchalantly, hoping like mad that he hadn't bulldozed too far over a firmly placed boundary.

'Hello, Jade,' Julia said, smiling at the stunned woman. 'I wanted to come and see you, but if it's not a good time, I can go.'

'Um … err … no, it's okay,' stammered Jade, not sure how to react to the estranged woman she'd thought was her mother for ten years, and her paternal aunt for another sixteen. Who was she now? Jade wondered.

Julia put her hand on Robbie's shoulder. He took her hint and stepped aside, letting his mother take his place. Julia bent and kissed Jade on the cheek, and then, instinctively protective of the child she'd reared, however badly, she put her arms around the still gaping young woman. After a moment of shock, Jade stood up and returned the hug, hot tears coursing down her cheeks.

'Oh, sweet baby,' Julia whispered hoarsely. A hard nugget of regret burned her throat, and a cloudburst threatened to destroy her makeup.

'I'm so sorry. I'm so sorry.' Overcome, Julia wept, rocking Jade in her arms as they reconciled.

The last few weeks had been a living nightmare as Julia reassessed her life, her values, and her priorities. Tom had been a wonderful source of emotional support, surprising her with his ongoing sensitivity and practical advice. She'd told him the story of how Jade had come to be a part of her family, and confessed all her sins of neglect as a selfish, apathetic mother. Tom had suggested therapy and Julia had taken his words to heart.

'You might learn some coping strategies, and figure out where you belong in this new picture of your life,' he'd advised.

They'd become more than just lovers; now they were also friends. It gladdened Julia to have someone trustworthy to turn to in her hour of need. Tom had encouraged her to get involved in the current proceedings. Until this opportunity arose, she hadn't been sure how to take part. The prospect frightened her. She'd taken a huge personal risk, fully expecting to be rejected when she arrived at the restaurant.

Fortunately, Jade had grown into a beautiful woman who, underneath her porcupine exterior, was also a caring, understanding and forgiving person. Julia melted at the sight of her. She looked so vulnerable.

Tears prickled Robbie's eyes and he joined the cuddle, enveloping the tattered remains of his family in his embrace. For several minutes, the trio clung together, blubbering and comforting each other, oblivious to the curious stares of other diners.

'Aren't we a cheerful bunch?' joked Jade, finally breaking the tension.

'Oh, I'm so happy we can talk,' said Julia, and kissed tears from Jade's cheek.

'Let's sit down before they get a Jerry Springer film crew in here,' chuckled Robbie, glad his dangerous gamble had paid off.

Jade was surprised by this turn of events. She'd assumed Julia would support her husband, and told her so in her usual straight-forward manner as she tucked into a tasty chilli lentil burger.

'Not in a million years,' Julia vehemently denied, putting her fork down. 'Even though I'm probably ranked the worst mother on the planet, I could never condone child abuse of any description. No, Jade,' Julia shook her head. 'I'm on your side. And he's going to rot in hell.'

'You are not the worst mother on the planet,' chided Robbie, grinning at his mother. She had her faults, he admitted, but he adored her. He stuffed another French fry in his mouth and winked at Jade.

The reunion went well. Julia confessed her sins. She was gradually coming to terms with her guilt, and expressed her wish to make it up to both Robbie and Jade somehow. Jade apologised for being an impossible child, and was instantly forgiven. Robbie apologised to Jade for being a terrible cad as a little brother, and, laughing, she clipped him under the ear. Once the portions of forgiveness had been dished out equally, they settled in to chat and chuckle, quickly relaxing into the role of family.

'Wanna know something funny?' said Robbie, looking at both women with arched eyebrows.

'Always,' answered Jade, smiling. 'As long as it's actually funny. Your last joke was atrocious.' She shook her head and grimaced in mock disgust.

'It's not that kind of funny.' Robbie smiled, pleased she felt comfortable enough around Julia to tease him. 'I was just thinking that if I'm your ... um ... brother, and you're my sister, and Julia is our mother, well, you know, um ... kind of, she was your mother for a while,' he said, fumbling awkwardly over the complicated reality of their situation. 'Then, err ... Well, anyway, I was thinking that our mother should probably meet your father.'

Flabbergasted, Julia stared at Robbie in disbelief. 'Her father?' She'd always assumed that Steve was Jade's father. 'But ... he ... isn't?' Did this mean her brother wasn't dead? Julia was confused. Robbie had never mentioned anything about Steve. Julia had assumed he'd told her everything. She gaped at Jade. 'Your father?'

'You know,' replied Jade, nodding, wondering where to start her explanation. 'That's probably not such a bad idea.'

55

Carl lay in bed, eyes wide, staring at the darkened ceiling. He couldn't sleep, was afraid to doze off again in case his recurring nightmare came back to taunt him. His mind clunked and whirred, tossing random thoughts backwards and forwards. Tired of cerebral tennis, Carl sat up and switched on the lamp. A pile of books sat on the sideboard. He read the titles. None of them looked interesting. Lately, nothing interested him, not even little girls. He was severely depressed. His usually voracious appetite for life had disappeared.

He'd tried to call Julia a few times but she wouldn't talk to him. Then, she'd changed the phone numbers at the house. The new ones were silent. He'd been issued a court order to stay away. Even her lawyer had refused to take a message to her.

'If it's not regarding the divorce settlement, we don't want to hear it,' the solicitor had sneered.

Carl couldn't get his head around a divorce settlement. He was mortified his respectable family had fallen apart. Unlike his friend, the police commissioner, who had been divorced twice, he was a good husband and father. It was a vital part of who he was. There was also the chummy mayor who had married beneath his potential. And some of the senators to whom he was closest confided their marital distress. Board members often commented approvingly on his harmonious personal life, and politely ignored his recently confessed indiscretions. His relationships with his wife and son were widely envied. Ironically, most of his business associates secretly applauded Carl for choosing a partner who seemed to emulate the Stepford Wife philosophy. Julia would have died laughing if she'd known.

' … Carl also has a remarkable wife, and is blessed with a highly intelligent son …' people would say in their introductory speeches when presenting him to new clients or potential business partners.

Divorce was an unthinkable tragedy Carl didn't think he could survive. An integral piece of himself was missing. He didn't understand why his beloved wife wouldn't talk to him. When Claire had died, he'd dutifully grieved and moved forward, but this new loss seemed unfathomable. His only solace came from the fact that no one knew about it. Julia didn't care for public scandal and hadn't told anyone. Carl wouldn't discuss it under threat of death. If the media got hold of the story, it would be markedly less painful to fling himself from the bridge.

'If I just had a chance to explain …' he lamented, gazing around the dark, sparsely furnished apartment, 'she would understand.'

He expected his usual suave charm to soften Julia, if he could just get near her. It was that lawyer who had poisoned her against him.

One afternoon, feeling uncharacteristically impulsive, he'd driven out to the house. Her car wasn't there, so he didn't go inside. Despondent, he'd driven back to the office to bury his morbid thoughts in paperwork. Loyal to her naïve core, Sarah thought her boss was dispirited because his wife was out of town, and considered it extremely romantic.

Out of the blue, Julia had shipped Carl's personal belongings to the newly rented west-side apartment, after slyly conning the address out of Sarah, who believed his wife was sending some surprise flowers to cheer him up.

'That's so sweet,' Sarah had gushed, happily giving Julia the information.

Carl had returned from the office late one night to find piles of packing boxes stacked haphazardly at the front door. There'd been no note. Disliking disorder intensely, he'd angrily hauled the boxes inside. The following morning, when he'd called Clarissa, his cleaning lady, to come and help him unpack and clean up, her number was disconnected. He didn't know her address. Carl was baffled. He didn't understand why his orderly world was suddenly crumbling at a time when he needed it most.

How could everyone abandon him? Couldn't they see they were nothing without him?

Scowling, Carl climbed out of bed and went to the kitchen. He took a bottle of scotch from the cupboard and poured a large double nip into a tumbler. He took the soda from the fridge and topped up his drink. Barefoot, and in pyjamas, he paced the living-room floor, sipping his scotch, and tried to figure out a way out of his dilemma.

So far, no one at the office, nor any of his associates, had got a whiff of what was really going on. There'd been some idle gossip after Alec's visit, but he'd quashed it with more excuses about a misunderstanding. Carl was expecting the axe to fall any moment, and he had to stop it. However, the closed court proceedings had afforded him a great deal of leeway. Colleagues believed Julia was on an extended trip through Europe. Since their only contact with her was through him, no one had yet discovered the lie.

'Greetings to your lovely wife,' a visiting executive had commented during a recent building industry conference.

Carl had beamed, exuding pride, thanked the man, and returned the greetings, even though he couldn't remember a single thing about his associate's family.

Carl also missed his son, Robert. He turned the name of his sole heir over in his mind a few times. Robert. Robbie. Rob. At his father's insistence, the boy had been named after his grandfather, as Carl had been. Father and son had never been close. Young Robbie was always off at school or holiday camp or sports events, sent away by his mother for a proper education, on holiday with other children, or to train in sports. Carl considered it her duty to raise the child, and he'd left her to it. But now that Robbie was at university, Carl had taken an interest. He wanted Robbie to come into the business, to learn the ropes, so he could take over when Carl retired. He wanted to get to know his boy. He recalled Robbie's face in the courtroom, awash with tears, hatred burning in his eyes. The memory gave him heartburn.

'He'll come around,' Carl muttered confidently as he went to refill his glass. 'He doesn't know the whole story about that girl.'

He thought about Juanita. Jade. This was her fault, he ranted internally. She'd blown it all apart. Who was she anyway? She wasn't his daughter. Wasn't his niece. She'd lived under his roof for sixteen years. He'd fed her, clothed her and educated her, and this was the gratitude she showed, after causing Julia so much grief.

'Little ingrate,' he mumbled, stopping in his tracks. 'I'll find her. She'll get what she deserves.'

Carl's mind worked itself into a rage. He stamped about, cursing and muttering, frequently refilling his glass. Before long, his brain felt fuddled and his thoughts became slurred. He slumped into the sofa, succumbing to the flood of gloominess. As he sat sipping his eleventh double scotch, the bottle now on the table in front of him, the soda abandoned, his thoughts wandered to the distant past.

'Prudence,' he whispered to himself, summoning fond memories of the little girl he'd once loved.

As a young child, he'd known her as Peregrine. Then, as a blooming teenager, she'd insisted on being called Prudence. She'd disappeared a few weeks before her eighteenth birthday and he hadn't seen her again until the committal hearing. His heart had leapt into his mouth. She'd be what … thirty-something, he guessed. She was still very beautiful. It didn't surprise him that she was now known as Ruby.

'Ruby,' he mused, clucking with amusement, his tongue heavy with scotch, 'where did you go, my precious Ruby?' He liked her new name.

Carl recalled their days together in his little downtown apartment. He'd taken her from high school and brought her home. After a few months, she asked if they could get married and have babies. She'd been sixteen then, and filled with romantic notions. He'd laughed at her. He was already married. Julia had been his wife for three years, and was pregnant with Robert.

'Besides, you're too young for marriage,' he'd told her, still chortling, 'this is a time to be having fun. I'll still be the Daddy, though.'

She'd pouted, and then agreed. Locked in his secret hideaway, Prudence was his mistress for two years. She loved him, she told him so often, but he quickly grew bored; she'd grown up, her body had ripened, and she wasn't fun to play with any more. Juanita was six years old by then, and more attractive with her bubbling youth.

Carl amused himself by inviting his friends to have sex with Ruby. During wild parties, he'd tie a white silk scarf over her mouth, strap her face-down to an A-frame in the bedroom, bent over with one of her long skirts tossed over her head. Then, he'd take money from anyone who wanted her. The boys took turns, assuming she was a kinky prostitute he'd hired for the night. They never saw her tears. Carl bought heroin with the money she'd earned, and injected it into her veins to help her forget the pain. When Ruby had fled, he'd taken an even keener interest in young Juanita.

'She'd have stayed if you hadn't been so naughty,' Carl chided himself gently, chuckling drunkenly at the memory of her delightful tantrums.

A wave of sorrow and anger suddenly washed over him. He slumped into sullen depression. Wallowing in self-pity, Carl made himself another drink. He sat back into the cushions, and recalled the other girls; Paula, Katie, Lizzie, and Carmine.

'Brrrr,' he blurted, disgusted, shuddering as he recalled Carmine. 'Dirty girl.'

She'd been the last one he'd taken from the club. He'd brought her into the apartment, showered, cleaned her face, then taken her clothes off, preparing her for the initiation ceremony. She was bleeding. A stained sanitary pad adhered to her panties. The recollection of his hideous discovery gave Carl the horrors. He'd thrown the girl's clothes back onto her prostrate body, pulled on some clean clothes and taken her back down to the street. Not willing to put her filthy body back into his car, he'd dumped her in an alley between the café and the boutique.

'Dirty girls should stay at home,' he'd spat angrily at her unconscious form, cursing her under his breath. Carl recalled the times his father had made his mother stay in an empty bedroom. He'd only ever done it when she was dirty.

When Carmine had woken up, she had no idea where she was or how she got there. She would never know of her fortunate escape.

Katie and Lizzie had been easy, he thought, fondly remembering the two young girls. It was clear they were neglected. Girls whose parents cared for them didn't go to clubs like The Blue Mango. Carl couldn't believe the terrible things they'd said about him in the courtroom.

They'd loved him. They'd called him 'Daddy'. They'd begged him to have sex with them. Both those sweet little girls had asked for the drugs, pleaded with him to bring their heroin, and hugged him adoringly when he'd complied with their requests. He'd only given them to Lenny to help them. It was sad, they liked the drug too much.

'They've been brainwashed by that little witch,' he slurred, pointing an angry finger at the wall opposite, as if Jade were there to accept the blame.

He'd gone looking for Katie to ask her to come back, but hadn't been able to find her. Probably for the best, he thought, she'd be too old now.

Paula had been lovely too, he recalled, picturing her silky blonde hair and peachy complexion. He'd grieved for her when she'd overdosed on crack cocaine a couple of years earlier. She'd talked to the police before she died too. Probably that wicked witch's fault, he decided, automatically blaming Jade for all his current woes. By some miracle, Paula had managed to get the case to go to court. Once the jury had seen the drug-addicted prostitute making wild unsubstantiated claims about the respected businessman, they'd dismissed her as crazy and found him not guilty. Distraught, Paula had returned to the streets and wiped herself off the planet with a cocktail of lethal narcotics. Her father, a local vicar, had been inconsolable. Her mother, who had run off with a surfer when Paula was still a toddler, had never heard the news.

Carl sat morosely on the sofa, wondering about the future. It looked grim. He thought about suicide, and pondered the various ways in which he could kill himself. Most methods were too messy. Carl hated mess. Sleeping pills seemed the most sensible way. They'd cause him no pain. He hated pain, too. Extremely inebriated, Carl stumbled around the flat, rummaging in the cabinets to see if he had any tablets. Halfway through his search, he chickened out and retreated to the safety of the sofa.

'I don't want to die,' he howled into his glass. 'I want my life back.'

Suddenly, Carl started crying, his tears dripping into the small tartan pillow on his lap. Overcome, he lay in a foetal position along the length of the cushions. Drunk and exhausted, he cried himself to sleep. The dream came back, haunting, taunting, and he slept fitfully, reliving the memory, mumbling, sweating, throwing cushions on the floor until there was nowhere to escape.

'Yes please, Father,' Carl intoned robotically, exactly as he'd been instructed, 'I'd love to, Father.' Severe punishment was offered if he refused.

Trembling, unable to protest, and terrified of a much worse fate, the eight-year-old pupil walked toward the huge mahogany desk. He dropped his trousers and pulled his underpants down to his ankles. He bent over, put his forehead on the leather topped table and waited for the pain to begin, teeth clenched, fists tightened.

Highly aroused, the priest lifted his long black robes and approached the young boy. He was delighted at the sight of the smooth, round, little bottom presented to him, and thanked God for the wonderful gifts on offer.

56

David collected plates from the table and took them to the sink where Ruby was washing up. He set them down on the bench next to her and went out for the salad bowls. Jade picked up the empty beer bottles and softdrink cans, tossing them in a large garbage bag she carried around with her. Alec swept the balcony, pulling chairs out as he reached under the table with the broom. Nick had gone to rendezvous with a colleague who needed help moving house.

'Phew!' said Ruby as she scrubbed her way through the huge pile of dishes. 'I haven't laughed that hard in ages. That was seriously entertaining.'

'We're always entertained with you around,' complimented David, dumping another stack of bowls at her elbow. 'But you're right, it was pretty funny.'

Despite the cold weather, Nick had suggested another barbeque. He wanted to gather everyone together again. It was important, he thought, that they all have some fun in the middle of this emotionally difficult period. Keeping up morale was vital, particularly as the trial date loomed closer.

Amanda and Gerard had welcomed the idea. Donna couldn't get Lizzie in the car fast enough. And, for a change, Ruby had arrived first, laden with music, madness and magic.

Nick encouraged Jade to invite Robbie, so she did. He'd happily accepted the invitation and, after seeking Jade's permission, he brought Julia with him. Robbie had asked Tom too, but he'd declined the invitation, pleased the young man would think of asking.

Tom wasn't sure if he was ready to be seen in public as Julia's partner, or even if being her partner was what he really wanted. He needed more time to process the new circumstances. For the moment, he was happy with the way things were. He'd refused to move into the big house, but now they romped upstairs in her enormous bed. He was glad it didn't squeak or rock when their frequent lovemaking got out of control. Tom had hired another young gardener to help out around the grounds, but continued doing the work he loved.

'I've got an assignment to finish,' Tom said, glad of the excuse to bow out.

'Assignment?' queried Robbie, wondering what bizarre task his mother had set for the gardener that he couldn't come to a party.

'Yeah,' replied Tom, enthusiastic about his current project. 'I'm doing another degree at uni. I'm a horticulturalist, and I want to start my own business, but I've got all this economics stuff to learn first. I'm a bit snowed under at the moment. But thanks for the invite.'

Robbie had been impressed. Julia was gobsmacked when he told her. She'd had no idea. Tom had never even hinted at such a thing. Suddenly, she was bursting with pride and newfound respect for her lover, her friend, and her wonderfully intelligent gardener. Tomless, she'd gone off with Robbie to the winter beach party.

Just as they'd planned, Robbie arrived half an hour late. Jade greeted them at the door, kissing Julia's cheek warmly, and winking at her smirking brother. Jade led them through the beach house and out to the balcony, holding Julia's hand as they went.

'Mum,' said Jade, struggling to keep a straight face as she presented Julia to the group sitting around the picnic table. She hadn't warned the gathering about the little surprise she'd saved for this moment. She continued with an animated flourish, 'I'd like you to meet Dad.'

Jaws dropped. Knives clattered to the ground. Forks bounced over the balcony and landed silently in the sand. Amanda dropped her glass of wine into her lap. Lizzie's elbow landed on her plate, which flipped up and tossed her lunch down the front of her shirt. Gerard couldn't speak, and sat staring at Julia and David in turn, as if he were watching the tennis. Katie snorted loudly, and clapped her hands over her mouth so she wouldn't spit food over the table. Her eyes met Robbie's as she chuckled. Donna gaped, frozen, her fork halfway to her mouth. David quickly recovered his wits, and stood up to greet the fiercely-blushing woman graciously.

'It's wonderful to meet you,' he said politely, trying not to chuckle. 'I'm David.'

At this, Ruby shrieked, laughing helplessly. Nick was pleased Jade had rediscovered her wonderful sense of humour. Alec giggled too. Jade's timing was flawless. So, the detective concluded, this is the infamous Julia Rutherford. He had some questions for her, but he'd wait until things settled down. Robbie grinned, delighted Jade had executed the prank perfectly. He shook hands with everyone present, proudly admitting his part in the conspiracy. Julia was welcomed, kissed and hugged, and the group continued their jovial little party.

'Why didn't you report her missing?' Alec asked as he strolled down the beach with Julia.

'I did,' she replied, then corrected herself. 'Well, I thought Carl had. I trusted him, and assumed he'd made the police report after we discussed it. When no news of her came, I thought she was gone forever.' A chill breeze nipped at her skin. She wrapped her arms tightly around herself. 'She was a difficult child, Alec. I was new to the motherhood game. It didn't come naturally. I had a hard time with her,' Julia explained, knowing it wasn't an excuse for her ignorance. 'Now I know why. It kills me that I didn't do something more.' Julia admitted her selfishness, and felt guilty all over again. She then detailed what had happened after teenage Juanita had run away. 'Carl regularly filled me in on what police had told him. I had no way of knowing none of it was real. I feel so stupid.'

Alec nodded, understanding. He'd been terribly deceived once too, and it had hurt him deeply. Empathetic, he forgave Julia. By the end of their long conversation, he found himself liking the forthright, still contrite woman.

When the kitchen had been tidied and the balcony restored to its usual neatness, coffee was made and handed around. David had gone off to have a nap. Jade sat on a lounge chair, her cup on the table beside her. Ruby and Alec plonked on opposite ends of the sofa and sipped their coffee.

'Are you two sleeping together?' Jade asked, posing the question she'd been mulling over all day.

Spluttering, Alec put his mug on the coffee table and stared at Jade, eyes wide. He couldn't believe she could tell. They'd been so careful. Ruby placed her cup on the floor at her feet and looked across at Alec with raised eyebrows. Jade stared him down, then looked into Ruby's dark brown eyes.

'I thought so,' she grinned, pleased they were together.

'It's a secret,' whispered Ruby. 'No one is supposed to know.'

'Grimshaw would kill me,' said Alec, 'if he found out.'

Jade moved across to the sofa and sat between them. She extended her arms, inviting them to snuggle against her. Hesitant at first, they slid into her embrace, and put their arms around Jade's shoulders. One by one, she took their hands, and put them on her lap, holding them down with her other hand as if they'd escape. As if she were completing a jigsaw, Jade intertwined their fingers until Alec's left hand was joined to Ruby's right hand. Neither of them spoke. Alec stopped breathing. Ruby's heart pounded in her chest. Jade put her hands over theirs and squeezed lightly.

Jade looked into Alec's eyes. 'Do you love her?' she asked.

Alec swallowed, met her steady gaze, and nodded dumbly. He smiled shyly, and silently acknowledged he'd been busted.

Satisfied, Jade turned to Ruby. 'Do you love him?'

Ruby nodded eagerly, grinning as if she would burst. She was pleased their blooming relationship was no longer something she couldn't talk about. Keeping secrets was not Ruby's forte. She'd longed to share this one with someone for months.

'Good,' Jade said, once again squeezing her fingers around their clasped hands. 'Because you are both so adorable, and you belong together.' She looked from Alec to Ruby, smiling broadly. 'I promise I won't tell anyone your secret.'

57

'I am not exposing my daughter to your ridiculous radical feminist attitude that excludes half the population on the planet just because you think they're all evil!' Donna was furious. Eyes flashing with anger, she railed at the young therapist.

'But … Missus …' Greta tried to explain.

Donna pointed at the closed door behind which Lizzie was sitting. 'My daughter needs to come to terms with what happened to her,' she yelled. 'And she needs to find a way to cope so she doesn't have nightmares for the rest of her life.' Donna glared at the young counsellor as if she were mad. 'One day, she's going to get married and have children. What you're suggesting is damaging, not healing. I won't condone it. Not now and not in the future.'

Greta Bunting hung her head. It was no use. Missus Lawrence had made up her mind. Greta thought Donna was wrong, but she knew that there was no point in arguing with an irate woman who'd already decided she was right. She let Donna rant for a few more minutes, and then concluded the meeting.

'Okay, Missus Lawrence,' she said calmly, her hands at her sides. She went to the door and closed her hand around the knob. 'Then, I guess we'll just see Lizzie next week for her usual therapy.'

'No, you won't!' shouted Donna, frustrated to distraction by the calm, smiling woman draped in tie-died cheesecloth, with beads threaded through her dreadlocks and rings on each one of her fingers and toes. Hell, thought Donna, feeling uncharacteristically critical, she even looks like she fell out of a hippie colony. 'I'm going to find a therapist who can structure a suitable management plan and sort out some coping strategies for my daughter.'

Greta took her hand from the door. She was feeling insulted, but remained silent.

Donna continued, 'I'm not having you fill her head with all your stupid anti-male nonsense. How dare you even mention it to her without talking to me first!'

'That's your choice,' said Greta, sad to be losing Lizzie as a client. She liked the deeply troubled girl, and had done her best to help. She looked at her watch pointedly and then opened the door. 'You must excuse me, Missus Lawrence, I have another appointment now.'

Donna stormed out of the office, grabbing Lizzie by the hand as she stalked out to the car. As she started the engine, she felt as if she could kill something. Lizzie said nothing, letting her mother rant and rave, mumble under her breath, and swear loudly all the way home. When they arrived, Lizzie still hadn't spoken. She went to her room, closed the door and lay on her bed. Donna stared after her. She didn't know what to think any more. She sat on the sofa and burst into tears. A few minutes later, she called Amanda.

'It's not that I'm against protesting against violence towards women,' said Donna, who was a veteran of many worthwhile protests, 'it's that they exclude men. I can't come at that. It doesn't feel right.'

Amanda listened to Donna's tirade. Greta had suggested Lizzie participate in a Reclaim the Night march taking place the following week. While she saw the merits of such protests, Donna felt if her husband Mattie were alive, he would agree with her objections.

Mattie abhorred abuse or violence of any description. He'd have been equally as heartbroken and angry after learning what Lizzie had endured.

'Their whole philosophy is about women being safe wherever they are,' Donna cried, 'and I totally agree with that. I really do. But Lizzie felt safe with her father too, when he was here. I believe women need to know that they can feel safe with men too. And there are so many supportive men in our circle right now.' Donna wiped her face with a tissue. 'If Mattie had been here,' she lamented, 'none of this would have happened in the first place.'

Mattie Lawrence had wholeheartedly supported the rights of women to walk safely in the streets, to work in safe environments, to dress however they liked. And yet, if he'd volunteered to march in the protest, Greta's group would have rejected him. All of the wonderful men in the current supportive group would have been rejected. The thought infuriated Donna.

Amanda listened to the angry woman for twenty minutes. 'Donna, you could do your own thing, in your own way,' she suggested, 'in a manner your husband would have agreed with and felt a part of if he was here today.' Amanda spoke softly. She was trying to be helpful, aware she needed to be sensitive. 'You could talk about it with Lizzie and come up with something that suits you both.' As a mother, and as a wife with a loving caring husband, she had heard the message Donna was getting across loud and clear.

Donna stopped in her tracks. 'You know, that's a brilliant idea.'

'I could help if you like,' Amanda suggested. 'Katie might have some input, too.'

'Oh, would you? Thanks,' said Donna, grateful to have a sounding board who knew where she was coming from. Before she'd spoken to Amanda, she'd wondered if Greta was right and she was being completely irrational. 'You are so amazing. That would be wonderful. Are you free right now?'

Donna got off the phone and went to Lizzie's door. She knocked quietly, hoping she hadn't upset her daughter with her furious outburst.

'Lizzie, can I come in?' Donna sniffed.

'Yeah,' she called, sounding sad.

Donna sat on the bed and stroked Lizzie's hair. For a long moment, neither of them spoke. Lizzie had heard Donna's side of the phone conversation after opening the door a crack to listen. She agreed with Greta. It might be a good idea to do something positive. But she agreed with Donna too; Daddy would have been hurt if he wasn't included, and so would David and Nick, and Alec and the others.

'Mum,' said Lizzie, breaking the tense silence. 'I love you. You're the best.'

'Oh, you're the best too, baby. I love you so much,' Donna replied, kissing Lizzie on the cheek. 'What are we gonna do? I feel so … I don't know … lost.'

'Wanna know what I think?' said Lizzie, moving to a sitting position.

Mother and daughter talked for a while, exchanging thoughts and feelings. An idea emerged. By the time Amanda and Katie arrived, Donna was enthusiastic. Katie made some helpful suggestions and Amanda added her own recommendations. Managing this ordeal had strengthened her. Amanda was no longer as fragile as she'd been when Katie first returned home. Lizzie was excited. She wanted to call Ruby and Jade, and invite them to participate.

'Great idea.' Katie grinned and picked up the phone.

After talking to Jade, Katie rang Ruby. The two women soon arrived at Donna's and tossed their two cents' worth into the forum. As the concept evolved, Jade realised they'd need a little extra help. Ruby made a few suggestions. After some discussion, they all agreed. Ruby called Alec.

After their brief conversation, Alec looked up some old files, and went to see Ryland Thomas.

'Do you think you can find this guy?' Alec asked, handing Ryland a piece of paper with a name on it.

Ryland looked at the note and asked, 'Where do I know this name?'

'A few years back,' said Alec, impressed at the man's memory. 'It was that case we did with …'

'Yeah. I remember now,' said Ryland. 'Give me an hour. I'll get back to you.'

Alec nodded. He patted Ryland on the back and left him to it. The computer guru was already at work, scanning files. The detective went down to the lab to talk to Jamie.

'There's something I think you should see,' Alec told him.

'What?' asked Jamie, exasperated. He was flat out on a forensic investigation for a murder case and the pieces weren't coming together quickly enough for the superintendent, who'd been riding his back all week.

'Not right now,' Alec explained. 'What are you doing Sunday evening?'

'Day off. Nothing, I guess,' said Jamie and shrugged.

'Can you bring Heather, and get a sitter for the kids?'

'What are you up to, Stonewall?' asked Jamie, suspicious.

'You'll see,' grinned Alec. 'It will be worth it. You'll have to trust me for now. I'm sworn to secrecy.' He put a piece of paper with an address on Jamie's workspace. 'Five sharp. Don't be late.'

Jamie looked up from his microscope. He looked at the address, then looked back at Alec. Saying nothing, he peered through the lens again, comparing the blood samples. Alec turned to leave, hoping Jamie would come. They'd never done anything together outside of work. It would be a first. Alec thought it would be good for Jamie.

'Okay,' agreed Jamie as his colleague neared the door. 'We'll be there.'

True to his word, Ryland called Alec an hour later with the information he needed. Alec grabbed his coat and went to make a house call. It was on company time, but Alec was sure if he explained it to Debra, she wouldn't mind. Come to think of it, Alec thought as he drove away from the police station, he should ask Debra if she wanted to come. When he returned, he called Ruby back, and then had a long discussion with Debra.

A few days later, everyone was gathered in the living-room at Nick's house, along with their specially invited guests.

Over the past few months, the sprawling cabin had become a kind of safe haven, a place they could meet to escape from the harsh reality of life. The Greens arrived first, a few minutes before Donna and Lizzie. Julia and Robbie brought Tom, who had readily agreed to come and show his support. Within fifteen minutes, cars lined both sides of the street. Alec introduced his colleagues, and went to find Jade. Jamie immediately introduced Heather. The newcomers were warmly welcomed. Spontaneously, a long hug-fest burst into life. Alec walked to Jamie's side, with Jade in tow.

'Jamie, do you remember this lady?' he asked.

Jamie looked at Jade for a long moment. At first, he didn't recognise her. Then, he remembered the photos Alec had taken of the scene. The unloaded gun. The empty bourbon bottle. The newspaper clippings. The trashed apartment. Jade stood silently, not sure who he was. Alec grinned. Heather watched her husband think.

'Yes. Yes, I do,' he said, smiling. 'It's a pleasure to meet you, Jade.'

'You know my name?' said Jade, surprised.

Alec laughed. He explained who Jamie was, what he did, and how he had come to know Jade's name. She blushed fiercely.

'So you're the girl with the roses,' Heather said to Jade with a huge smile.

'Roses?' Jade asked, confused. Jamie explained it for her. Again, Jade's face became crimson with embarrassment.

Heather reassured her. 'It's okay,' she whispered, 'we all do stupid stuff.' She showed Jade the jagged scars on her wrists, where she'd slashed them two years before.

While Jade and Heather talked, Jamie went in search of the infamous Lizzie Lawrence. He wanted to talk to the teenage genius and convince her to study forensics at university. They were still head to head when Bob Tompkins arrived.

'Hi,' he said after Gerard let him in. 'I'm looking for Alec Stonewall.'

'Over there,' said Gerard, pointing toward the balcony door.

Alec was deep in conversation with Tom and Robbie, the latter of whom kept sneaking glances at Katie. The detective saw the man approaching and went to greet him. Bob was nervous. When Alec had explained the plan, he wasn't sure it was a good idea. Alec had convinced him to give it a shot. Bob decided he had nothing left to lose, and agreed to come.

'Hello,' he introduced himself to Ruby when she approached the pair. 'I'm Bob. Paula's father.'

Teary-eyed, Ruby embraced him, applauding his courage, conscious of how difficult it would have been for him to lose a daughter to drugs, after she'd gone through so much tragedy. Ruby kissed his cheeks and welcomed him, then took him by the hand and introduced him to everyone else. After a few minutes, he wondered why he'd ever doubted what he'd first thought was a crazy idea.

Debra, taking up the role of emcee, announced that the ceremony would begin in ten minutes. Jade, Ruby, Lizzie, and Katie raced upstairs to change. Julia helped Donna light the candles and set them out in a large circle on the floor, warning everyone not to step on them. The night was chilly. Wind lashed at the windows. Earlier that day, Nick and David had cleared the furniture from the living-room.

When the four girls were ready, Debra announced they would begin. Everyone except Debra assembled in a circle, each standing in front of a candle. Donna quickly rearranged those who were standing in the wrong place. Between each woman stood a man. The four girls were dressed in the long white robes that Amanda and Donna had hastily designed and sewn. They each had a wreath of jasmine intertwined with baby's breath resting on their heads. Jade, Ruby, Lizzie, and Katie each stood in the circle with two men and one woman between them, as a symbolic guard of honour. Donna looked around the symmetrical arrangement of men and women, and was pleased. Mattie would have been proud of her. Greta and her friends, she thought with a light smirk, would probably have been horrified.

Standing outside the circle, Debra began the short speech she'd prepared for the evening, proud to have been invited to participate in the Healing Ceremony. The statements she'd taken from the girls, had haunted her, taken back to her own painful childhood. She appreciated being given the unique opportunity to begin healing the scars within herself, as well as those within the four stalwart girls.

'Healing is a long, and often traumatic process for anyone who has been wounded,' she began, conscious that everyone standing on the perimeter had been terribly hurt in some way. 'But it is a journey that begins from within.'

As Debra spoke, everyone joined hands, linking their grief, their pain, their trauma, as if they were one. United, they felt stronger. The Senior Sergeant spoke eloquently of suffering, and of healing. She talked directly to the girls of their ordeals, and the effect they'd had on her, not only as a policewoman, but also as a mother, a daughter, a sister and as a woman. She sympathised with the families and friends, and emphasised the importance of putting a stop to all kinds of violence. Debra acknowledged the men in the group, and thanked them for their presence and their support.

'Men can help to educate other men by setting an example, and by teaching each other that violence against women is not acceptable behaviour and that it won't be tolerated. There are no excuses for violence and abuse. Both women and men are responsible for spreading that message as far as they can.'

Gerard squeezed Julia's left hand and Jade's right hand. Jade squeezed Bob's hand, and the ripple of support ran from hand to hand in both directions around the circle. With a tear in his eye, David listened to Debra. Julia cried openly, making no sound. Tom was deeply moved. Jade gazed across the emotionally charged circle at Nick, who stood between Ruby and Heather. I love you, he mouthed with silent lips. Jade blinked her tears away. Alec sent telepathic encouragement to Ruby who was overwhelmed by the love flowing through the circle. Her cheeks were wet. Her eyes were closed. Her face looked both angelic and anguished. Both Lizzie and Katie and their parents were in tears, too. Bob stood stony-faced, grief written clearly across his features.

'It's a terrible tragedy that this ceremony is necessary in the first place,' continued Debra, her voice on the verge of breaking. She spoke softly, but powerfully. 'But by reporting their abuse, these women have helped to prevent others from suffering the way that they have. These beautiful, strong, courageous women deserve the best we can offer in terms of love, support, encouragement and healing. And so here we are, reclaiming their childhood innocence, and helping the healing process begin so that they, and their loved ones, can move forward and live in peace.'

On cue, Debra pushed the play button on the CD player. She stepped into the circle, and held hands with Donna and Robbie, closing her eyes while John Lennon sang Imagine, the song Lizzie had chosen to send a message of peace into the universe.

When the lyrics faded out, Jade, Ruby, Lizzie and Katie released the hands of men on either side of them and took a step forward, into the centre of the ring, so as to form an inner-circle. They held each others' hands, and stepped into a long embrace, surrendering to their emotions. The hands they'd let go reached out to make the outer-circle complete. Debra stepped back and spoke again, addressing each of them.

'Jade, Ruby, Katie, Lizzie, we welcome you to our healing circle.'

The four girls turned around, facing the people in the outside ring. Each held a small piece of paper bearing a handwritten message. Lizzie's fingers trembled, the paper fluttered in her hands. Each message was the same. In turn, the girls recited, beginning with Katie.

'My name is Katie Green,' she said, standing tall. Katie glanced at the message in her hands. 'I am strong. I am brave. I am proud to be a woman. No man has the right to harm me. I embrace my sisters as we unite as women against violence against women. I embrace my brothers, and acknowledge their love and support in this safe environment. I send this message out to the world in the hope that I will be heard. I reclaim my innocence, and I accept that within myself I hold the power to heal my wounds.'

As Lizzie read her message, Bob's hands flew to his mouth. He mourned his daughter all over again, praying for her damaged soul, thankful that others had found the road to redemption that Paula had so desperately sought. David swallowed the lump in his throat, his pride for his indomitable daughter immeasurable. A tear fell from Gerard's eye and trickled down his cheek, his heart bursting. He felt awed, and honoured. Nick and Alec each experienced an intense combination of grief, hope, and pride. Donna and Amanda wept, dabbing at their faces with sodden tissues. Robbie gazed at Katie, admiring her courage. Tom sought out Julia's moist eyes. She gazed back, and smiled through her tears. At that moment, Tom realised he loved her. Heather looked across at Jamie, filled with regret. Her sorrowful blue eyes apologised for the pain, for the stress, for the damage she'd caused. Instantly, Jamie's resentment melted. In its place, the familiar warm rush of love flowed through him, a love he had not felt toward his wife for a long time. A charge of complicated emotions shot through Debra, filling her heart. Sniffing quietly, she was proud she'd been asked to participate.

When the brief readings ended, Debra pushed play on the second CD. Elena Higgins's Powerful Women rang out; the song Jade had chosen as her anthem, singing it to herself every day. While everyone listened to the moving, soulful lyrics, Debra summoned Bob, Gerard,

David and Tom to instruct them briefly in the roles they would play in the ceremony.

Then, the four men stood opposite the four girls in the centre of the circle. Each man held a white teddy bear. Debra nodded, and Bob stepped forward, clutching the bear in his hands.

'This bear symbolises your lost innocence. I return it to you to hold close to your heart.' He placed the teddy in Jade's hands and wrapped his arms around her shoulders. She accepted his embrace, thanked him and stepped back. Gerard gave his bear to Ruby. David's went to Katie, and Lizzie received hers from Tom.

It had been Ruby's idea to present teddy bears. 'It doesn't matter how old you are, every woman needs a teddy bear to hold when she's alone at night,' she'd insisted. Katie had agreed, and suggested they should be white.

As the ceremony drew to a close, Ruby, Jade, Lizzie, and Katie, draped in their white robes, white flowers in their hair, and each holding a fluffy white bear, huddled together near the window. Outlined by the clear, dark-blue sky, stars winking brightly in the distance, they each recited a verse of Maya Angelou's famous poem, Phenomenal Woman. Her voice echoing lyrically through each corner of the hushed room, Ruby began the first verse:

Pretty women wonder where my secret lies.
I'm not cute or built to suit a fashion model's size
But when I start to tell them,
They think I'm telling lies.
I say,
It's in the reach of my arms
The span of my hips,
The stride of my step,
The curl of my lips.
I'm a woman
Phenomenally.
Phenomenal woman,
That's me.

Awed by the dramatic backdrop of bright stars, the gathering listened to the poem intently, hearts filled with love and pride for the four women. As Ruby's voice fell into silence, Jade stood tall, locked eyes with Nick and, with a tinkling musical tone, recited the second verse:

I walk into a room
Just as cool as you please,
And to a man,
The fellows stand or
Fall down on their knees.
Then they swarm around me,
A hive of honey bees.
I say,
It's the fire in my eyes,
And the flash of my teeth,
The swing in my waist,
And the joy in my feet.
I'm a woman
Phenomenally.
Phenomenal woman,
That's me.

58

Emma wanted to throw her head to her knees, put her hands over her ears, and sing loudly to shut out the dreadful words. It was as if she'd gone to sleep four days previously and had woken up in someone else's never-ending nightmare. The young woman glanced to her left. Three men, middle-aged to elderly, and two thirty-something women sat gazing toward the centre of the room, unmoving. Their expressionless features gave nothing away. Heads frequently bowed, they scribbled on notepads. Emma glanced right. A man of twenty or so sat next to her. His jaw worked occasionally as he listened, and fastidiously took notes. Adam, or was it Andrew? She couldn't remember. They'd met earlier that week when the jury had been assembled, but Emma, still shell-shocked, couldn't remember what any of them were called.

'Hello, good morning. How are you?' Emma smiled at the little group of twelve each day, hoping like mad she wouldn't be forced to rack her brain for a long-forgotten name.

The twenty-two year old sous chef looked at the backs of the heads in front of her. Two older women and three men – one in his late twenties, the other two fortyish – sat in the shortest row. She couldn't see their faces. Emma sat with her fists clenched tightly in her lap, trying to absorb, albeit reluctantly, every sordid detail. She looked across the courtroom and caught the witness's eye. She noted Jade's deeply troubled expression, and saw her hands shaking as she spoke, her fingers constantly fiddling. Emma admired her courage, and was profoundly moved by the woman's story. She brushed away the tears which threatened to cloud her vision, bowed her head, and listened.

'What happened next, Miss Randall?' asked Stephen Frederick. He glanced at the faces of the jury, trying to gauge their reaction to his third witness. Aside from the young woman at the back who was visibly upset, the rest of the jurors wore poker faces. There was no way of telling what they were thinking.

'We went under the greenhouse,' said Jade, her voice quavering, her fingers stroking the little purple stone. Ruby had shoved the little amethyst into her hand as the bailiff had led Jade from the witness room. 'He told me to take my clothes off. I didn't, and he yelled at me. He said, "You'll do what Daddy says", and he threatened me. He said he would kill me. I was afraid, so I got undressed.'

'Errm ... how old were you at that point?' interjected the prosecuting barrister.

'I was twelve,' answered Jade, her voice cracking a little.

Emma gasped under her breath. She felt like she couldn't breathe. Her ears rang. Her heart was beating too fast. She'd been listening to horrific stories for most of the week. She couldn't take any more. She wanted to run home, screaming all the way. To stifle her selfish feelings, Emma focused on the defendant. He sat smirking, tapping his toes on the rail at his feet, as if he were a spectator at a barn dance. Hatred simmered in Emma's gut. There was no doubt in her mind that he was guilty.

'Thank you,' said Stephen, 'please continue.'

'The room was freezing. Aside from some old gardening stuff, there was nothing there.' Jade scanned the faces of the jury. She could sense their discomfort. It made her nervous. Her words tumbled over each other. 'He told me to lie on the cement floor. I said it was cold, so he threw a hessian sack on the floor. I lay there, not moving. He walked around me, and then told me to spread my legs. I was afraid and started crying. He shouted at me to stop. I couldn't stop, I was so scared.' Jade sounded small and frightened. 'I didn't want him to hurt me,' she whimpered. 'He got angry and told me to roll over so he could spank my bottom. When I didn't move, he kicked me, flipping me onto my stomach with his boot.'

Emma closed her eyes. Her youngest sister was twelve. She couldn't imagine what would possess someone to sexually abuse a child. When Carl yawned, and twirled a bored finger through his hair, Emma wanted to crucify him.

'I lay on my belly, crying,' continued Jade. 'Then, I felt him lying on top of me. He was still dressed, but his trousers were open. His penis was hard. I could feel it against my buttocks. He pushed my face into the floor. Then, he held me down and he sodomised me.' Jade gasped and swallowed hard. She reached for the glass of water at her elbow and took a sip. She closed her eyes and took another deep breath before she went on with her testimony.

Emma glowered at the defendant. Out of the corner of his eye, Carl noticed her angry stare and refused to look at her. She imagined a thousand ways to cook his filthy penis and serve it up to him, with his balls as a side-dish.

After a few more questions, the barrister concluded his examination of the witness. The defence barrister got to his feet and acknowledged Judge Leonard.

'Miss Randall, who is Carl Rutherford in relation to you?' he asked, hoping to trip her up somewhere.

Jade gazed at Richard Gregson for a long moment. In her peripheral vision, she could see Carl staring at her from around the screen. She realised the defence was clutching at straws.

'Nobody,' she answered calmly. 'He is nobody in relation to me.'

'But …' the defence blustered, 'according to your statement, he's your uncle. He raised you, fed you, clothed you, and educated you, beginning from when you were a small child.'

'No, he didn't,' Jade countered, 'his wife did.' She began telling the jury how he'd pretended to be her father for ten years, all the while molesting her, insisting she call him Daddy. Then, she learned he was her uncle, who continued sexually abusing her. But, she told them, he wasn't even that. 'He's not related to me at all. My real father is sitting over there.' Jade pointed to David, who beamed with pride through his tears.

Carl blanched. The barrister was stunned. This unexpected twist was news to both of them. Carl hadn't had a chance to ask Julia about the strange questions the detective had asked him. It took a moment for Gregson to recover. He adjusted his wig, flipped his robes about, and gradually regained his composure.

'Miss Randall,' he said, glaring patronisingly over the top of his spectacles. 'When did you first give a description to anybody about what had happened to you so far as Carl Rutherford was concerned?'

'I never told anyone until I made my statement last year,' Jade answered. 'That was the first time I'd ever talked about it in detail.'

'I see,' nodded the barrister. 'Well, you certainly made an allegation in general terms to Detective Stonewall.'

'Yes, I did,' replied Jade. 'I told Detective Stonewall that Rutherford had raped me. But I didn't tell him the details.'

'Oh, you are very aware of the importance of not contaminating evidence, aren't you, Miss Randall?' he sneered, tapping at the papers in his hand with a pen.

Emma narrowed her eyes and listened closely to the defence barrister. She didn't like his tone. Sharkish eyes flashed under his horsehair wig. His nose twitched, as if sniffing the room for easy prey. Emma looked across at the witness. She looked composed, ready to do battle. Good for you, thought Emma, as she leaned back on the hard bench. The young juror wanted to kick Gregson's butt. How did he sleep at night, defending scum like that? she wondered.

'Contaminating evidence?' Jade repeated. 'I told Alec I'd been raped, and then cried my heart out. He advised me to report the crime. I went to see Detective Senior Sergeant Debra Lazarowitz two weeks later and made a detailed statement.'

'Alec?' the barrister pounced, grinning. 'You're very close friends, aren't you? I put it to you, Miss Randall, that your friend, the detective, put these wild allegations in your head, because his last case against Mister Rutherford was unsuccessful, and he plotted revenge against the defendant, and enlisted your help.'

'That's ridiculous,' snorted Jade, her eyes flashing angrily.

Gregson cut her off. 'And you agreed because he threw you out when you were a teenager, and cut off your lavish lifestyle. You were angry and wanted revenge too. Isn't that right, Miss Randall?'

Jade glared, but refused to take the bait. 'I made my statement because Carl Rutherford repeatedly raped and abused me from when I was a small child until I was a teenager. Long before I knew Alec.'

'How long have you known Detective Stonewall?' asked Gregson.

'Objection!' called Stephen, leaping to his feet. 'Relevance?'

Stephen wondered if Gregson was aware of Alec's drunken past. He was afraid the defence barrister had found out and would try to discredit the detective's testimony through Jade. The judge overruled. Gregson was, however feebly, trying to prove a conspiracy.

'About four years,' said Jade, 'but we've only become friends since I made my statement. He's helped me to cope through a difficult time. But I have never discussed my statement with him.' Gregson tried to butt in, but Jade overrode him. The judge put up a hand to silence the barrister and allow her to finish. 'Aside from telling Debra, and testifying twice in this witness box, I've never discussed the details of my statement with anyone. It's disgusting.' Jade screwed her nose up and shuddered. 'I certainly don't want to talk about it with anybody. I'm sure no one wants to hear it either, including most of the people in this room.'

'Okay,' conceded Gregson, realising she wasn't quite the meek little mouse he'd hoped to catch in his trap. He tried another tack. 'If something this terrible was happening to you as a child, Miss Randall, why did you take so long to report it?'

Frantically rubbing her little rock, Jade rallied. 'Because, Mister Gregson, it was too horrific. It was something I wanted to forget about. I ran away because I wanted it to stop, and I never wanted to think about it again. Most of the time, I succeeded, until,' she said with a wry smile, 'Alec Stonewall came crashing into my life.'

Emma smiled secretly. Jade had brought the barrister full circle.

For the remainder of the afternoon, after Jade was dismissed and Lizzie took the stand, Emma struggled with the emotions flooding through her. In the middle of the teenager's harrowing testimony, she wanted to run home and dive into bed so she could cry her heart out. She knew she was in for yet another sleepless night.

59

Stephen Frederick billowed in the door, with Ellen Johnson following closely on his heels. He wasn't a particularly tall man, but his elegant poise, contagious confidence, and booming voice added height to his personality. Ellen was a tiny woman, and spaghetti thin, which added to the perceived largeness of the Crown Counsel. Ellen headed towards the bar, while Stephen approached the crowded table in the beer garden. The bar across from the courthouse was quiet in the middle of the day. A few regular patrons rested against the bar. Stephen took a seat and praised the four women for their clear, concise testimonies.

'You were all wonderful,' he boomed. 'Really, you couldn't have done any better.'

'How long will the jury take to decide?' asked Ruby, a double scotch and coke in her shaking hand.

'I think we're in for a long wait,' Stephen said, accepting an orange juice from Ellen's fingers. 'They'll need to examine each piece of evidence thoroughly, and they have a lot to get through.'

'I'm scared,' said Katie, wringing her hands.

'Don't be,' reassured Stephen, who had also been worried about her history as a streetwalker. 'You were terrific. Once you laid it out for the jury, Gregson had no recourse on the cross. You stumped him by telling the ugly truth. I think the jury was impressed by that.'

'What do you think they'll decide?' asked Ruby nervously, after draining her glass. She hopped from one leg to the other, setting Ellen's teeth on edge.

'There's no way of telling until we go back in,' replied Stephen calmly, aware of how fickle juries could be. 'But I feel very confident.'

Jade's leg bounced double-time under the table. She drank two shots of tequila in quick succession and tried to shut down her mind.

What if they don't believe us? What if they think he's innocent? What if he gets away with it? She didn't dare articulate her doubts.

Ruby got herself another drink, then came over and sat beside Jade, squeezing her shoulder in support, and trying to calm herself. On her other side, Lizzie sat gazing at the wall, absently sipping lemonade.

'Take it easy,' Jade whispered to Ruby. 'You don't want to be pissed when we go back in.'

'I'm too stressed out to get drunk,' Ruby replied, downing half of her scotch.

Alec and David went to the bar to buy another round. Donna and Amanda chattered, while Gerard listened. Robbie sat next to Katie, reassuring her that the jury had seen the truth. He'd seen their tears, he told her. Since they'd met, Robbie and Katie had become close friends. Everyone expected that, when this was over, they'd get together. Gerard liked the sensitive young man, and openly approved. Nick and Julia were head to head in murmured conversation. His wife's presence in the courtroom on the last day had rocked Carl's world. By the time they'd adjourned for the jury to deliberate, he looked quite unwell.

'I'm not a fan of public scandal,' whispered Julia, as she brewed up a little scheme with the stockbroker. 'But I think this time around it'll be worth the trouble.'

'Yeah,' said Nick, nodding agreement. 'I have some mates in the media industry; one in particular. Jade has been doing some work for him. We were buddies at university. We've kept in touch over the years.' Nick took a mouthful of beer. Julia sipped her white wine. 'His wife was sexually abused, but the paedophile died before she got justice, so it's a subject close to his heart. He's the News Editor at the Daily Tribune. What say I give him a call? Then, I'll talk to a few others, too, if you like.'

'Sure, go ahead,' said Julia. 'I'm sure I can weather the storm. Things will settle down pretty quickly, especially as they can't publish names.'

That annoying little protection law had bothered Julia at first. She wanted Carl Rutherford's name to be plastered over the front page of every newspaper in the country. It would serve him right to be publicly labelled a paedophile. But, she conceded, it was probably better for the girls to remain anonymous. They had to try and rebuild their lives. She'd changed her own name back to Juliana Randall. After today, the divorce proceedings would go ahead, regardless of the verdict.

Nick walked to the edge of the outdoor area and dialled a number. After two rings, his call was answered. 'Hello?' said Nick, adopting his most pleasant tone. 'Is Mel Dempster available, please?'

Inside, Stephen was wrapping up his little pep talk with the four women. 'Now,' he said, 'I want you all to write Victim Impact Statements. The judge will need to read them before he decides on sentencing.'

Ellen handed out legal pads and pens. She would stay with them in the pub while Stephen went to sort out a few details regarding another case.

'What if he's found not guilty?' asked Ruby, voicing Jade's fears.

'I don't think that will happen,' smiled the barrister, 'but we will cross that bridge when we come to it. For now, it would be prudent to have these statements ready. The judge will want them handy.' With that, he left.

'What do we write?' asked Katie, staring at the blank notepaper, not exactly sure what Stephen wanted.

'This is a statement about how the abuse affected your life,' explained Ellen. 'You can write about your feelings; how you felt when you were being abused. How you feel about it now. It's to give the judge some idea of the impact this crime has had on you and your life.'

Katie nodded, still not sure she understood. Ruby suggested moving to another table where they could concentrate. Lizzie agreed. They sat at the furthermost table from the bar, and put pen to paper. Katie surprised herself. Once she began, she discovered there was so much to say. Lizzie wrote with her head down, arm wrapped around her pad. Ruby chewed her pen while she thought about how Carl Rutherford had warped her perceptions of romance, love and sex. When her thoughts finally melded into coherent sentences, she scribbled them down. Jade struggled with the task, crossing out words, rereading each sentence over and over as she wrote about the devastation the abuse had caused in her life.

Ellen smiled encouragement as Ruby looked over at her, the pen stuck between her teeth. The rest of the gathering spoke quietly, autopsying what they had heard in court, the reactions of the jury, and the testimony of Carl's eternally loyal secretary, Sarah. Ellen sipped a glass of wine, and joined in a lengthy discussion between Amanda and Julia on parenthood. From time to time, she looked up at the clock, its minute hand circuiting once while the group chatted. Another half an hour later, when the girls finished writing, Ellen gathered their statements and returned to the courthouse, promising to phone Nick the minute the jury was ready.

Two and a half hours later, just as the bar was beginning to fill with after-work patrons, Nick's phone rang. Everyone jumped.

'They're ready,' he whispered, and led the procession of jangled nerves back to the courthouse.

The four women filed in and sat on the bench in the front row. Jade clutched Ruby's left hand. On her other side, Lizzie held Ruby's right hand. On the end near the wall, Katie clasped Lizzie's hand. They sat rigid, nervously waiting for the judge and the jury to enter the courtroom. Katie's parents sat behind her in the middle row, with Donna beside them. Alec and Nick took up the other two seats. On the bench along the back wall, David sat with Julia and Robbie. This was the first time they'd all been in the courtroom together.

Tension bounced off the walls. Emotions ran high. Despite the air-conditioning, the little group felt as if they would spontaneously combust. Stephen turned to survey his witnesses, and winked encouragement. Gregson buried his head in papers.

The courtroom shook violently for a moment as a small tremor rumbled up from the center of the earth, shifting plates far below.

"Hear that? That's the gates of hell opening," whispered Robbie.

There was silence as everyone sat with heads bowed, each focusing on their own muddled thoughts. Finally, the clerk announced Judge Leonard's arrival.

'All rise!'

As one, everyone leapt to their feet. The judge settled himself, indicated everyone should retake their seats, and called for the jury to be brought in. The bailiff crossed the room and opened a door in the panelled wall. The twelve jurors stepped through and marched slowly toward the jury box, faces impassive. As she passed the benches in the gallery, Emma caught Lizzie's eye.

Ruby saw the look pass between them and her heart stopped. 'Bloody hell,' she whispered under her breath. She burst into silent tears and squeezed the hands on either side of her.

The head juror handed a piece of paper to the clerk. In turn, she handed it to the judge. He opened the folded note, read it, and handed it back to the clerk. She returned the page to the head juror. The judge gestured for the reading to begin.

'On the first charge of maintaining a sexual relationship with a minor, a unanimous jury finds the defendant guilty …'

Ruby gasped. Jade inhaled sharply. Then, all four girls burst into tears. Donna clutched Amanda's hands and cried. Gerard put his arm around his wife. Robbie held his mother's hand as she sobbed into a hankie. Her other hand instinctively reached out for David's. He held it and wept. Fighting tears, Nick patted Alec's leg. Relief flooded in as the group was overcome with emotion. Gradually, the tension began to unravel.

The head juror continued, 'On the second charge of maintaining a sexual relationship with a minor, a unanimous jury finds the defendant guilty …'

'Oh my!' breathed Jade, crying louder. Overwhelmed, she held Ruby's hand tightly. In the back row of the juror's box, Emma let her tears flow unchecked.

The head juror continued, his voice breaking from time to time, as he read out a unanimous guilty verdict for each charge.

By the time he'd read the long list of guilty verdicts, Jade, Ruby, Lizzie and Katie were huddled together on the bench, their arms around each other, each woman weeping loudly. Ruby didn't notice Jade's hair in her mouth. Katie ignored Lizzie's foot pressing down on hers. Lizzie pressed her forehead into Jade's shoulder. The younger girls' parents reached over to touch their children, patting backs, stroking hair, as they absorbed their victory. David put a hand on Nick's shoulder and squeezed.

After a moment the bailiff approached the girls. 'Quiet, please,' he said gently, conscious of their enormous relief.

When his court was restored to order, the complainants sniffing, the families gathering themselves together, the defendant staring dumbly at his shoes, seeing and hearing nothing, Judge Leonard thanked the jury and dismissed them. The four men and eight women filed out of the room slowly, accepting the murmured thanks of the grateful girls as they passed.

After several minutes of quiet discussion about dates and cases between the barristers and the judge, sentencing was adjourned for a fortnight hence. Satisfied that justice had been served, Judge Leonard took his leave.

Carl was handcuffed by the attendant prison officer, and led from the defendant's box.

Turning to face his father, Robbie yelled, 'I hope you rot in hell, you twisted pervert!'

Carl hung his head as he stepped through the door.

The jubilant troupe walked out of the courtroom, and into the jury's arms. An emotional hug-fest ensued, the teary jurors whispering messages of admiration and pride. They applauded the girls' fortitude, and acknowledged the strength they had needed to come forward and testify.

Finally, most of them ready to get seriously drunk, the victorious little group walked out of the court and across the street to the pub.

Behind the courthouse, as Carl was escorted to the armoured police van, three newspaper journalists, two television news crews and a freelance photographer harangued the disgraced man. They threw a rabble of personal questions, snapped off dozens of pictures and shot footage that would be heavily pixelated for the evening news. Carl, mortified by the media ambush, tried to hide his face and refused to comment.

60

Sausages sizzled on the barbeque, popping and squeaking as they were lined up on the hot plate next to a steaming pile of fried onions. A tray of marinated steaks sat next to the grill, ready to be cooked. A plastic bowl of sliced potatoes rubbed edges with a stainless steel bowl of large, green king prawns. Gerard snapped his tongs and hummed as he turned the sausages, then pushed the well-browned onions toward the back to make way for the chips. A small plate of tofu kebabs also waited on the side. As he lay out thick slices of potato, Gerard surveyed the scene in his back yard.

'Want another beer?' called Nick, reaching into the esky to get one each for himself and Tom.

'Love one,' called Gerard, feeling the diminished weight of his empty can. 'Thanks.'

Lizzie played pole tennis with Alec. She giggled every time he missed the ball, which was attached to the top of the metal post with a length of string. She whacked a strong backhand, flinging the ball into an anticlockwise orbit, then reversed it with a hard forehand when it came back to her. Waving his bat ineffectively at the flying green ball, Alec stumbled sideways and tumbled to his knees.

'C'mon, Alec,' laughed the teenager. 'How could you miss that?'

'I'm much better at cricket,' the out-of-shape detective admitted, wondering if his hand-eye coordination had taken a holiday without telling him.

Ruby and Katie sat at a round, cement, garden table, a game of Jenga between them. Ruby stuck her tongue out the side of her mouth as she concentrated on pulling the block of wood out of the teetering stack. Katie watched, holding her breath, as her opponent's steady fingers carefully extracted the block and put it on the table. Triumphant, Ruby grinned.

'Wow,' said Katie, examining the remaining blocks of wood. 'I was sure you'd lose that. Okay, here goes.'

She gently manoeuvred a block out of the pile and put it down. Once again, Ruby's tongue found its way out to rest on her bottom lip while she thought about her next move.

On the verandah, David played chess with Robbie, muttering as the younger man gradually pushed the black king into a corner.

'Checkmate,' laughed Robbie, collecting his opponent's pieces from the side of the board. David played well, but Robbie was highly skilled, and almost invincible.

Nearby, Donna and Amanda took their usual places at the picnic table, cutting up fruit and vegetables, preparing salads and side dishes. Jade and Juliana had offered to take over, but the gossiping pair refused. They were happy to chat and chop, while chaos reigned around them.

Tom and Nick walked around the garden, discussing business strategies. As they strolled, sipping cans of beer, Tom inspected each of Gerard's plants, checking them for bugs and diseases, noting their position in the garden and growth patterns. During a long pause, when Tom had bent to examine more closely the thin trunk of a young tree, Nick looked around the yard for Jade and saw her through the kitchen window. She was deep in conversation with Juliana as they prepared dessert. He smiled, pleased she was now happy. It had been a long, rocky road.

'I'm stoked he got twenty-five years,' said Nick, as Tom straightened up.

'Yeah,' agreed Tom, 'that was an excellent result. I hope he rots and dies in prison.'

'Yeah, but he's eligible for parole in twenty. That'll make him what? Seventy-four when he gets out. I was expecting the judge to go lightly,' added Nick. 'You know, because of his age.'

'He didn't look well at the sentencing. I reckon your little publicity stunt knocked the wind out of his sails,' chuckled Tom.

News of the sex abuse scandal had spread across the media like a bushfire. Although Carl was never named, or shown clearly in pictures, there were enough clues in the news reports for those who knew him to identify the businessman. As word spread from company to company, the directors began damage-control campaigns, while several of the boards called emergency meetings.

After seeing the devastating ripple effect of the guilty verdicts on television, Carl was a broken man. By the time sentencing came around, he'd aged ten years, and wished he'd had the courage to kill himself when he'd had the chance.

'I think it did him good,' countered Nick, pleased Mel had come through for him. Even better, impressed with the work he'd outsourced to her, the editor had also offered Jade a permanent job. She had a job interview with him on Monday.

'Lunch is ready!' called Gerard, flipping the last steak, cooked exactly as David like it, just scared, onto a plate.

Bats and balls, chess and Jenga, and all deep discussions were abandoned as everyone gathered at the table. For several minutes, the only sounds were the clattering of crockery and cutlery, and murmurs of praise for the sumptuous feast laid out before them. Everyone tucked in, enthusiastically smacking their lips, enjoying their meal, the company of their friends, and the warm spring sunshine.

'What are you gonna do now, Lizzie?' asked Jade, pulling a tofu square off the bamboo stick. She had been wondering if any of the others had thought about the future yet. She'd tried, but still felt a little lost. Even though Nick's friend had offered her a great job, she was still operating on automatic pilot.

Lizzie looked up and smiled proudly at Donna. 'We were just talking about that yesterday,' replied the girl. 'I've decided to repeat this year at high school because I missed so much. Then, in the future, I'm going to study forensic science, if I can get in.'

'Jamie will be very pleased to hear that,' praised Alec. Other murmurs of encouragement and approval floated across the table.

'He talked me into it,' she admitted with a shy smile, proud of her choice. She looked across the table. 'What about you, Jade?'

'Don't know. I feel … I don't know. I feel amazing,' replied Jade, knitting her eyebrows as she tried to articulate her complicated feelings. 'It's like there's this inner-calm deep inside me. I've never felt it before. It's great. I'm lovin' it. I feel like I could take on the world. But when I think about the future, I feel … lost, I guess.'

'Last night, I asked her to marry me,' said Nick, butting in.

Jade's eyes widened as she turned to face him. She hadn't been going to mention that. Gasps of surprise and delight fluttered around the table like butterflies of joy. Nick looked into Jade's eyes, his love for her written on his face in large bold letters.

'What did she say?' asked Amanda, turning to Jade. 'What did you say?' Her shrill voice hushed the celebratory racket into breathless anticipation.

'She hasn't given me her answer yet,' Nick confessed, wondering if, by telling everyone, he was pushing too hard. A moment of panic pierced his heart. What if she doesn't want to marry me? he asked himself, feeling momentarily crushed. They'd been through so much; marriage seemed like the logical conclusion.

There was a long gulp of silence at the table as everyone took this in. A dozen faces turned to stare expectantly at Jade. She had told Nick she needed time to absorb this new information. She'd wanted to think about what marriage meant to her, and then decide if she was ready for it. She'd spent a sleepless night wondering what it would be like to be Nick's wife, and the mother of his children. Yesterday had been the second time he'd proposed. She still didn't know if she was ready for such a binding commitment.

Jade looked at the gathered crowd and smiled. She gazed into Nick's eyes and instantly knew what she wanted. 'Yes. I said "yes".'

There was a round of applause. Juliana dabbed at her eye with a tissue. The newly engaged couple kissed as everyone offered congratulations.

'How about you, Katie?' asked David when the furore finally settled down. 'What does your crystal ball tell you to do?'

Katie glanced at Robbie. Gerard smiled, thrilled his daughter was happy at last. Amanda put her hand on Donna's arm and was about to blabber the news about her daughter's two-day-old relationship with Robbie when Katie cut her off.

'I'm going back to school when the term starts,' she said decisively. 'I'm thinking of studying psychology at university. We'll see.'

'That's a great idea,' said Donna, nodding and smiling. Gerard and Amanda beamed with pride. Under the table, Robbie reached for Katie's hand.

'And,' continued Katie, holding her hand, clasped in Robbie's, above the table for everyone to see. 'I'm going to try and make this thing with Robbie work out.' She grinned at him. He kissed her cheek.

'Oh, sweetheart,' gushed Juliana, smiling at her son. 'I'm so pleased for both of you.'

'It was never going to be any other way,' said Tom, chuckling. 'That boy fell head over heels in love the second he laid eyes on Katie.' He winked at Robbie, who grinned back happily.

'And you're head over heels in love with Mum,' Robbie countered.

'That's right,' agreed Tom, putting his arm around Juliana. He kissed her forehead. She kissed his cheek and blushed slightly, hot with love for her new man. They'd decided to sell all the Rutherford houses, move to the beach, and start up a nursery on the outskirts of town.

'So, Ruby,' said Nick. 'That leaves you. Any plans?'

'A few,' grinned Ruby secretively. 'There are a few things up my sleeve.'

Ruby and Alec had been talking about their plans every day for the last two weeks. She'd slept for four days after the sentencing, emotionally and physically exhausted, while Alec took care of her, cooking and bringing food to her bed. Then, when she was fully rested, they'd discussed the future, and what it held in its palms for them.

'Spit them out, girl!' coaxed Gerard, waving his fork at her. 'Don't leave us hanging in suspense.'

'Well,' she said, clearing her throat. 'I do have an announcement I'd like to make.'

She stood up, her glass of wine raised above her head. Heads turned to see her face, Ruby had everyone's attention. Alec chuckled to himself. She was going to be a handful, he thought, delighted with the prospect of his new life.

'Alec and I are going to Antarctica,' she told the stunned faces. 'We're booked on the November cruise out of Argentina.'

Jade laughed out loud. 'That's wonderful,' she chortled with glee, pleased they were able to operate openly as a couple. 'Sounds like the perfect honeymoon trip.'

Alec beamed. 'It might be that,' he said. 'We're still in negotiations.' Everyone started speaking at once. He silenced them with an authoritive hand. 'I promise,' he continued, 'that when a decision is made, you will be the first to know.'

'So, you're going on holiday. Is that it?' asked Lizzie, still a long way from thinking about boys and relationships, and their implications. She still faced years of counselling, and had accepted that. She wanted to know what would happen after the holiday. 'And then what?'

'Okay,' said Ruby, resuming her seat, and rising to the challenge of revealing all. 'First, let me say that I've been bumming around the world, chasing unicorns for a long time. Now, I've caught one. An important one.' She smiled at Lizzie and took in the faces of the people she'd come to love like family. This was her first experience of family since her mother had died. 'There are others, of course,' she went on, 'but this one was vital. I needed to find it so I could get on with the rest of my life.' Ruby held the floor. 'Now, after a lot of thought, tossing ideas around, and bouncing them off Alec, I've decided I want to write the story of our experiences. But only if it's okay with all of you.' She looked around the table at the smiling faces. Alec held her hand and squeezed, knowing if they said no, it would break her heart. In turn, as she met each person's eyes, they nodded, giving her permission to write her book. Ruby breathed a sigh of relief. She'd thought they'd say no. Pleased, she told the gathering, 'I'm thinking of calling it *Chasing Unicorns*.'

There was a hush as the book title was absorbed. Once again, the collection of nodding heads approved.

'Ruby?' Lizzie wanting to ask the burning question. 'What happens after you catch the unicorn? I mean, what do you do with it?'

'You let it go, Lizzie, doll,' smiled Ruby, lowering her voice to a whisper. 'You just let it go.'

Acknowledgments

I would like to thank the following people who all gave so freely of their time by answering my endless, sometimes inane questions, elaborating on their answers at length, and for providing me with the rare opportunity to experience intensive hands-on research, and for following through on their promises and convictions.

Psychologists Karen Harris from Victims of Crime and Margaret McDonald from Queensland Health restored my belief in myself, guided me down the right path, and helped keep my feet on the ground.

Senior Sergeant Greg Kelly and Detective Kathy Richardson from the Queensland Police provided invaluable assistance regarding the law and police procedures. I thank them for their ongoing support.

Frances Chatterton at the Queensland Justice Department generously gave up time to show me around the judicial maze and assisted in deciphering incomprehensible legal jargon.

Special thanks goes to Inspector Rob Gunton from the Tasmanian Police for his dogged persistence in helping me to achieve the justice I so desperately needed.

I am also deeply indebted to Mike Stoddart of the Tasmanian Justice Department for finally allowing me to be heard, despite the department's initial reluctance, and to Gail Leeson for just being there. Both of you have changed my life immeasurably.

And finally, inexpressible gratitude goes to those members of my immediate and extended family who believed in me, who fought alongside me, and who held my hand when I needed it the most. Thank you. I love you.

Roni Askey-Doran

About the Author

Tasmanian born Roni Askey-Doran has spent her life seeking adventure, happiness and inner peace, in spite of her tumultuous and traumatic history. A gypsy at heart, Roni has maintained a wonderful sense of humor which shines through in her writing. Filled with passion, sometimes fueled by rage, and powered by her desire to tell her stories using vivid lexiconic imagary, Roni writes from her heart and from her own experiences.

Roni has lived or traveled in 46 countries over the past three decades and frequently lives under the radar and off the grid. Despite her nomadic tendencies, she's an accomplished chef, talented wordsmith, avid gardener, and her wandering feet dance to more than one beat.

Like a cat with nine lives, Roni has survived, even thrived on everything destiny has thrown her direction and, through storytelling, has found a way to share her adventures with a great sense of humor and a writing style that has readers breathlessly turning the page.

Now a full-time beachbum, Roni currently resides in a bamboo shack on a remote beach in South America with three cats, two opossums, a non-venomous Granadilla snake, some tree frogs, a large green iguana and several species of tropical birds and butterflies. A large huntsman spider named Horacio resides in her bathroom. She's addicted to bananas, loves to cook fresh seafood with coconuts, is passionate about her tropical garden, and makes her own chocolate.

Webpage: https://booksbyroniaskeydoran.wordpress.com
Facebook: @booksbyroni

Books By Roni

ANNUS HORRIBILIS: DIARY OF A NOBODY

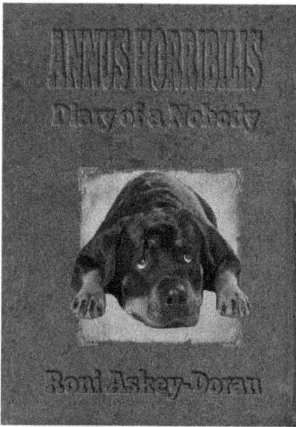

ISBN: 978-1501016547

Fiction, Women's Fiction,
Contemporary Fiction
Genre: Comedy, Humor

At the lowest point in her life, Kirsten Smith wakes up under a lantana bush on New Year's Day. Determined to reinvent herself, she vows to rise above her worst moment.

Throughout the year, Kirsten and her best friends are flung into a hysterical romp through life; their mishaps and adventures ultimately force them to question themselves and their perceptions of love, beauty, sex, men and even their friendship.

Hilarious and heart-breaking, Kirsten's year of self-renovation culminates in an enchanting love triangle, an unexpected new family, and a surprising new career.

Warning: this novel is slightly naughty.

PHEW! ARGH! EWWW! TRAVEL TALES I NEVER TOLD MUM

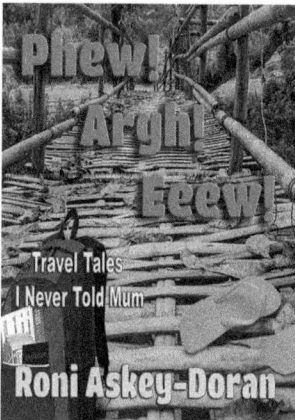

ISBN: 978-0975760093

Non-Fiction, True Stories
Genre: Travel, Adventure

Phew! Argh! Eeew! is a fantastic collection of short travel tales so enthralling, so gripping, and so chilling to read that you'll never leave home again.

When this intrepid young backpacker first embarked on her adventures around the globe, even her own wild imagination could not have conjured up some of the unforetold events that took place in her thirty-five years of travel.

Despite being hijacked in Bulgaria, nearly dying of Malaria in India, being imprisoned in Ecuador and almost blown to pieces in Turkey, Roni lived to tell her stories in the vivid and humorous style for which she is known. The only person she never told was her mother….

Books By Roni

BROKEN

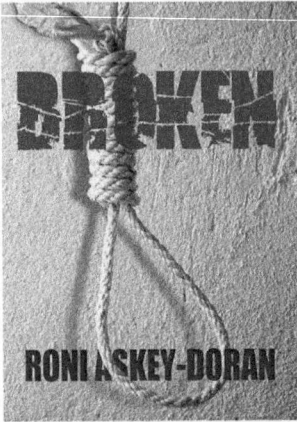

ISBN: 978-0975760055

Fiction, Women's Fiction,
Contemporary Fiction
Genre: Drama, Suspense
*Trigger Warning

Today is Emily Zylaz's birthday. This is the day that she chosen to kill herself. After struggling for many years to cope with the roller-coaster of mental illness, a devastating failed marriage, and a soul-destroying career that is going nowhere, she's giving up.

Feeling like the only solution to all of her problems is to take her own life, Emily plans to hang herself at midnight. She believes no one will care that she's dead, that she won't be missed, and that everyone will be better off without her and her fickle moods.

As we journey alongside Emily, counting down the hours on her last day alive, we explore the twisted labyrinth of her troubled mind and learn why she so desperately wants to die.

PENDULUM

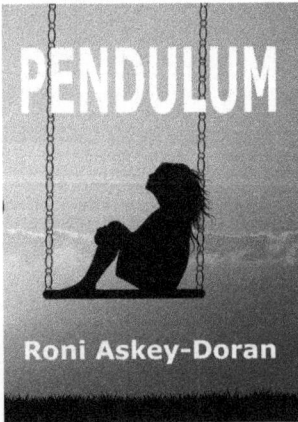

ISBN: 978-0975760000

Fiction, Women's Fiction,
Contemporary Fiction
Genre: Drama, Suspense
*Trigger Warning

Zara Kaplan has been sexually abused by her grandfather since she was a child. At sixteen, Zara runs away. In the city, Jay Thorndyke rescues Zara from the streets, and the unlikely pair become fast friends. In the heart of the red-light district, Zara is plunged into a whirlwind of wild parties, alcohol, and drugs.

Zara's friends have no inkling of her tormented past, or her checkered present. She can't find the words to tell them her horrific story. Wrapped up in their own troubles, Zara's friends are oblivious to her plight.

Seeking relief from her tortured memories, Zara sinks deeper into an abyss of reckless oblivion, heading down an ominous road littered with sex, drugs, and death.

Can her friends save her in time?.

Books By Roni

I'M BIPOLAR AND I KNOW IT: IT WORKS OUT!

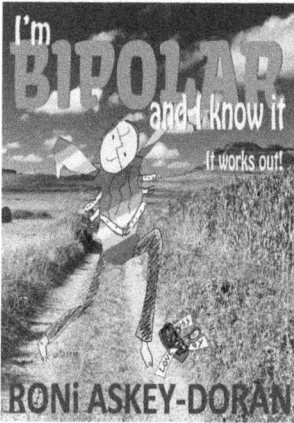

ISBN: 978-0975760062

Non-Fiction, True Stories
Genre: Self-Help; Mental Health–
Bipolar Disorder

Determined to treat her Bipolar Disorder with compassion, awareness, love, and understanding, instead of prescription medications, Roni embarks on a dangerous solo mission to salvage her sanity and somehow create the balance in her life that she desperately needs to survive.

I'm Bipolar And I Know It tells her amazing story in vivid colors, the challenges and triumphs, the almost insurmountable odds, and her ultimate success in learning to live alongside her terrible mental illnesses with true inner peace and eventual happiness.

Roni describes the steps she took towards healing. A no-holds-barred tragi-comedy, her successes and failures are outlined in detail, with some very surprising outcomes.

STRINE: THE LANGUAGE OF AUSTRALIA DECIPHERED

ISBN: 978-1519734488

Non-Fiction
Genre: Languages, Guides,
Dictionaries, Humor

"G'day mate! Onyergaan? Ya' orright, or what?"

For those who don't get the drift, at last, here is the ultimate all-in-one guide to the bizarre spoken language of Australia! Ever spoken to an Aussie and wondered what they're rabbiting on about? This book will help to decipher Strine so all youse will be able to twig on and join the yabbering!

"Yeah mate, no wuckers!"

Whether you're at home, out with Aussie friends, or headed Down Under to go walkabout, this little phrasebook is the answer to your all your ridgy-didge language strife. Over 250 pages of definitions and entertaining illustrations will make a bonzer difference next time an Ocker crosses your path.

Books By Roni

MOMPICHE: A FOREIGN PERSPECTIVE

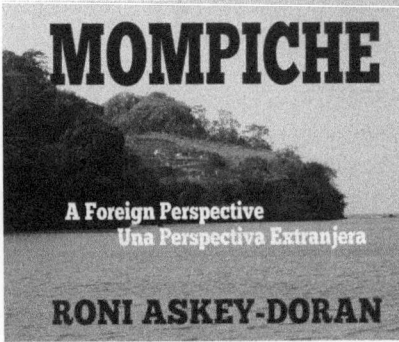

ISBN: 978-1502894885

Non-Fiction
Genre: Arts & Photography,
Photography & Video, Travel

A sleepy fishing village on the north coast of Ecuador, Mompiche is home to around one thousand people, including a foreign journalist and photographer.

In this book, Roni Askey-Doran shares her unique perspective of the village, with its people going about their daily lives, through a series of evocative photographs that she has taken during her years in residence.

With captions in English and Spanish, this book is a great gift for anyone traveling around, or living in Ecuador.

GOING FREAKING BANANAS:
101 THINGS YOU DIDN'T KNOW A BANANA COULD BE

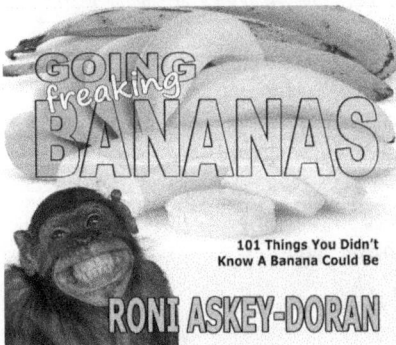

ISBN: to be determined

Non-Fiction
Genre: Cookery, Cookbooks, Travel

Status: Work in Progress
Watch this space...

Half blog, half cookbook, *Going Freaking Bananas* provides an insight into the many different ways in which bananas can be consumed, 101 ways to be exact. Several types of bananas, both green and yellow, and even purple feature in this book with easy to read recipes and fun stories.

If you thought just peeling and eating was the only thing you could do with a banana, think again. This lovely little book will enlighten and entertain with delicious new ideas about how to eat your bananas.

Books By Roni

YA MISMO: THIRTY MINUTES NORTH OF ZERO

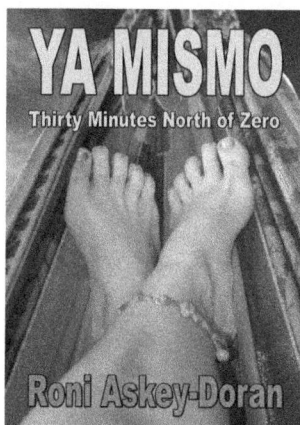

ISBN: to be determined

Non-Fiction, True Stories
Genre: Travel, Biography

Status: Work in Progress
Watch this space...

After more than thirty years on the road, Roni Askey-Doran abandons her nomadic lifestyle to set up house in a remote coastal village in the middle of the world. A tiny fishermen's haven nurtured by the Pacific Ocean, Mompiche barely earns its dot on the Ecuadorian map. Pursuing her dreams to design her own eco-friendly home and get her hands dirty in rich topsoil, Roni easily settles into the small community but quickly finds herself challenged on many levels.

In a culture far removed from her own she encounters some unique problems; from bathing in buckets of cold water every day to frequent power failures, doing battle with flesh-eating parasites to almost dying of dengue fever, and enduring the daily harassment about being unacceptably single to machete-wielding lunatics threatening to kill her. Not to mention the lack of chocolate and marshmallows in the store, the disappointment of discovering the once-a-week fruit and vege truck is out of garlic, and struggling to survive the leanest times on five dollars a week. As the bamboo shack rises from sticks in the mud to take shape and the first organic tomato plants begin to bear fruit, the neighbors begin a relentless campaign of terror to force out la gringa loca – even resorting to witchcraft.

Ya Mismo: Thirty Minutes North of Zero is a crazy story that unfolds from the moment Roni steps off the bus and follows a winding trail through a complex and mystifying culture that first embraces her but then chews her up and spits her out. Wheedling the recipes of traditional dishes from the local women, Roni learns to feed her soul as well as her body, losing over thirty kilos (70lb) along the way. She learns to dance like a Latina, speak like a Mompichera and celebrate the unique traditions of her adopted culture, simultaneously despairing the mindless exploitation and destruction of precious natural resources, and waging war on the army of land crabs that chomp on her vegetable seedlings.

Ya Mismo is a gritty rollercoaster of a tale about what can happen when you force a square peg into a round hole. This amazing story is still being written.